Historic
South Edinburgh

BY CHARLES J. SMITH

VOLUME THREE

CHARLES SKILTON LTD

DEDICATION

For My Family

Made and printed in Great Britain
by C. I. Thomas & Sons (Haverfordwest) Ltd
Haverfordwest, Pembrokeshire
and published by
CHARLES SKILTON LTD
Whittingehame House
Haddington, East Lothian
and
Balmoral Publishing Works
Cheddar, Somerset

SBN 0284 98739 5

VOLUME III

CONTENTS

iv

INTRODUCTION

IN my earlier volumes, I sought to provide a general history of South Edinburgh, in a very wide sweep, researched and presented at various levels, in certain instances at some depth, in others for reasons of space, lack of source material, relevance or simply according to my personal interest, at a more superficial level. It was always my assumption and indeed hope that if I simply "opened up the ground" over a wide area readers might be stimulated to pursue further their particular sphere of interest from the bibliographical sources cited or indeed even to make a systematic study for publication. It was most gratifying therefore that Malcolm Cant in his well-researched and highly successful work *Marchmont in Edinburgh* kindly attributed some of his original inspiration to the necessarily brief treatment of the district in my Volume I. Again, it has been a source of special pleasure to learn that many young people at various levels in a number of schools have found my work a useful source of reference in their local history study projects, thus bringing a fresh approach to a subject sometimes the object of perhaps overmuch nostalgia and the regretful sigh that, alas, "things are not what they were"! That my earlier volumes have also proved useful to those working in the more rarified atmosphere of academic circles in Edinburgh and beyond has been most encouraging, confirming that local history is a continuous ongoing process and work of collaboration. It is now earnestly hoped that the further two volumes which Mr Charles Skilton has kindly decided to publish will duly prove of similar interest and stimulation, providing an introduction, where needed, to the rich variety of people of such widely ranging character and distinction who have resided in or been associated with South Edinburgh.

People's interest in local history differs greatly. For some it lies in the architecture of houses or institutions; how a district originated and the factors which influenced its development; the life-style of people of different achievements and social background; local occupations and leisure patterns; or the origins of the area's institutions, hospitals, schools, colleges. Yet again, it may be the archaeology or natural history of a district which appeals. From considerable correspondence I have received and the response to lectures, it is clear that there is virtually no limit to the many aspects which attract attention. Whereas my earlier volumes provided some treatment of most of the above facets, the work now presented is in a sense more specific. It is concerned with people. While I am obviously interested in the general history of South Edinburgh, what has always appealed to me most is not primarily the architecture of a particular house, its precise age or for that matter the condition of its fabric and how well it was looked after — but rather who resided there, or was associated with it. What were they like as people?

What did they do or achieve or leave behind to enrich the area's or the city's, or on occasion, the world's heritage in the arts, literature, science, medicine or other spheres? If history is shaped by people who in turn are shaped by it, South Edinburgh has had many examples. Most certainly there has been an abundance of such people prominent in the above spheres and others who have resided in South Edinburgh. That my interest in such people is widely shared by others was encouragingly confirmed by the response to a course of lectures on "Historic South Edinburgh: People and Places" which I was kindly invited to give by Mr Basil Skinner, Director of Edinburgh University's Department of Extra-Mural Studies, some few years ago, and which provided the original inspiration for these volumes.

The choice of people selected for presentation is my own. Many more might have been included and some perhaps left out. Certain reviewers of my earlier works suggested — not without a certain tone of accusation — that I was "pre-occupied with the landed gentry" or "the famous and distinguished" to the exclusion or disregard of "the ordinary people" of the area. This, if it appeared to be so, was certainly not my intention. "The ordinary people", a rather vague phrase of course, form the majority of the population, South Edinburgh being no exception, and while in the "ordinariness" of their lives and from their humbler dwellings they perform day after day the services invaluable to the community or the city and are the "backbone" of such, their worth and the value of their lives goes without

saying. There is perhaps scope for another different type of book on this sociological theme and i hope someone may produce sufficient material to meet this need. The people whose lives are presented in these two volumes have simply, by general consensus, merited or have at least been given a special place in the annals of South Edinburgh and indeed far beyond and very many have, without any sense of condescension contributed to the welfare, physical, cultural and spiritual of "the ordinary people".

The biographies are presented in the same geographical sequence as followed by the chapters in my earlier books, proceeding from what for long was South Edinburgh's northern boundary, the South or Burgh Loch, now the Meadows, southwards with detours east and west ultimately to Swanston. Unfortunately it was not feasible to make volumes 3 and 4 correspond exactly in their geographical coverage with volumes 1 and 2. The reason was simply that, in historical context, since the development of South Edinburgh residentially south of the Jordan Burn at the foot of Morningside Road, the dividing point for my first two volumes, was relatively recent, the great majority of people of historical interest lived north of the Jordan which was also for long the city boundary. To have chosen the same dividing line therefore for these biographies would have resulted in an imbalance in size between the two volumes. Hence people associated with Tipperlin and Canaan are to be found in volume 4, which I rather regret.

As regards the biographies themselves, when the person concerned

vi

has been the subject of fairly lengthy treatment in my earlier volumes or appears in biographies accessible in lending or reference libraries, then they are presented rather briefly. Where my researches have brought new material to light concerning someone who, although well known, has hitherto received no or sparse attention in published sources, then I have treated such people at some length. Special attention has been given to tracing and publishing portraits never previously published or even seen and perhaps having been thought not to exist, and it is hoped that these illustrations may form the not least interesting feature of these pages. I have been specially grateful to the many art galleries, publishers, authors, photographic libraries and agencies, as also the descendants or relatives of many of the subjects, who have kindly provided portraits and granted permission for their reproduction.

Meeting of Robert Burns and young Walter Scott at Sciennes Hill House. Professor Ferguson is seated extreme left beside fireplace, behind Burns

Painting by Charles Martin Hardie, A.R.S.A.

(See page 18)

ACKNOWLEDGEMENTS

IN seeking historical material for biographies, especially of people in the rather remote past, recourse must normally be made in the first instance to various libraries, usually of specialised resources, and this indeed was essential for most of the subjects presented. I must therefore express my deep indebtedness to the following people from whom more assistance was required from some than from others.

As always, research into Edinburgh's history, whether of people or places, must indeed lead one immediately to the vast and it seems always increasing and increasingly invaluable resources of the Edinburgh City Libraries Edinburgh Room, which so widely range from rare volumes and manuscripts of scholarship to the nonetheless important and carefully-filed programmes of some school's opening ceremony or a theatrical first night, all constituting the story of the city's past. Here Miss Sheena McDougall's and her staff's professionalism and patient and painstaking assistance was as indispensable as it was kindly given. Likewise Miss Meg Burgess and her staff in the adjacent Scottish Department were extremely helpful. Mrs N. E. S. Armstrong, Head of the City Libraries Reference and Information Services seemed to have a most valuable subconscious reflex instinct, upon hearing a name, to know immediately just where much rare and essential material on the person might be found. But one also had to search further afield in other specialised libraries and I am most grateful to Miss Margaret Wilks, Superintendent of the Map Room of the National Library of Scotland and her colleagues, and Mr Patrick Cadell, the library's Keeper of Manuscripts; to the staff of Edinburgh University Library and Dr John Hall and his colleagues in the Special Collections Department; to Mr George H. Ballantyne of Edinburgh's Signet Library; to Miss Joan Ferguson, Librarian to the Royal College of Physicians, Edinburgh; to the late Miss Dorothy Wardle, Librarian to the Royal College of Surgeons, Edinburgh; to Miss Jean Adams, of Edinburgh University's Erskine Medical Library; to Mrs Catherine Strang, Librarian to Edinburgh District Council's Department of Architecture, and to Mr W. Howard of Edinburgh University's New College Library.

Furth of Edinburgh, I have been greatly indebted to Mr Peter Grant, Aberdeen City Librarian and his staff; to Miss Karen Middleton of Aberdeen University Library's Special Collections Department; to Mr D. M. Blake of the British Library's India Office Library and Records Section; and the Library of the House of Commons. As regards portraits and photographs, I am grateful for much patient assistance from Miss Julie Murphy and Miss Claire Stewart of the Scottish National Portrait Gallery and Miss Pearl Sutherland of the latter's sales department. The invaluable help of Miss Elspeth Yeo, Publications and

Exhibitions Officer of the National Library of Scotland, was also much appreciated as likewise that of Miss Sheila Fletcher, Secretary to the University of Edinburgh Pictures Committee. Dr. Walter Makey, formerly Edinburgh's City Archivist, was most helpful. I have been greatly indebted to numerous authors, publishers, and individuals — in many cases descendants or relatives of the subjects of the biographies — as acknowledged in the captions. As in my earlier volumes, I have depended very greatly indeed upon the much-appreciated professional skill and patient assistance of Mr Bill Weir of the Photographic Department of the Edinburgh University Library and his assistant, Mr Malcolm Liddle, who frequently vastly improved upon quite un-promising original material. The assistance of Mr James Paul and his staff of Edinburgh University's Medical Illustrations Department has been most helpful. Although because of the nature of these two volumes, few of the photographs by my brother, Mr William R. Smith, appear, nevertheless I am greatly indebted to him for very much direct and indirect assistance and support in many other ways.

In the research for material, in addition to the resources of the many libraries I have also been greatly assisted by very many individuals, firstly in drawing upon the special-ised knowledge and information of Mrs Sheila Durham, who in colla-boration with the Scottish Genealogy Society and assisted by a number of her Morningside friends, carried out a most valuable survey of those interred in Morningside Cemetery, which provided data of great value in my studies; Mr Ian Gow of the Royal Commission on the Ancient and Historical Monuments of Scotland who also assisted me greatly in tracing and providing lesser-known portraits; and Dr Ian Campbell of Edinburgh University's Department of English Literature, who is an authority on the Carlyles. Absolutely essential was the kind and invaluable assistance I received from very many descendants and relatives of the subjects of the biographies either in providing information never pre-viously published, or portraits which existed only in family circles, and much help from other people specially knowledgeable concerning various individuals. I must therefore express my appreciation to the following as regards Volume 3: Mr Fred Whalley of Groves-Raines Nicholas, Architects; Dr J. E. Phillips, Senior Lecturer, Depart-ment of Veterinary Pathology, Edinburgh University Royal (Dick) Veterinary College; the late Mr George Cramb, formerly manager of Robert Middlemass & Co.; Mr John R. Webster, Session Clerk, Salisbury Church of Scotland (formerly Newington United Presbyterian Church); the Reverend Edwin S. Towill; Messrs A. C. and D. W. Kirkwood; Mr R. J. Shepherd; Dr N. A. Hood, Consultant Physician, Longmore Hospital; Mrs C. Jamieson, relative of James C. H. Balmain; Mr John G. Gray; Mr John C. Bartholomew; Miss Margaret Buchanan; Sister St Ignatius of St Margaret's Convent; Reverend Father Mark Dilworth, O.S.B., Archivist to the Roman Catholic Church in Scotland; Colonel the Honourable John Warrender; Mr Douglas F. Stewart, concerning the Warrender archives and much else; Mr Maurice Berrill of the Edinburgh Merchant Company; Mr Donald M. Craig, of the Barclay Bruntsfield Church; Mr William Anderson, formerly Free Church of Scotland College Officer; Mr Logan Kirk, grandson of Mrs Eliza Kirk; Mrs Yvonne Hillyard, concerning the discovery of a portrait of Hippolyte Blanc; Mr Terence M. Ryan, New Zealand, archivist to the Forbes of Pitsligo family; the Reverend A. Ian Dunlop; Mr Stuart Harris; Mr Gilmour Main; Dr Margaret Oliver of East Morningside House; Mr W. Knight of Yule Catto & Co.; Professor Emeritus Neil Campbell; Mr James C. Allan; Major Alexander Deuchar, descendant of David Deuchar of Morningside House; Mr Stewart Foster; and Mr Watson Kerr, grandson of "the Canny Man".

BIBLIOGRAPHY

Unlike my earlier volumes, for reasons of space a slightly less comprehensive bibliography is provided, and this appears in Volume 4. Much biographical and basic material was obtained from the following source books: the *Dictionary of National Biography*; the *Biographical Dictionary of Eminent Scotsman*, edited by Robert Chambers (3 volumes); *Silences that Speak* by William Pitcairn Anderson, an invaluable record of Edinburgh's ancient churches and burial grounds and of those buried there; *Old and New Edinburgh* by James Grant; *Memorials of Edinburgh in the Olden Time* by Daniel Wilson; *The South Side Story* edited by John G. Gray; *Book of the Old Edinburgh Club: Volume 24*, for much on Newington residents; *The Grange: a Case for Conservation* by the Grange Association; *The Lord Provosts of Edinburgh*; John Kay's *A Series of Original Portraits*; *Edinburgh*, by John Gifford, Colin McWilliam and David Walker, Penguin Books in association with the National Trust of Scotland; and *Marchmont in Edinburgh* by Malcolm Cant.

For many of the people presented, standard or several biographies exist and these may be borrowed or consulted in most public libraries, consequently the bibliographical material relative to most of the subjects and kindly compiled by Mrs N. E. S. Armstrong, Head of Reference and Information Services of Edinburgh City Libraries, is selected from special sources or from biographies considered particularly relevant. I am also greatly indebted to Mrs Armstrong for compiling the index which appears in Volume 4.

Finally, typing of the rather voluminous manuscript was no light task and I am most grateful to Mrs Anne Craigie for her invaluable assistance in undertaking it. The considerable research involved proved costly and I therefore express my sincere appreciation to the Scottish Arts Council for their financial assistance.

1 · THE MEADOWS

SIR THOMAS HOPE OF RANKEILLOUR

Dutch-style house, now No. 6 Hope Park Square, beside East Meadows, built by Sir Thomas Hope of Rankeillour in 1770.

By courtesy of Edinvar Housing Association Ltd
Photographed by Stewart Guthrie

THE MEADOWS, once the ancient Burgh or South Loch, which over a period of nearly two hundred years was gradually drained and in stages converted into one of the city's most pleasant and popular green spaces, is synonymous with the name of one man, Thomas Hope of Rankeillour. At the east end, a number of streets and a secluded little square, along with Rankeillour Street to the east, are named to commemorate Hope's major contribution to the drainage and landscaping of the area and his residence on the north bank of the loch.

Although described by certain writers as "a public-spirited citizen" and well known, in fact little is to be found concerning Hope in the city's printed records. Nor could a portrait be traced. The only relatively detailed biographical material which could be found was a 4-page handwritten document headed: "Memorial Thomas Hope of Rankeillour", dated 27th May 1761, and held in the Special Collection Department, Edinburgh University Library. Written by an unidentified third party and drawn up four years prior to 1761, the Memorial is an appeal to George II for a pension to be paid to Hope because of the financial hardship resulting from his public services. From it the following information about Hope may be obtained. In places, the handwriting is illegible and the phrasing somewhat confusing. Certain passages are therefore presented here in the original.

Thomas Hope of Rankeillour whose age, in 1761, is given as 81, is described as having become an advocate in 1702, continuing at the Bar until 1715, "after which date he never put on the gown". He was "the last chosen in Scotland to the Union Parliament", as one of the four Members for the county of Fife where he had succeeded to the estate of his father, Sir Archibald Hope, Senator of the College of Justice, "who predeceased that Parliament". Thomas Hope was elected "without

1

a contradictory vote", although "a county candidate had been set up against him".

Hope "voted every vote against the Union because he thought the prerogative was too easily parted with". He insisted that England should pay £2 million stg. to enable Scotland "to carry on its own manufactures and trade so that in some measure it could keep pace with England and pay the English burdens and duties to which Scotland was liable by the Articles of Union". Hope served Fife so satisfactorily in Parliament that, until after the 1715 Rebellion, he was always the county's first choice as candidate.

In 1719, Hope left his farm improvements at Rankeillour, an estate near Cupar in Fife, and came over to Edinburgh to educate his numerous family and "observing how conveniently that spot of ground lying so near the city and fitt for publick works lay, then a perfect bog and loch, he gave a scheme to the Lord Provost and Magistrates, of the said field, being proprietors thereof, and after arguing every article, they agreed to the same and soon after, exposed to public roup for 30ty years tack in August 1721". Hope seemed so doubtful as regards obtaining the "tack"(lease) that he went back to his farm in Fife for the harvest.

When he later returned to Edinburgh, Hope was informed that while several men had bid for the lease of the Burgh Loch, none was prepared to maintain the hedges, trees and policy. The Town Council therefore prevailed upon Hope to undertake the improvement of the loch, which, the writer of the Memorial continues: "You see now in its beauty and they called Hope

Park after his name". Hope's lease was taken out in 1722, and was for 57 years. The memorial goes on: "He no sooner finished this in a twelve-month, but projected and assisted to form a Society for the improvement of the Knowledge of Agriculture and to meet and dine at a public house in the said park upon a Saturday every fortnight for the above purposes". Apparently after their business sessions, the committee members of the above society answered questions on agriculture raised by the public who were admitted.

Hope had in earlier years travelled in Europe, studying farming methods, and the society which he helped to found seems to have been so successful that "in the space of three years our number exceeded three hundred and fifty of the first nobility and gentry in the nation, to whom is owing our great success at agriculture, manufactures and fisheries". The society gained royal approval and had some influence on parliamentary legislation as regards agriculture and fisheries. Little concerning this early society could be traced in the available records.

After Hope's numerous children had completed their education he returned once again to Fife but soon afterwards was informed that the society which he had helped form was no longer meeting regularly and was losing its influence. Hope was begged to return to Edinburgh but replied that through his public services his estate in Fife had suffered and that he could not be active in both places. He was promised a financial settlement by "the ministry" if he would return to Edinburgh. This he did but since the financial payments were not forthcoming, once more he returned to Fife.

Next it appears that Sir Robert Walpole and "most of the Scottish nobility" undertook to ensure the financial support promised if he would assume responsibility for what appears to have been considered a very important society. Hope agreed to return and, "giving over his farm to his son, flitted bag and baggage to Edinburgh for the third and last time". He remained responsible for the society for nearly twenty years but, during all this period, still received no payment. "It might be said that he wasted his estate upon the good of his country and has retired only with these last few years of his time to spend with his three daughters in his house at Hopepark, receiving a small annuity from his son".

The Memorial, actually written in 1757, was also submitted on behalf of Hope's eldest son and grandson who had suffered from financial hardship. The appeal to the King, however, was principally on behalf of Hope's daughters. A pension of £150 was sought so that during Hope's remaining short years he and his daughters "would look upon his Kingly benevolence with great honour and as a remembrance of his past services". The appeal ends with the Latin words, difficult to decipher:

SPERAMUS QUOD VOLUMUS
SED QUOD ACCIDERIT
FERAMUS

Loosely translated:

We hope for what we want
But we take what we get.

It is not known if the pension was ever paid.

During his lease of the Burgh Loch, Hope had apparently made some progress towards converting "the perfect bog and loch" into a more pleasant area but at the time of his death the work was far from complete and the city authorities had to take over the final stages. In fact it was not until 1863 that the Meadows finally came to resemble the present-day appearance. Hope had effected considerable drainage and laid out a walk all around "the meadow", 33 feet broad and with an inner ditch five feet broad. Each side of the walk had to have a hedge and row of trees. The early stages of what became the Middle Meadow Walk leading to the Marchmont district were completed. For a period of seven years Hope had excluded the public from access to the area while work was in progress but through "universal complaint" this was revoked.

The east end of the Burgh Loch was the deepest part, and here in 1770 Hope had built himself a house where he resided with his daughters. The house, No.6 Hope Park Square, has a Dutch-style frontage, which was rather fashionable in the houses of people of means at that period, probably resulting from the considerable trade then carried on with Holland. A house with similar Dutch-type gables for long stood on the Prestonpans-Tranent back road. This was Bankton House, once the residence of Colonel Gardiner of Prestonpans, supporter of "Johnny Cope", and killed in the battle there during Charles Edward Stuart's great victory in the 1745 Rebellion.

Thomas Hope's house on the diminishing waters of the Burgh Loch was pleasantly situated. It is believed to have served also as a bath house and boat house, there being a

3

little jetty on the loch at this point from which a boat could take off for fishing, mainly for perch and eels. The house was sold in 1851 to a builder who erected the surrounding houses to form a square. After a period of ownership by the University, the house was sold to Edinvar Housing Association in 1976. During restoration in 1978 it was discovered that alterations had taken place in earlier years and that in fact Hope's original house had been built on the site of a very much older one, possibly dating from the 16th century. No. 6 Hope Park Square now consists of three separate flats which are let under special conditions.

Any pleasures which Thomas Hope may have enjoyed as relaxation from his many public services in his pleasant loch-side residence were short-lived, for he died there in 1771, only a year after completion of the house. The date when he was awarded a knighthood could not be traced.

The former South or Borough Loch becomes The Meadows

From Grant's "Old and New Edinburgh"

WILLIAM BURNESS

WHEN Robert Burns first came to Edinburgh in 1786, his father, William Burness, had already resided there briefly nearly thirty-seven years before, in about 1749. The poet used this spelling of his surname until 1786 when it last appears above his signature to a letter. Thereafter he adopted the version without the "e" and the second "s".

The father of Scotland's national bard was born at Clochnahill Farm, Dunnottar, in Kincardineshire, in 1721 and trained as a gardener, as was his father, at Inverugie Castle in Aberdeenshire. In 1748 William Burness sought references from three Kincardineshire landlords. Perhaps he did so because of the possibility that his father had been regarded as a Jacobite supporter in the 1745 Rebellion. Certainly, Robert Burns himself liked to think that his grandfather had been loyal to the Stuart cause. At any rate, after the rebellion, the economic hardships in the north were such that the Burness family split up.

William Burness, armed with his references as an assurance to any future employer of his political "good name", came to Edinburgh. As a trained gardener he was engaged by Thomas Hope in the early landscaping of the partially drained Meadows. If Burness was thought to have had any family Jacobite background, this would not have influenced Thomas Hope who had been a severe critic of Scotland's absorption into the United Kingdom. William Burness was probably engaged in the laying out of the various "Walks" round the diminishing Burgh Loch and

4

planting of the lime trees which Hope was required to plant.

After about two years work at the Meadows, Burness left Edinburgh for Ayrshire, where the Laird of Fairlie employed him on his estate. Next he feued some land from Dr Alexander Campbell at Alloway, amounting to about eight acres, and set up as a nurseryman. This was not a success. He next became head gardener at the Doonholm estate of the Ayr Lord Provost, William Ferguson, while retaining his nursery land and on this, with his own hands, built himself a cottage. On 15th December 1757 he married Agnes Brown, a farmer's daughter, and in the small cottage on 25th January 1759 Robert, their first son, was born.

William Burness, hard working and conscientious, was entirely devoted to his family's physical and mental welfare. Indeed, he did everything possible to ensure good educational opportunities for his children both at school and in a home background of books and lively discussion. After his death at Lochlea on 13th February 1784, aged 63, his life shortened, it has been suggested, by his arduous labours for his family, Robert Burns wrote of him: "The best of friends and the ablest of instructors". Thomas Carlyle wrote of William Burness: "A silent hero and poet without whom the son had never been a speaking one".

Unfortunately, a portrait of William Burness could not be traced. While many of the innumerable books on Robert Burns and his family carry illustrations of various other members, his father does not appear. One reason for this, suggested by an authority on Burns, was that when his father died in 1784 Robert had not yet achieved renown and thus the poet's parents were not of sufficient importance or social standing to merit public interest or attract the portrait painters.

WILLIAM MILLER OF MILLERFIELD

William Miller of Millerfield

From "A Catalogue of Engravings" by William Miller

MILLERFIELD PLACE, one of several rows of terraced villas leading off southwards from Melville Terrace to the rear of Sciennes Primary School and close to the Royal Hospital for Sick Children, commemorates the notable Edinburgh Quaker family who resided here in the early 19th century in a fine secluded villa originally named Hope Park. The house was to become the residence of William Miller, one of the foremost engravers of his time and scarcely surpassed.

William Miller was born in Nicholson Street on 28th May 1796. His father, George Miller, was a devout Quaker, as had been several other of his ancestors. One of these had been hereditary master-gardener at Holyroodhouse, another a prosperous seed merchant at the foot of the Canongate, and a third William Henry Miller, a notable book collector who acquired the estate of Craigentinny and is buried in the impressive mausoleum to be seen prominently on the north side of Portobello Road.

George Miller, father of the engraver, was born near Holyrood, educated at the High School, under Dr Adam, and the University, where he became something of a classical scholar. He did not, however, pursue an academic career but opened a shawl maker's business in Bristo Street, moving later to Nicholson Street where William was born. He acquired the property at Hope Park in 1800.

William Miller was educated in England and at Edinburgh University. While it was intended that he should enter his father's business, his early interest in art led him instead to become apprenticed to William Archibald, an Edinburgh engraver. After four years training with him Miller went to London and became a pupil of George Cooke, an engraver of some note. He returned to Edinburgh in 1821 and established a successful practice as a landscape engraver with his studio at Hope Park. His first significant commission was a plate for Edinburgh artist "Grecian" Williams' *Views in Greece*, subsequently completing eighteen more pieces from this work.

In 1824 Miller executed an engraving which was the beginning of his earning the greatest notice and fame. This was a plate after Turner of the famous painter's Clovelly Bay, which with a further two pieces appeared in Turner's *Antiquarian and Picturesque Tour round the South Coast* of 1826. While now called upon to make engravings from the work of other artists, it was his reproductions of Turner's painting which earned his highest reputation. Dr John Brown, the celebrated Edinburgh doctor and author, assistant to Professor James Syme in his private surgical hospital in Minto House in Chambers Street, whose classic work *Rab and His Friends* had been illustrated by Miller, wrote to the engraver: "Through your engravings, the power and the beauty and touch of Turner have been made known and impressed in quarters, and upon multitudes who otherwise would never have known his name or benefited by his wonderful genius—". Turner himself considered Miller to be "unequalled in his art".

Amongst the other artists whose work was reproduced by Miller was Sir George Harvey, President of the Royal Scottish Academy, who had the highest opinion of his art and in his 1843 Disruption picture *Leaving the Manse* introduced a view of part of the old-world garden at Hope Park. Other illustrations of this most pleasant secluded house remain. Miller's studio was in his house and Sir Daniel Wilson, author of

6

Memorials of Edinburgh in the Olden Time, who resided with his brother George at Elm Cottage at Blackford Road, wrote from University College, Toronto, where he became the Principal, giving a vivid recollection of Miller at work at Hope Park with his pupils gathered round him at the large studio window.

Miller was also constantly in demand by authors to illustrate their work. A catalogue of his engravings exhibited in 1886 provides an indication of his prolific and varied output. In the comprehensive lists are many books of special Edinburgh and general Scottish interest in which his work appeared. He illustrated Lockhart's *Life of Scott* and many of Scott's own editions of prose and poetry. Miller also illustrated books for the Stevenson engineers on the Bell Rock and Skerryvore lighthouses. The variety of subjects for which authors sought his art is very wide indeed, ranging from *The Castles, Palaces and Prisons of Mary, Queen of Scotland* to *The Edinburgh Journal of Science,* edited by Professor D. Brewster and treatises on anatomy by Dr Alexander Monro, along with other medical text-books and journals. They also encompassed sketches of "The Retreat" at York, an early Quaker establishment for the treatment of mental illness and of great interest to Edinburgh psychiatrists pioneering the then new branch of medicine in 1828; entrance tickets for the lectures of the famous anatomist Dr Robert Knox of Burke and Hare fame, and plates for the *Encyclopædia Britannica.* The celebrated Edinburgh pioneer of early calotype photography, David Octavius Hill, also

called upon Miller's services in his landscape and portrait work. The list of the engraver's commissions seems almost endless.

William Miller received many distinguished visitors at Hope Park, including Ruskin and leaders of various peace movements, which, as a devout Quaker, he supported ardently. His home was always open to refugees, especially from Poland. Having a most prolific and highly praised body of work to his name, Miller eventually retired from active work and found pleasure and relaxation in painting in water-colours. During his semi-retirement, he increased even further the philanthropic work which had characterised his life. In 1861 the lands surrounding the villa at Hope Park began to be feued out and the erection of new houses began to encroach on its seclusion. He himself feued out the field between his house and the then almost completely landscaped Meadows, and in 1863, the first house was built on what commemoratively became Miller-field Place. On 20th January 1882, during a visit to his daughter in Sheffield, William Miller died, in his 86th year. His remains were brought back to Edinburgh and interred in the burial ground attached to the Society of Friends Meeting House in the Pleasance.

THOMAS NELSON

A DETAILED historical account of the celebrated Edinburgh publishers, Thomas Nelson & Sons, is outside the scope of this book. However, the firm and its founder merit a place in

Thomas Nelson

From Grant's "Old and New Edinburgh"

the chronicles of the Meadows under two heads. Firstly, the firm at one stage occupied premises at Hope Park, and secondly, the twin stone pillars which stand at the east end of Melville Drive were erected by Thomas and William, the founder's sons who succeeded to the business.

Thomas Nelson, the founder, was born in the small village of Throsk near Stirling in 1780. At the age of twenty he went to London where he worked for a publisher in Paternoster Row. There he first developed an interest in the standard works of traditional theology which were to characterise much of his subsequent work. Returning to Edinburgh, Thomas Nelson set up in premises in a small corner shop at the West Bow. With the entry of his sons, Nelson's began to publish a wide range of work including cheap editions of

popular books and the classics. The firm developed steadily and, in 1846, moved to very large premises at Hope Park, in size surpassing any other similar establishment in Edinburgh, employing 600 workers. Then in 1878 tragedy struck, through a disastrous fire. Such was the reputation of the firm and so important to Edinburgh's trade, that the magistrates of the city offered them temporary premises at the east end of the Meadows near their previous building.

In appreciation of the city's sympathetic gesture, Nelson arranged for the erection of the stone pillars at the Melville Drive. The pillar on the south side, surmounted by a unicorn, has a scripted shield which is inscribed: "Presented to the City of Edinburgh by Messrs Thomas Nelson and Sons". On the north side the pillar, surmounted by a lion, is also inscribed: "The Rt Honourable Thomas J. Boyd, Lord Provost, 1880".

Within two years of the fire, extensive new premises were built at Dalkeith Road, in the little street leading to the King's Park, anciently known as Gibbet Loan, where the gallows once stood, but renamed Parkside by John G. Bartholomew in 1889, when his firm of cartographers was also established there. Indeed, at Parkside, Nelson's, which had long published maps, entered into partnership with Bartholomew's whose premises adjoined. Thomas Nelson, founder of the famous firm, was an invalid in the last two years of his life and died in 1861. He was buried in Grange Cemetery near the grave of the Cromarty stonemason and author Hugh Miller.

8

SIR JOHN MELVILLE

Lord Provost Sir John Melville

WHEN, at last, after the long-standing and sporadic efforts over two centuries to drain and landscape the Meadows were completed, with its pleasant tree-lined pathways around the perimeter, and southwards towards Marchmont and Bruntsfield, the roadway giving access from Tollcross by Brougham Street to Hope Park Crescent and Buccleuch Street was opened during 1858-59. This important and soon busy thoroughfare was named Melville Drive in honour of Edinburgh's civic head of that time, Lord Provost Sir John Melville.

John Melville was born at Kirkcaldy in 1802. He studied law in Edinburgh and became a Writer to the Signet in 1827, soon afterwards building up the highly successful legal firm of Melville and Lyndsay, and in due course became Crown Agent for Scotland. He was elected Lord Provost in 1854, succeeding Duncan McLaren, who had been elected Member of Parliament.

Lord Provost Melville played an important part in obtaining the legislation required for the city's annexation of the hitherto separate burgh of the Canongate in 1856. He was also closely involved in the extension of the city's boundary southwards. He held the Provostship for five years and was awarded a knighthood on retirement. A man with a strict sense of fairness and objectivity in discussion he was greatly in demand as a chairman of many civic bodies and important public meetings. He was also of scholarly interests, his speciality being Greek.

Sir John died at his home at 15 Heriot Row on 5th May 1860, aged 58, and was buried in Greyfriars Churchyard in the family tomb near the south-west end. The monument is a mural consisting of a fine sandstone tablet and pediment. Sir John's only son, George F Melville, an Oxford graduate, became an advocate and Sheriff of Linlithgow. He died in 1917 and it was believed that he bequeathed a very large sum for the endowment of a cancer hospital in Edinburgh.

WILLIAM DICK

AT the east end of Melville Drive, one of south Edinburgh's best-known landmarks and historic institutions rises high above the districts of Hope Park and

William Dick

By courtesy of the Faculty of Veterinary Medicine,
University of Edinburgh

Summerhall, familiarly known as the "Dick Vet". Professor O. Charnock Bradley, a former Principal of the college, introduces his detailed, definitive biography of William Dick with these words concerning the college which commemorates him: "No wealthy man endowed it: no public subscription list brought it into being: no appeal was made to or support given by the State; a famous university could not help. A poor man, the son of poor parents, started out on a venture supported by nothing more than a promise of £50".

In modern times, new institutions, whether colleges, schools, or hospitals, are normally established by official bodies, provided the funding is available. William Dick belonged to an era when very many such institutions resulted from the pioneering vision or generosity of an individual. Such, in south Edinburgh's history were Dr Sophia Jex-Blake, David Ainslie, and in more recent times Dr Ratcliffe Barnett, who are the subjects of later biographies. Dick's long determined campaign for the establishment in Edinburgh of a much needed veterinary college provides a classical example of the singlemindedness and perseverance which so often have been features of the Scottish character. It is certainly most fitting that the official title of the Royal (Dick) School of Veterinary Studies should immortalise his name.

William Dick was born in White Horse Close in the Canongate in May 1793, one of eight children, of whom five died in infancy. His father, John Dick, had come to Edinburgh from Aberdeen when aged eighteen. Precisely when he acquired the house where he set up a blacksmith's forge in White Horse Close is not on record. He was a man of strong character and considerable intelligence, who, it was said, "If he had had fuller educational opportunities would have gone far". As is not uncommon, perhaps on account of his own restrictions, he made sure that his children received every encouragement.

An entry in the baptismal register of Trinity College Church in Leith Wynd, now the site of Waverley Station, records: "A son born 6th May 1793 — William". William Dick's education began at the school attached to the historic Paul's Work also in Leith Wynd and later at a small school in Shakespeare Square. While still quite young he began assisting his father at his forge in White Horse Close, and here he first acquired his love for horses and a concern for the welfare of animals. His father's methods of treating horses was advanced for his time.

By 1799 the blacksmith's business had moved to Rose Street, soon afterwards to Nottingham Place and then, in 1815, the Edinburgh directory records: "Dick, John: Smith and farrier — 15, Clyde Street". William Dick had begun to look for some means of learning more of the scientific approach to animal ailments and this led him to attend the lectures of the noted Scottish anatomist and Edinburgh medical teacher, Dr John Barclay. Barclay was greatly impressed by his young pupil and indeed became Dick's staunch friend, exercising a deep influence on his ambition and development.

There were many veterinary schools in various European cities prior to 1800 and the London school had been opened in 1791. William Dick had heard about it from a friend, and in the autumn of 1817, aged 24, "he boarded the lang road coach" to the south. In London, he lived at Somer's Town. The lectures at the London Veterinary School were almost exclusively on horses and after only three months Dick felt he could be learning just as much in Edinburgh. He therefore applied to the directors of the London College for his diploma, and when this was awarded he returned to Edinburgh. Dick began giving lectures at an unfurnished shop which he rented in Nicholson Street, at that time attended by only one student, and the lecture room was illuminated by candlelight. Next he gave a series of lectures at the Calton Convening Rooms and then in the Freemasons'

Hall in Niddry Street. By 1822, wherever they might be held, an average of 20 students, frequently farmers, attended. His syllabus included: diseases of horses, black cattle, sheep and other domestic animals, illustrated by the relevant anatomical diagrams.

In 1823 formal education in veterinary science became properly established and William Dick's long struggle and efforts "in the wilderness" were more formally recognised. In that year, through the influence of his great friend and supporter, Dr John Barclay, the Highland Society gave Dick £50 to inaugurate a systematic teaching course in veterinary science. The Society also appointed a Board of Examiners and awarded certificates to successful students. By 1833 Dick's "College" had become so successful and was attracting so many students that his father's premises at No 15 Clyde Street were enlarged, at a cost ultimately of £10,000, which Dick himself bore, the Society providing £50 for furnishings and equipment. Dick was appointed the first professor. He, of course, received fees from the students, which was for him a source of income.

A description of the Clyde Street college is on record. "On entering from the street, there was delightful confusion. Skeletons of all descriptions, from horses to apes — higglety-pigglety — animal heads looking in all directions — vast quantities of diseased bone — no order — no arrangement". The former stable became a hospital. There was a lecture room, library and dissecting room. Dick and his elder sister Mary lived on an upper floor. His sister, in fact, had been Dick's most devoted supporter from the beginning. She looked after accounts, her brother being rather unconcerned about money. An austere lady of Calvinistic principles, she kept an eye on the "moral tone" of the college and "delinquent students" had to appear before her. Indeed it has been said that from the beginning until Dick's death the veterinary college was very much a joint enterprise. Even after her brother's death Mary Dick exercised an influence on the establishment he had created

Although so dedicated throughout his life to veterinary science and being single-minded in purpose, Dick in fact had wide interests and took part most vigorously in the affairs of many public bodies. He became Deacon of the Hammermen, an ancient Edinburgh craft guild, Deacon Convenor of Trades, Dean of Guild with a seat on the Town Council, a Justice of the Peace and Moderator of the High Constables. He was also involved with Heriot's Hospital and the health of Edinburgh's citizens, especially the work of the then Morningside Lunatic Asylum.

William Dick, the visionary who by taking every possible practical step was in his lifetime to see his dream become a reality, died on 4th April 1866 and was buried in the New Calton Burial Ground. In his will he vested his college in the Lord Provost and Town Council of Edinburgh as trustees. A representative board of management was later formed which continued until 1905. At that time, the Clyde Street college proving inadequate, new premises were sought. The Summerhall site was acquired in 1913. At the time of the First World War the present-day building was opened and the transfer from Clyde Street completed in 1916. This latter building which had been Dick's creation and home was demolished when the bus station was opened in St Andrew's Square. Modernisation and additional building at Summerhall in more recent times, and the opening of the Field Station and centre for Tropical Veterinary Medicine at the Bush Estate, signify the importance attached to veterinary science and the continual developments in diagnosis and research.

Very many mementoes of William Dick and his achievements remain. Most obvious is the fine stone sculpture of a horse standing prominently above the entrance to the College's out-patient department in Summerhall Square. This was transferred from the original Clyde Street premises. In the quadrangle is a stone-sculpted seated figure of the founder, while in the college entrance foyer is a fine stained-glass window in three parts: William Dick in the centre; on the left a representation of the Clyde Street College, and on the right one of the present-day college. This window was provided by students of the Clyde Street College. In 1839, at a special banquet, former students presented Dick with an epergne. He was presented with a coffee pot by the Royal Physical Society in 1851, and these items, along with a claret jug which he won in a competition of pistol shooting from horseback in 1831, Dick, as the first College principal, bequeathed for the use of his successors. They remain in the custody of the University and are still displayed on appropriate occasions.

2 · SCIENNES/ CAUSEWAYSIDE

WALTER CHEPMAN

BEFORE Sciennes was so named, Walter Chepman, with his partner Andrew Myllar, co-pioneer of printing in Scotland, was associated with the district. Indeed he is the earliest known person to merit a place in its chronicles. Myllar had been familiar with the printing trade in Rouen where he had had books printed for himself. In 1507, through the active interest of "Good Bishop Elphinstone" of Aberdeen, patron of so many new spheres of learning in his day, James IV, who also was always enthusiastic in supporting new developments, granted a royal patent to Myllar and Chepman. Attached to this privilege there was also the right to prevent the importation of books into Scotland.

Chepman was a burgess merchant in timber for ships, and in wool, cloth and velvet imported from abroad. He was the businessman in the printing partnership. Their early productions were of short pamphlets, notably of the works of Scottish and English poets, including Dunbar, Henryson and Lydgate. In 1508 they produced the first printed book in Scotland. This composite work included the famous *Lament for the Makars.* In 1509-10 Chepman published the important Aberdeen Breviary, using black and red print, a major achievement.

Walter Chepman lived from 1473 to 1538, although the exact dates are not known. One of his special enterprises was the selling of land. In 1505 he obtained the freehold of Ewerland at Cramond and also extended his dealings to Perthshire.

He enters the chronicles of South Edinburgh through his acquisition, on an unrecorded date, of Prestonfield and there are references to his having property "near the Boroughmuir". This is believed to have been a small piece of land with a house at what became Sciennes, on the site of which, in relatively recent times, rather appropriately, were built the premises of Bertrams Ltd, manufacturers of paper-making machinery.

Seal of Walter Chepman

13

Chepman's principal residence was at the top of Blackfriars Wynd and the printing presses used by Myllar and himself were at the lower end of this street. In his latter years, he gave up printing to concentrate on his trading as a merchant. In 1513, the year of Flodden, and James IV's death in that tragic battle, Chepman erected an aisle on the south side of St Giles. Fifteen years later he erected a mortuary chapel in St Giles' graveyard in which prayers were to be constantly said for the soul of his friend and royal patron James and his faithful subjects slain at Flodden. Chepman himself was interred in the aisle which he had built. Since no portrait of him could be traced, the illustration is of his printer's seal.

LADY JANET HEPBURN

SCIENNES, in early documents spelt "Sheens", takes its name from Scienne, the French version of Sienna, or Siensis, the Latin form, used for the convent established in the district in 1517 and dedicated to St Catherine of Sienna. The year of the convent's origin has historical significance. It was one of the many consequences, albeit indirect, of Scotland's disastrous defeat at Flodden on 9th September 1513. Details of the decimation of the Scottish army under James IV are only too well known. Not only did the most fascinating and enigmatic of the Stuart kings fall in the battle, so too did bishops, including James' natural son, the Archbishop of St Andrews, abbots, thirteen earls, fifteen lords, and numerous clan chiefs with countless ordinary men,

"the Floers o' the Forest". It was as a consequence of the large number of the nobility who did not return that the convent at Sciennes was built.

Very many titled ladies were thus left widows, notably of the families of Angus, Douglas of Glenbervie, Lauder of the Bass, Auchinleck, Bellenden and Seton. It was the widow of the last, Lady Janet Hepburn, eldest daughter of Patrick, first Earl of Bothwell and widow of George, fifth Lord Seton, who was primarily responsible for establishing the convent, and with other ladies of similar rank, became the first sisters to enter. Sir Richard Maitland in his *History of the House of Seton* describes Lady Janet Hepburn's part in the foundation. Written in Scots, his own words best sum up the story.

"George Seton was bot five yeiris Lord and was slane in the feild of Flowdoune and was brocht hame furth of the said feild and erdit (buried) in the queir (choir) of Seytoun, besyd his fader". Seton chapel, now known as Seton Collegiate Church, is near Tranent in East Lothian. "Efter his deceis, his ladye remanit widow continualie IV years. She was ane nobile and wyse ladie. Sche gydit her sonnis quill he was cumit to age and thair efter sche passit and remanit in the place of Senis, on the Burrow Mure, besyd Edinburgh. Quhilk place sche helpit to and big (build) as maist principale. She did mony guid acts.".

Maitland continues, describing how Lady Hepburn had waited until her other children were married or their future ensured before she became a sister at Sciennes. "She leiffit to gud age and deit in the yeir of God 1558 in the said place of Senis, her body was transportit honorablie, and was bureit in the cheir (choir) of Seytoun besyd her husband. The cause that I set furth, the speciall actis and deidis of this ladie is to gif occasioun till all ladyis in tyme to cum that happinis to be in the said hous, or ony other hous, to follow the said Ladie in honest conversation and chastity: and in kyndness and liberalitie to the hous to which they are allied and have thair leving".

Such appears to have been the character of Lady Janet Hepburn who played a principal part in the foundation of the convent of St Catherine of Sienna in Sciennes in 1517. And perhaps it was on account of her exemplary life, and likewise of the other sisters from notable Scottish families who had joined her there, that Sir David Lyndsay in his great masterpiece of the Scottish theatre, *Ane Satyre of the Three Estates,* first performed before the Scottish Court in Linlithgow in 1540, and revived in the early and more

recent years of the Edinburgh International Festival, chose to exempt them from his strictures upon the many religious orders in Scotland which prior to the Reformation had merited severe censure and urgently required reform. No portrait of Lady Janet Hepburn could be traced but an illustration of her seal is reproduced.

PROFESSOR ADAM FERGUSON

Sciennes Hill House
All that remains of Professor Ferguson's home where young Scott met Robert Burns

Photo: Alexanders
By courtesy of Mr John G. Gray

MANY people deserving well enough in their own right to occupy a place in history have nevertheless enjoyed added fame or become much more widely known for some quite incidental reason or association with someone more famous. Professor Adam Ferguson, distinguished historian, moral philosopher, author, and one of that renowned group of *literati* of Edinburgh's 18th century "Golden Age", is a case in point. Not far from the building

Seal of Lady Janet Hepburn
From "The Convent of St Catherine of Sienna"
by George Seton

15

named after him in Edinburgh University's George Square complex, in his home, Sciennes Hill House, there took place in the winter of 1786-87 the only recorded meeting of Robert Burns and Walter Scott, who were among his guests.

To include in this collection of relatively short biographies an inevitably much abbreviated account of Professor Adam Ferguson's life and achievements would be quite inappropriate. What is presented is largely within the context of his residence in South Edinburgh and the circumstances of the historic meeting. Adam Ferguson was born on June 23rd 1723 at Logierait in Perthshire, youngest of the large family of the parish minister. From Perth Grammar School he went to St Andrews University where he specialised in classics, mathematics and metaphysics, graduating Master of Arts in 1742. Under his father's influence he then studied for the ministry at Edinburgh University. Here he became a close friend of future minister John Home, author of the controversial dramatic play *Douglas*, and of William Robertson, celebrated University Principal from 1762 until his death in 1793.

In 1745, as an ardent opponent of Prince Charles Edward Stuart and his attempt to regain the British throne for the Stuarts, Ferguson enlisted as deputy chaplain in the Black Watch. His continued army service gave rise to certain controversies. By 1754 he had abandoned the clerical profession and soon afterwards succeeded David Hume as librarian of the important Advocates Library.

Ferguson was one of several prominent Edinburgh literary figures who took part in the amateur rehearsals of Home's *Douglas* before its professional staging at the theatre in the Playhouse Close in the Canongate. The Kirk tended to regard the theatre and the influence of the Devil as synonymous so that a clergyman had committed a serious offence in writing and producing a play. However, in spite of the fierce controversy which followed the presentation of *Douglas,* Ferguson wrote a pamphlet on *The Morality of Stage Plays* in which he defended Home.

In 1759, Adam Ferguson was appointed Professor of Natural Philosophy at Edinburgh University which drew ironic comment from David Hume as regards his friend's rather rapid acquisition of a sufficient knowledge of physics. Six years later he was appointed to the Chair of Moral Philosophy, for which he was very much better qualified. Indeed his lectures on this subject, presented with great sincerity and eloquence, drew very large attendances. His *Institutes of Moral Philosophy,* published as a textbook, was highly successful and used widely in Europe and in Russia. His most famous work, *History and Termination of the Roman Republic,* illustrated with maps, in five volumes, published in 1782, and again the subject of many translations, was widely acclaimed. In 1785 Ferguson resigned the Chair of Moral Philosophy and was succeeded by Dugald Stewart, to whose vacated Chair of Mathematics he in turn was appointed.

Many publications on the Scottish Enlightenment have recently appeared, and at least one author has placed Adam Ferguson alongside his friends and contemporaries, Principal William Robertson, David Hume and Adam Smith, as the group at the centre of the 18th century "Golden Age" in Scottish letters when the country enjoyed its highest literary and artistic reputation in Europe and beyond, unequalled since.

Professor Ferguson's home in Argyle Square must have been a mecca for Edinburgh's literary coterie but especially so was the house to which he moved early in October 1786, shortly after his retirement from the Chair of Moral Philosophy. This was Sciennes Hill House, the remains of which may still be seen in Sciennes House Place, formerly Braid Place. At that time the house in Sciennes was quite remote from the city, so much so that his friends who had to make their way out to it surrounded by fields south of the Boroughloch, later the Meadows, called it "Kamchatka". This is the name of a small village on the peninsula of north-eastern Siberia discovered in 1698 and, apparently even in Edinburgh, considered synonymous with extreme remoteness and isolation. The nearest houses to Professor Ferguson's new home in Sciennes were the Grange of St Giles in Grange Loan, for some time the residence of Principal William Robertson, and the house of Lord Cockburn's father, situated in what is now Gladstone Terrace.

Perhaps Adam Ferguson preferred the remoteness of his Sciennes house as congenial to further writing, and especially perhaps for reasons of health. Until around the age of fifty he had enjoyed great conviviality of life-style and his company and his own liberal hospitality were much sought after and enjoyed by a wide circle of academic colleagues and friends. However, in his early fifties he suffered from some form of paralysis. He placed great faith, quite justifiably, in the medical advice and skill of his wife's uncle, Dr Joseph Black, distinguished physician and notable chemist with several important discoveries to his name. Ferguson returned to good health but only through adopting a quite austere life-style, becoming a vegetarian and a total abstainer, drinking only water and milk. His health, indeed, became an obsession. His paralytic illness had left him with a deep sensitivity to cold and he regulated the temperature of his house very carefully. Outdoors, and frequently indoors, he wore a fur coat and hat, and his friend and neighbour Lord Cockburn referred to him in jest as "the philosopher from Lapland".

Professor Ferguson's attire on that historic occasion in the winter of 1786-87 is not on record, when during one of his celebrated literary dinners and conversations at Sciennes Hill House, Burns and Scott met. Burns, who had only recently arrived in Edinburgh, had been brought to the gathering by Professor Dugald Stewart. Amongst the company were James Hutton, noted geologist, the Reverend John Home, author of *Douglas*, Dr Thomas Blacklock, the blind poet who encouraged young Walter Scott's excursions into Edinburgh's literary circles, and, of course, Dr Joseph Black, Ferguson's medical adviser, who was seldom far away.

The sequence of events is well known. Walter Scott was years later to describe them in a letter included in Lockhart's *Life*. "As for Burns, I may truly say, *Virgilium vidi tantum*. I was a lad of fifteen in 1786-87, when he first came to Edinburgh, but had sense and feeling enough to be much interested in his poetry, and would have given the world to know him; but I had very little acquaintance with literary people, and less with the gentry of the West Country, the two sets he most frequented. I saw him one day at the venerable Professor Ferguson's, where there were several gentlemen of literary reputation, among whom I remember the celebrated Dugald Stewart.

"Of course, we youngsters sat silent and listened. The only thing I remember which was remarkable in Burns' manner was the effect produced upon him by a print of Bunbury's, representing a soldier lying dead in the snow, his dog sitting in misery on one side; and on the other his widow, with a child in her arms. These lines were written underneath:

Cold on Canadian hills, on Minden's plain,
Perhaps that parent wept, her soldier slain
Bent o'er her babe, her eyes dissolved in dew,
The big drops mingling with the drops he drew,
Gave the sad presage of his future years,
The child in misery baptised in tears.

"Burns seemed much affected by the print, or rather the ideas which it suggested to his mind. He actually shed tears. He asked whose the lines were and it chanced that nobody but myself remembered that they occur in a half-forgotten poem of Lang-horne's called by the unpromising title of *The Justice of the Peace*. I whispered my information to a friend present, who mentioned it to Burns, who rewarded me with a look and a word, which though of mere civility, I then received and still recollect, with very great pleasure."

Another account of the incident relates that Burns fixed a look of half-serious interest on the youth (Scott was then only sixteen) while he said—"You'll be a man yet, Sir!" The historic meeting in Professor Adam Ferguson's house has been recorded for all time—at least in an imaginative reconstruction of it—in the painting by Charles Martin Hardie, R.S.A. This was not completed until nearly a century after the event, in 1887, and was first exhibited in 1894. It is not certain where the original is now. Hardie was not born until 1868 and Sciennes Hill House was converted into flats in 1867. Even if the artist had visited the original house, or rather what remained of it, in order to reconstruct the scene and the guests present, the original drawing room would have been greatly altered. Certainly in 1867 the house was almost literally turned back to front. The handsome wide flight of stairs leading to the main entrance door was removed and the door bricked up. Some of the fine moulding and other decoration on what was originally the front of the house remain. A long avenue ran due south to the house from the east end of the Meadows.

Today, entrance is given through a passage-way at No. 7 Sciennes House Place, off Causewayside, and from the back green the original frontage can still be seen. In 1926 the Sir

18

Walter Scott Club and the Edinburgh Burns Club installed a plaque which reads simply: "This tablet commemorates the meeting of Robert Burns and Sir Walter Scott which took place here in the winter of 1786-87." Those residing in the small flats into which the original house was subdivided have various relics in their rooms such as pieces of the original ceiling cornice and remains of fireplaces. With some imagination the present walls may seem to vanish, the original spacious room reappears, and figures seen and voices heard again as they were two centuries ago.

In 1795 Adam Ferguson's wife died and he moved from Sciennes Hill House to Neidpath Castle, but finding its state of disrepair rather uncongenial he removed to Hallyards nearby. Here he farmed the area for fourteen years. Perhaps there was something to be said for the austerity of life prescribed for him by Dr Joseph Black, for he lived into his ninety-third year, dying at St Andrews in February 1816, having outlived the doctor himself by seventeen years and his celebrated guest of Sciennes Hill House, Robert Burns, by twenty years. He was buried beside St Andrews Cathedral, and on the monument over his grave an elaborate inscription was composed by his other, then young and unknown, guest on that same evening who was to become the famous Sir Walter Scott.

LORD HENRY COCKBURN

AS WITH regard to several other biographies included in this volume,

Lord Henry Cockburn
by Sir Henry Raeburn R.A.

so much has been written about the persons concerned by recognised authorities and so well are they known that their inclusion here arises simply from their association with South Edinburgh. So for one of Edinburgh's great immortals, Lord Henry Cockburn.

Cockburn was born at Hope Park on the south side of the Meadows on 26th October 1779. His family home was a fine villa which stood at what today is the junction of Gladstone Terrace and Sciennes Road, approached from the Meadows by a beautiful avenue of lime, elm and horse-chestnut trees. In such most pleasant surroundings young Henry Cockburn spent his school and university student days. In his classic work on Old Edinburgh, *Memorials of His Time*, published two years after his death in 1854, there are many interesting and colourful recollections of the district in which he grew up.

19

Lord Cockburn's father, Archibald, was well known in the city and this enabled his son to visit very many interesting houses in the South Edinburgh area. He knew well and was fascinated by the atmosphere of the Grange of St Giles in Grange Loan, a house with ancient origins, which young Henry Cockburn could visit simply by crossing the open ground towards what is now Lovers' Lane, still leading to the site of the mansion house, long since gone.

Principal William Robertson of the University, who resided for some time at the Grange House (its later name), was a friend of young Cockburn's father, hence the garden was available to be explored. Sir Thomas Dick Lauder, owner of the Grange lands who had the mansion house restored by W. H. Playfair in 1827, giving it a fairy-tale castle-like appearance, was also another close friend of the Cockburn family. Henry Cockburn often joined the Dick Lauders in excursions to the Pentland Hills with breakfast at Habbie's Howe at Nine-Mile Burn. Just beyond the Grange estate was Blackford House, and Lord Cockburn was a friend and great admirer of Miss Meenie Trotter who resided there, often visiting her and paying amusing tribute to her character and eccentricities in his writings.

The last remains of the Convent of St Catherine of Sienna stood near the Cockburn family home and in open ground which in fact Cockburn's father had rented from Sir Andrew Lauder of Grange, whose land it was. References to these ruins; to his visits to Prestonfield House, whose owner Sir Alexander Dick allowed young Henry Cockburn to use his boat on Duddingston Loch; his recollections of the ruined remains of the early 16th century chapel of St Roque in the Canaan district; the heyday of George Square and Buccleuch Place as Edinburgh's fashionable quarter rivalling and then giving way to the emergence of the New Town elegance — all are but part of Lord Cockburn's fascinating, faithfully recorded recollections, interspersed with characteristic comment of the distinguished judge who included a great deal of South Edinburgh in his *Memorials.*

As Lord Cockburn gained increasing distinction in the legal world, eventually becoming Solicitor-General, he moved to the New Town and eventually to the beautifully situated Bonaly Towers on the verge of the Pentlands. It was his knowledge of and love for the pleasant amenities and architecture of South Edinburgh which developed into his wider and constant concern for the preservation of the best features of the city itself. Most appropriately he was chosen as the patron for the important and eternally vigilant association which bears his name.

THE REVEREND MOSES JOEL

SCOTLAND'S first Jewish community consisted of twenty families living in Edinburgh in 1816, who founded a "Kehillah" or Congregation of Jews. The actual beginnings of this pioneer community are obscure, since no contemporary records now remain. Early Jewish immigrants came from Russian Poland,

Reverend Moses Joel

Germany, and the Baltic ports. If records did exist concerning the origins and development of the Edinburgh community, and certain Jewish historians believe they did, they may well have been buried in a grave, as was Jewish custom, in the little Jewish cemetery in what was Braid Place, now Sciennes House Place, before it was closed in 1867, at about the time the Edinburgh congregation, then growing, were moving from their original synagogue in Richmond Court to their larger new one in Park Place. Even Jews from Glasgow were brought for burial in the little Sciennes cemetery beside the Jews Close in Causewayside where the first Edinburgh community may have originated.

In the *Edinburgh Evening Courant* of 28th September 1820, it was reported that "On Friday evening the Jews settled here commenced holding the Feast of the Tabernacles for the first time in Scotland in a temporary building near the Pleasance". This building, the first synagogue, described as being in a lane off Nicholson Street, was in Richmond Court at the corner of 22 North Richmond Street, and was opened in 1816. A writer in the *Edinburgh Evening Express* in 1883, in a historical article, indicates that the Jews may have met prior to 1816, without the aid of a minister.

Edinburgh's Jewish historians have differed as regards who was the first minister of their earliest congregation. One writer believed that the first was the Reverend Moses Joel who came to Edinburgh from London in 1816 and was in office for forty-six years. Another authority, however, was of the opinion that there was an earlier pastor, named Meir Rintel Cohen, author of various Hebrew books and something of a controversialist.

The *Edinburgh Street Directory* for 1813 lists "Moses Joel, Eating House, North Richmond Street", and for 1825: "Moses Joel, clothier, 19 Pleasance". In 1832, however, the entry after Moses Joel's name is: "Priest of the Jews". Since the directories for 1825, 1826 and 1827 also give "M. M. Rentle, Minister of the Jews' Congregation, 19 Richmond Street", it is suggested that in fact the Reverend Meir Rentle was the first duly appointed Jewish minister in Edinburgh (though his service was short, about four years) and that in 1831 he was succeeded by the Reverend Moses Joel.

21

It is believed that the Reverend Moses Joel became a teacher of Hebrew and religion to the children of Edinburgh's small Jewish community, and would have been the minister officiating at the second of the synagogues opened at Richmond Street in 1825, and thus would probably have conducted the funerals of the small number of Jews buried in the little cemetery at Sciennes.

In the Edinburgh Room of the City Public Libraries there is a collection of engravings by J. G. Howie of Edinburgh personalities, known and unknown, between 1830 and 1860. These show the costume or uniform of the period of people in various occupations, e.g. policemen, water caddies, a whey wife, etc. Amongst them is a portrait of Moses Joel with the inscription: "High Priest of Jews Preaching. Also Butcher and Baker to the Jews of Edinburgh". This illustration forms the frontispiece to the late Abel Phillips' valuable *History of the Origins of the First Jewish Community in Scotland*, Edinburgh 1816.

James Goodfellow

From booklet of Jubilee Celebrations of Newington
United Presbyterian Church, 1898
By courtesy of Mr J. R. Webster

JAMES GOODFELLOW

AROUND 1850 the Causewayside, which extended from West Preston Street to Mayfield Loan, was described by one writer as "the worst bit of Edinburgh". The fine mansion houses, villas, and the picturesque red tiled two-storey cottages with their little outside stairs, once the workshops and homes of a bustling and thriving community of weavers and other skilled craftsmen, had become deserted and the properties had deteriorated seriously. Here to this "deprived area" had come poor and often large families from houses and conditions little better in the overcrowded High Street and its adjoining closes. In Causewayside overcrowding became even more acute, and amidst unemployment with its attendant poverty and despair, leading to heavy drinking, the scene was a pathetic one. Infectious diseases spread like wildfire. At the Causewayside entrances to Salisbury Place and Duncan Street wooden barricades were erected to prevent the "undesirable elements" having any access to the fine new residential district around Minto Street and Blacket Avenue. Running battles took place between the "New Road puppies" as the Newington young people were described by their rivals, the Causewayside "keelies". The latter area had become a ghetto and its inhabitants left largely to their own devices.

Nearly a century before the significant advent of the professional community worker, the title of social worker might well have been given to a man who, certainly with no financial incentive and not at all confident in his own ability for the task, nevertheless readily moved into the challenging Causewayside scene. He was James Goodfellow and the book which he wrote, *The Print of His Shoe*, published in 1906, the year of his death, describing the district and his tireless labours there for nearly forty years, provides a unique and invaluable record of the late 19th century social history of part of southern "Old Edinburgh".

Biographical details of Mr Goodfellow himself are sparse. While his book gives a fascinating account of the Causewayside and of his work amongst the people there, it is written with characteristic self-effacement and reveals little of the author himself. Fortunately, the early records of Newington United Presbyterian Church, for which Goodfellow worked as a lay missionary, have been preserved and from these certain basic data, while scattered, can be pieced together. James Goodfellow appears to have been a native of Hawick, where he was ordained an elder of East Bank Church in 1850, and from which he carried out lay missionary work. In 1863 Newington United Presbyterian Church, then in Duncan Street, wished to appoint a missionary to work not only in Causewayside but also in the outlying hamlets of Echo

Bank, at the foot of Dalkeith Road, Powburn at the foot of Mayfield Road, Parkneuk, Greenend and Bridgend of the Inch estate near Cameron Toll—a far-flung parish. Goodfellow had previously applied for this post but had been considered to be in need of more experience. However, the man who was appointed had found the work too demanding, and in September 1863 the Newington Church board wrote to Goodfellow offering him the appointment. In November he accepted but humbly expressed his possible unsuitability and offered to come on probation. This certainly proved unnecessary. His impact on the challenging Causewayside conditions seems to have been almost immediate. And when, through ill health, he did retire after nearly forty years' service, no praise seemed too high for his work.

The "job description" given to Goodfellow on his appointment required him: "To visit for five hours per day, except Saturday, which you will be allowed for the purpose of rest and relaxation. To conduct two meetings per week in different places (including the outlying hamlets). Take charge of the mission hall and library, and report regularly to the committee". The salary fixed was £70 per annum. His removal expenses with his family from Hawick would be met. At first, lodgings were obtained for him at 3 Gladstone Terrace, though subsequently he resided at No. 4, then No. 10.

In one of the many tributes later paid to him, it was said that Goodfellow took with him into the stark realities of the Causewayside mission "something of a poet's sensitivity", and this is clearly evident in the narrative of his book, finely written. First he describes the Causewayside of former, more prosperous, days. He had visited the long-since-vacated Broadstairs House, or Wormwood Hall, a great mansion on the east side of the ancient thoroughfare to the south, a house of majestic exterior proportions and interior splendour, but by Goodfellow's time subdivided into overcrowded apartments. He provides a fascinating picture of the thriving, bustling Sciennes and Causewayside community of weavers in their picturesque two-storey red-tiled cottages — "the clanking of the looms and the whirr of the shuttles". There had been at one time four linen manufacturers with Dutch bleachers from Haarlem. Also produced in the district was plush silk for "tile hats" — their first place of manufacture in Scotland — and making of the then famous Edinburgh shawls. Leatherwork, especially harness, was yet another craft. A colourful and prosperous scene. The craftsmen, Goodfellow wrote, "were skilled and intelligent men, of good character. The masters and men resided together in the same district and the whole community had a fine spirit of neighbourhood and a high tone".

Then around 1850, there was a slump in trade and before long the once thriving work-places closed down and the craftsmen left the district. Into their empty houses came poor and often large families from other parts of Edinburgh, especially from the High Street and its adjoining congested closes. The social problems began and rapidly increased. Overcrowding, wide-spread drunkenness, unemployment, neglected children, infectious disease. In Grange Court, the opening of a slaughterhouse brought workers "of a rougher element". The Court, once with its picturesque well-kept houses of the craftsmen, rapidly deteriorated. It was here in Grange Court, with its special problems, that James Goodfellow began his work amongst twenty-nine families. A mission hall was opened in the Court and regular meetings were held for mothers, with talks on family and housekeeping problems, to help them make the most of their poor circumstances. There was a sewing and clothes-making class, a penny savings bank, a health clinic in the evenings with free medicines, under the charge of Drs Pridie, Brodie, and later Dr Catherine Urquhart. Meetings for young people and older men were also provided.

But Goodfellow's approach was not simply to wait on the people coming to the Grange Court hall and its facilities. He went out among them, into their homes in other parts of Causewayside, — about five hundred families living in Wallace's Close, Gow's Close, Stewart's Close and Amos Land. Amidst the regular epidemics of infectious disease, especially the frequently fatal typhus, only Dr Pridie and Goodfellow dared to enter the affected houses. Stewart's Close was eventually demolished in the interests of hygiene by Edinburgh's famous Medical Officer of Health, Dr Henry Littlejohn.

Goodfellow constantly attributes much of the deprivation to a vicious circle of unemployment, depressing conditions, and heavy drinking as an escape. Often the parents and

24

relatives were too drunk to attend a small child's funeral, with Goodfellow making the arrangements and being the only mourner at the grave-side. Yet in such a depressing scene he praises many of the people for their good spirit and neighbourliness. He gives numerous amusing anecdotes of the people's humour in the midst of adversity.

Again, despite the gloom and harsh realities of it all, the poetic and literary interests of Goodfellow shine through, also providing valuable historical side-lights on the district. He finds the remaining ruins in St Catherine's Place of the early 16th-century Convent of St Catherine of Sienna, which gave its name to Sciennes, reminding him of the Sisters, many from the leading aristocratic families of Scotland, going about the district and having a beneficial influence on the community of that day. He recalls Sciennes Hill House, the residence of Professor Adam Ferguson, where Robert Burns and young Walter Scott had their only recorded meeting. Indeed he remembered from his Borders childhood witnessing the funeral procession of Sir Walter Scott to Dryburgh Abbey. Visits to the empty villa at the top of what became Gladstone Terrace, once the family home of Lord Cockburn, also gave him much pleasure. The Jews Close, in which he had once worked, swept away during the building of the large police station, and the tiny Jews Cemetery are colourfully described. His book also has valuable photographs of the area.

In the conclusion of *The Print of His Shoe*, a record of his life's work in Causewayside, James Goodfellow readily records his failures but, with modesty, also his many successes. Undoubtedly, this man who undertook the work only on a probationary basis and continued for nearly forty years, had a tremendous impact. While he attributes his successes to the response of the people and to his prayers, his sincerity, courage, perseverance and charisma must have been pretty well unique.

At the Jubilee Celebrations in 1898, of Newington United Presbyterian Church, then at its new building at the corner of Grange Road and Causewayside, special tributes were paid to Goodfellow. In December of the next year he retired from active work, but still gave much support to the Mission, although suffering from "physical weakness". He died in June 1906. The church's offer to Goodfellow's daughter, his long and active supporter, then residing at 3 Gladstone Terrace, to defray the funeral expenses was graciously declined. The place of this great man's burial is not on record.

ELIZA WIGHAM

Miss Eliza Wigham (left) with her sister, Mrs Edmundson

25

IN the middle of last century many members of Edinburgh's community of the Society of Friends rendered great service in various spheres of public life, especially amongst the socially deprived. A lady of a notable Quaker family, Miss Eliza Wigham, was one of James Goodfellow's closest and most valued collaborators in his missionary labours amongst the people of Sciennes and Causewayside, and Goodfellow provides an illustration of her in his book *The Print of His Shoe*. The late Edinburgh Bailie, Elizabeth M. Mein, compiled valuable notes on Miss, Wigham, who was involved in many of the important national and indeed world issues of her day and yet who still gave of her time to work in "the worst bit of Edinburgh".

Eliza Wigham was born in Edinburgh in 1820. Her father, whose family had their origins in Cornwood in Northumberland, had been converted to Quakerism. He was a shawl maker with premises in Sciennes alongside others of the same trade or who carried on other forms of weaving. In the early 19th century, Edinburgh shawls were quite famous and much in demand. In 1816, John Wigham gained the highest award and a sum of £30 from the Scottish Board for the Encouragement of Manufacturers for his production of shawls of Indian design. He and other members of his family in this trade were websters, as weavers were named, and there are references to their craft in the proceedings of the Incorporation of Trades of Edinburgh. John Wigham's address in 1851 was No. 10 Salisbury Road and in this year, on the basis of his Quaker principles, he published a paper calling for the enlightened treatment of juvenile delinquents. His concern about this problem may well have resulted from his working in Causewayside where, from its reputation at that time, the issue would have been very real.

Miss Eliza Wigham was obviously greatly influenced by her father's concern with social problems. She was deeply involved in the anti-slavery movement and was a close friend of the notable English Quaker, Lady Elizabeth Fry, and many of the other prominent leaders in the movement in Britain and the United States. Florence Nightingale was another of her close friends. A strong supporter of the women's suffragette cause, she believed that Christians should become deeply involved in politics, bringing their principles to bear on the important issues of the day. She was concerned with medical treatment for women and a staunch supporter of Dr Sophia Jex-Blake, pioneer in the campaign for the admission of women to graduation in medicine.

Among the many activities promoted by James Goodfellow to assist the families in the Causewayside district to retain their dignity and indeed rise above the hardships of their environment were meetings for mothers, with classes in what would now be termed "home economics", and also the establishment in 1859 of a "Penny Savings Bank" to encourage thrift even among poor people, enabling them to pay their rent, purchase clothing and other necessities. Miss Wigham was in charge of many of these activities for nearly forty years. Her organisation of "trips" to the country for mothers and their children were eagerly looked forward to, and partly paid for from their modest savings. Roslin and Cramond were popular venues.

Miss Wigham's home at No. 5 South Gray Street, where she lived with her step-mother, was a hospitable centre for the distressed and the homeless, with people constantly calling day and night for help. There was deep regret among the people of Causewayside and Sciennes when, in 1897, she announced her retirement, due to ill-health. After having spent nearly seventy-six years of her life in Edinburgh, and for more than half of it with a deep commitment to the Causewayside Mission, Miss Wigham went to live with her sister in Dublin. There she died on 3rd November 1899. At a meeting of the Session of Newington United Presbyterian Church a week later, the news of her death caused a deep sense of loss, and the highest tributes were paid to her memory.

Robert Middlemass

By courtesy of the late Mr George E. Cramb

ROBERT MIDDLEMASS

FOR just over a century, the most prominent and familiar landmark in Causewayside was the large factory of Robert Middlemass & Son Ltd, the celebrated biscuit and cake manufacturers, which extended along Salisbury Place to Upper Gray Street. While other long-established firms in the area, notably printers such as Ballantyne, Banks, and Neill, had at various times closed down, Middlemass remained in business until 1974. In 1983 the vacated factory which for some time had housed the National Library of Scotland's Map Section was partially demolished to make way for the erection of the Scottish Science Reference Library, part of the National Library. Only Messrs John Bartholomew & Son Ltd, the world-famous firm of cartographers, a short distance off Causewayside in Duncan Street, still continue the district's manufacturing traditions.

Robert Middlemass, founder of the biscuit firm, was born in Peebleshire in 1819 and began work as an apprentice baker when only twelve years of age. After training in Edinburgh and London he returned to Edinburgh and in 1853 started a business in partnership with Robert MacKenzie in premises at the north corner of West Preston Street and Clerk Street. There biscuits were made by hand. In 1869 Mr Middlemass, by then the sole proprietor, built a small factory at the north-west end of Upper Gray Street around which the larger premises were eventually built. A number of small villas in the immediate vicinity were purchased and demolished. In 1892 Middlemass was involved in negotiations with the city authorities concerning the widening of Salisbury Place to permit increasing traffic.

Biscuit making in Edinburgh originated with the manufacture of the large substantial "ships biscuit" by a firm in Leith. At Causewayside Robert Middlemass began to introduce sophisticated products and to achieve fame and added prosperity with his "Albert Biscuit" during Queen Victoria's reign. The firm also proudly claimed to have "invented" the widely popular "Digestive Biscuit", which became an almost worldwide household name. From the original hand-making processes at West Preston Street the greatly improved facilities at Causewayside permitted great advancements in baking methods, and production was vastly increased.

Robert Middlemass died in 1904, aged 85. The family home was a large villa at No. 12 Dalrymple Crescent. In the records of Newington United Presbyterian Church, when situated in Duncan Street and eventually at the west corner of Grange Road and Causewayside, there are many references to the practical interest taken by members of the Middlemass family in the welfare of the people living in the late 19th century conditions of great poverty and hardship in Causewayside, and their generous financial support of many enterprises to improve the quality of life in the area.

3 · NEWINGTON

DR BENJAMIN BELL

IN the history of the Newington district of South Edinburgh, Dr Benjamin Bell merits a special place. Not only was he a surgeon of great distinction, but it was he who initiated and planned the development of Newington within relatively modern times as a most pleasant residential area.

Benjamin Bell was born on April 6th 1749, in Blacket House in the parish of Middlebie in Dumfriesshire. His parents came of several generations of farmers and landowners in the area. They were of

Dr Benjamin Bell medallion after James Tassie dated 1792

By courtesy of National Galleries of Scotland, Edinburgh

Covenanting stock, and noted for their longevity, one of Bell's forebears having reputedly lived to the age of 116. Some of the family had been doctors. Bell was the eldest son in a family of fifteen. At Dumfries Grammar School he showed great promise, and on leaving became apprenticed to Mr James Hall, a local surgeon.

In 1766 Benjamin Bell came to Edinburgh University to study medicine, then carried out in the old Royal Infirmary in Drummond Street and in the surgical hospital in nearby High School Yards. He was appointed a dresser in the Infirmary in 1767. During his medical studies Bell was the pupil, and eventually the colleague, of many of the famous teachers, notably Professor Alexander Monro, *secundus,* in anatomy, and Dr William Cullen in the Practice of Medicine, who were among those to earn world renown for Edinburgh's medical school in the early 19th century, and in turn to be duly enhanced by Bell's own reputation.

In 1771 Bell sought his parents' approval and financial support for two years' study of surgery in London and Paris, writing that while training to be a clinician in Edinburgh was excellent, in surgery wider experience was essential. On his return to Edinburgh he gained the Fellowship of the Royal College of Surgeons and obtained a post in the Royal Infirmary where he remained for twenty-nine years. Dr Bell has been described as "the 'first (foremost) operator of his time". His

29

skilled services were in great demand, in the hospital and privately, in Scotland and elsewhere in Europe. He was one of the first to seek some means of anaesthesia, sixty years before Sir James Simpson's historic discovery of the powers of chloroform. Bell's *System of Surgery*, in six volumes, was a major work and translated into French and German.

The wealth that accrued to Bell from his profession was considerably enhanced by his inheritance of property and land in Dumfriesshire. He was a great humanitarian and in his medical practice gave the utmost attenion to every patient regardless of class. Frequently at the end of a long working day he would climb high tenement stairs to visit poor patients in their homes. As a teacher he had the art of making less distinguished colleagues think they were instructing him. He also took an active interest in the fair treatment of those employed in his inherited Dumfriesshire properties. In 1775 he married Miss Grizel Hamilton, of a notable and influential family. He had a succession of residences in Edinburgh, including ones at Niddry's Wynd and Nicholson Street, and he also acquired the estate of Hunthill in the Borders.

Bell never lost his boyhood love of the countryside and especially of horse-riding. His letters frequently acknowledge the arrival of another horse from Dumfriesshire. In the same year as his marriage, he was thrown from his horse and seriously injured. He made a partial recovery under the skilled care of his great friend and colleague, the much loved Dr Alexander ("Lang Sandy") Wood, who had once treated Sir Walter Scott for his lameness. Bell's love of riding was now confined to being driven into the city from Liberton farm, which he had rented, in a stately carriage. *En route*, even by the light of the oil lamps, his ever active mind was engaged in reading or writing articles, often on agricultural topics, which he addressed to members of Parliament. At the height of his career he was offered a baronetcy, which he declined.

In 1778 Bell was appointed surgeon to George Watson's Hospital in Lauriston. Five years later he suffered a serious deterioration in health, and although largely housebound he devoted his still active mind to property development. In August 1803 he obtained the feu charter for the entire, and yet undeveloped, lands of Newington and began to sub-feu these for the building of high quality villas with specially preserved amenities. He built Newington House in Blacket Avenue as his own residence, and he died there on April 8th 1806, being buried in Canongate Kirkyard.

Benjamin Bell's son, George, continued the development of Newington begun by his father. When building was completed on the east side of Minto Street, the streets enclosing Newington House were named Blacket Avenue and Blacket Place, to commemorate Benjamin Bell's birthplace, as also was Middleby Street. Bell merited inclusion in *Kay's Portraits*. He was the great-grandfather of Dr Joseph Bell, another Edinburgh surgeon of note, one of whose pupils was Arthur Conan Doyle who, it is said, was so impressed by his teacher's eloquence and keen powers of perception and diagnostic skill that he used him as the prototype for his creation, Sherlock Holmes.

Dr ROBERT KNOX

A simple memorial stone is placed on Robert Knox's grave in Brookwood Cemetery, Woking, by a group of Edinburgh medical men just over a century after his burial

Photograph by courtesy of Professor Eric Mekie F.R.S.(E)

WHILE in the early decades of the 19th century an increasing number of professional people were bringing an air of finesse and culture to the rapidly developing Newington district, one such resident in No. 4 (now No. 17) Newington Road rather surprisingly perhaps, and a little out of keeping with his neighbours' life style, was providing a link between this respectable southern suburb and one of the seamiest, sleaziest areas of old Edinburgh. This was Dr Robert Knox, whose name is forever associated with the notorious West Port murderers, Burke and Hare.

To all appearances Knox would seem to have brought considerable distinction and graciousness to life in Newington. He was a most competent anatomist and became the foremost lecturer on the subject in Edinburgh, at its extra-mural medical school. After a period abroad as an army surgeon, he returned to Edinburgh and in 1823 was elected a Fellow of the Royal Society of Edinburgh, becoming two years later a Fellow of the Royal College of Surgeons of Edinburgh. He acted as curator of the College's museum of comparative anatomy and pathology, to which he donated many items brought back from his travels abroad. In his leisure time Knox was a most hospitable and entertaining host. A devotee of the arts of painting and music, he gave dinner and evening parties in excellent style. An attractive and even quite fascinating personality, a noted social success, it was said of him: "Knox at home was Knox triumphant".

But Knox was not always at home in Newington. Perhaps he was most truly himself in his other home — his lecture and dissecting rooms in the original Surgeons' Square at High School Yards, in the house he had acquired from his former great mentor and friend, Dr John Barclay. This house, long since demolished, was the scene of Knox's brilliant lectures to his admiring students who crowded the lecture rooms. While steady and indeed dramatic progress was being made in the training of medical students in Edinburgh with its world renown in this sphere, many

Dr Robert Knox

Photograph by David Octavius Hill and Robert Adamson
By courtesy of National Galleries of Scotland,
Edinburgh

32

anatomists (and Knox was certainly one of them) felt that very much more progress could be made with special relevance to and consequent advancement in surgical techniques, if one urgent need were met, — the availability of many more fresh bodies for dissection. Such as were legally available were limited in number, and in Edinburgh went to the University's Professor of Anatomy who had the bodies preserved in spirit and used very carefully and many times over. Very much aware of this need for more fresh corpses and of the financial gain involved were the "Resurrectionists", who stole newly-buried bodies from their graves and sold them to the anatomists.

On 29th November 1827, in a lodging-house in Tanner's Close in Edinburgh's West Port (the Close has long since gone to make way for government offices), an old man called Donald died. He owed £4 rent to his landlord William Hare. Determined to recover his money, Hare persuaded another lodger, William Burke, to help him take old Donald's body to Surgeons' Square, where it was hoped Dr Monro, the University Professor of Anatomy, would purchase it for his dissections. However, Burke and Hare were misdirected, or perhaps not really so, by a student who sent them instead to Dr Knox's premises in the same Square. Knox paid £7.50 for the precious cargo and promised the same rate for any others available.

No doubt back in the West Port lodging-house, or at a local hostelry, while celebrating their little windfall, Burke and Hare considered future possibilities. The "Resurrectionist" approach they felt was rather tedious and a little risky. They could meet Dr Knox's needs more directly and rapidly. Hence began the infamous series of murders, sixteen in all. Their method was one which resulted in little evidence for suspicion. Selecting their victims, the partners plied them with ample drink, part of the capital outlay which eventually made death by smothering quite simple. Their victims were mainly, but not all, old and infirm people. The regular delivery to Surgeon's Square began. Dr Knox himself did not actually receive the bodies. This was done by his colleague Dr William Ferguson (later to become President of the Royal College of Surgeons of London). Burke and Hare were duly paid cash on delivery. No doubt Knox's anatomical dissection lessons became much more instructive and realistic.

Supplies might have continued regularly and indefinitely. But on Halloween 1828, the dedication of the two gentlemen from the West Port was just a little too much. A passer-by heard cries of "Murder! Murder!" from one of the closes. It was no Halloween guiser's cry or hoax. The police were informed. In due course the body of a lady, Margaret Docherty, was found, newly unpacked from a box, in Dr Knox's dissecting rooms. Burke and Hare were arrested, along with their accomplice, Helen McDougal, Burke's common-law wife. The trial took place in December 1828. It was headline news. Hare turned King's Evidence and for him and Helen McDougal, the verdict was "Not Proven". Both eventually made their way to England. Burke was condemned to death and was hanged near St Giles Cathedral on 29th

January 1829, before a vast and angry crowd, estimated at nearly 30,000.

During Burke's appearance on the scaffold, the great crowd roared out for the others they considered also to be guilty—"Hare! Hare! Bring out Hare", and "Hang Knox! Hang noxious Knox!" But only Burke paid the supreme penalty for his part in the West Port murders. The Edinburgh populace's angry mood remained smouldering for some time afterwards. There was a distinct anti-medical feeling, but this was directed specifically at Robert Knox, and on February 12th, just two weeks after Burke's death, a great mob indeed surrounded Knox's house in Newington Road. They threw a barrage of stones at the doorway and then hanged an effigy of the anatomist, believing that he deserved the same fate as Burke. Failing to tear the effigy to pieces, they set it alight. Before they could storm the house and lay hands on Knox, he had escaped by the back door, disguised, and sought refuge with friends elsewhere in the city.

But if Knox escaped the mob's vengeance he could not so easily escape the spotlight and publicity constantly directed on him. The Edinburgh *Evening Courant* considered him a guilty accomplice of Burke and Hare. Lord Cockburn, who had been a counsel in the trial fully defended and vindicated the anatomist's "most proper behaviour". Sir Walter Scott, however, accused him of "trading deep in human flesh" and avoided every occasion of being in his company. Eventually Knox was acquitted by a special committee which exonerated him from any

knowledge of how Burke and Hare had acquired the bodies which they had supplied but considered that he should have tried to find out! Nevertheless he never really shook off the stigma of it all. He was the subject of insulting caricatures and cartoons. Despite all this, his great reputation as an anatomist and brilliant teacher remained. In the spring following the Burke and Hare trial, 504 students enrolled for his classes, the highest number ever. With his brother, John Frederick, he even bought a large rorqual whale which had been washed ashore at North Berwick, and together they dissected and studied it. The skeleton may now be seen in the Royal Scottish Museum in Chambers Street, Edinburgh.

After a number of unsuccessful attempts to obtain a University professorship and to uphold his reputation, his long-standing enmity towards the University authorities went against him and he steadily lost face. His wife died in childbirth and he was shattered, although a great deal of assistance in his entertaining and social life in fact had come from his sister. His four-year-old son died of scarlet fever and this drove him into deeper despair. His classes began to attract fewer students. He fell heavily into debt. He travelled in the north of England but his anti-Semitic views caused trouble. The Royal Society of Edinburgh struck him off their roll. In 1856 he obtained a London post at the Cancer Hospital in Brompton and settled in Hackney with his sister. Despite so much failure, his strong personality made him very popular and won him many London friends. On 20th December 1862 he died from an attack of apoplexy. As he had wished, he was buried in Brookwood cemetery, Woking, in Surrey. But, although over thirty years had passed since the Burke and Hare trial and the sensation of that time, Robert Knox's grave remained unmarked. It was all, even then, still too much within living memory for his body to rest undisturbed. Just over a century later, in May 1966, a group of members of Edinburgh's Royal College of Surgeons led by Professor Eric Mekie, Knox's successor as Curator of the College's important museum, gathered at the Woking grave and a commemorative tablet of Aberdeen granite was placed there, simply inscribed, "Robert Knox. Anatomist. 1791-1862." Seldom behind so few words can such a sensational story have been concealed.

EUGENE MARIE CHANTRELLE

FORTY years after Dr Robert Knox had escaped from the angry mob surrounding his house at Newington Road, chanting their angry accusations that he was equally to blame with Burke and Hare for the infamous West Port murders, the district (indeed the same street) was again to be associated with a murder trial, described in the legal records as "one occupying a conspicuous position in the annals of Scottish criminal justice" — and surely also one of the saddest. This was the case of Eugene Marie Chantrelle, found guilty and hanged for the murder by poisoning of his wife, the former

Elizabeth Dyer, a pupil of Newington Academy at 3 Newington Road.

Eugene Marie Chantrelle was born in Nantes in 1834. His father, a wealthy shipowner, had provided the son with an excellent preliminary education, followed by a course at Nantes Medical School. Forced to give up the latter due to his father's bankruptcy, though managing to continue studying medicine at Strasbourg and Paris, Chantrelle did not qualify as a doctor. He had become very politically involved as a Communist and had unsettled views about his future. He moved to America for a few years, and then, in 1862, came to England, proving

M. Eugene Chantrelle
photograph c. 1867

From " Trial of Eugene Marie Chantrelle" (notable Scottish Trials). Edited by A. Duncan Smith

himself a proficient teacher of French at Newcastle, Leicester, and other large cities. In 1866 he arrived in Edinburgh, succeeding a Monsieur Fourby as a French tutor and soon gaining a high reputation as a linguist and a man of considerable culture and polished manner, not to mention a most handsome appearance. His text-books in French were widely adopted and his teaching of Latin, German and Greek was also highly praised.

One of Chantrelle's teaching commitments was at Newington Academy, a private school at No. 3 Newington Road. Here an acquaintanceship began with one of his pupils, Elizabeth Cullen Dyer, aged fifteen, whose house was at 5 Buccleuch Place, then a quite fashionable street. Their relationship deepened and Elizabeth Dyer became pregnant. Then aged sixteen, she reluctantly agreed to marry Chantrelle. The marriage took place on 11th August 1868. It was said that never was a sadder story of married life related to a court of justice.

The first of their four children was born two months after the wedding and already, at their home at 81a George Street, Chantrelle had begun to treat his young wife with unkindness, infidelity, and indeed violence, which were to become steadily worse. During his assaults, the police were called on several occasions. Increasingly his wife sought refuge with her children at her mother's house. Any possibility of suing for a divorce she dismissed on account of the scandal this would cause—certainly very likely to be so in 19th-century Edinburgh — and also because she felt too sensitive and was concerned for the children's sake.

Chantrelle's drinking was now seriously affecting his teaching performance and his class attendances dwindled steadily, with consequent loss of income. Heavy debt became an increasingly serious problem. He now faced an urgent financial crisis. On many occasions he had threatened his wife with poisoning, boasting that he could use a foolproof method beyond police detection. Originally these were perhaps just idle threats under the influence of drink; now another factor accentuated their possibility: his increasing debt and precarious financial situation. He needed to obtain money urgently.

In October 1877 Chantrelle insured his wife for £1,000, then quite a considerable sum. He took special care to obtain a policy according to which the benefits would be paid only as a result of accidental death. He took great pains to be clear as to what this would involve. His wife was opposed to the insurance policy on her life — perhaps indeed because she was suspicious. But the policy was duly taken out. Little time was to elapse before its benefits were being claimed.

On New Year's Day 1878 the Chantrelle family were at home. Their servant, Mary Byrne, who had been on holiday, returned to the house at 10 p.m. She was called by Madame Chantrelle who was in bed with her baby beside her. Complaining of feeling unwell, she asked the servant for a drink of lemonade and orange. She then seemed to settle down for the night. Early next morning the servant heard sounds of moaning from her mistress's room. Entering, she found her unconscious and groaning loudly. Eugene Chantrelle came into the room and remarked to the servant about a strong smell of gas and the former turned off the supply tap. Chantrelle himself then went to call Dr Carmichael, the family doctor. After examining Madame Chantrelle, Dr Carmichael sent for Dr Henry Littlejohn, Edinburgh's medical Officer of Health, who was also the police surgeon and an expert toxicologist. On his arrival, Dr Littlejohn was informed of the gas leakage, by Eugene Chantrelle, who probably suggested it as the cause of his wife's condition.

Madame E. Chantrelle
(née Elizabeth Cullen Dyer)

From "Trial of Eugene Marie Chantrelle (Notable
Scottish Trials). Edited by A. Duncan Smith

Madame Chantrelle still remained unconscious and her mother, who was sent for, agreed that she should be taken to the Royal Infirmary. On arrival there she was examined by Professor Douglas MacLafan, who held the University Chair in Medical Jurisprudence (or Forensic Medicine). Professor MacLagan confirmed the view already held by Dr Henry Littlejohn that the patient's symptoms were not of gas poisoning but of narcotic poisoning. Madame Chantrelle died on the afternoon of 2nd January 1878 without having regained consciousness. The Procurator-Fiscal was informed and next day he ordered that a post-mortem examination be performed. The result of this showed no evidence of gas poisoning but neither did it show any trace in the body of narcotic poison. All chemical tests for the presence of poisons were negative and these results were confirmed by the two authorities, Professor Alexander Crum Brown, in chemistry, and Professor Fraser. However, although no evidence was found in the body, opium was detected in the vomit stains found on Madame Chantrelle's nightdress and the bed sheets.

Madame Chantrelle was buried in Grange Cemetery on 5th January 1878, her grave being unmarked. During the burial ceremony Eugene Chantrelle showed great emotional distress. After the funeral, he was arrested and taken to Calton Jail. The charge was that on 1st or 2nd January 1878 he did murder his wife at their home in George Street by the administration of opium in orange juice and lemonade. Parliament Square was crowded on 7th May 1878, when Chantrelle's trial began under Lord Justice Clerk Moncrieff. It lasted four days, three being taken up by the hearing of evidence and the fourth by the concluding speeches and pronouncement of the verdict. There were 115 witnesses. A full account of the proceedings was eventually published with specially detailed reports of the crucial medical and scientific evidence of the experts called for the prosecution. The latter's principal case was the finding of opium in the vomit stains in Madame Chantrelle's night-clothes, along with the testimony of so many witnesses of the accused's frequent threats to poison his wife and his generally aggressive behaviour towards her. He pleaded "Not guilty" to the major charges; his defence was conducted by Mr Trayner. The accused's submission that his wife had died from gas poisoning from a fractured pipe in her bedroom was quickly dismissed, from the reports by two gas fitters who had examined the room. Defence argued strongly that no trace of poison was found in Madame Chantrelle's body and that the presence of opium stains on the bed-clothes was not proof that her husband had administered this to her. Indeed a strongly supported public memorandum to this effect and alleging lack of conclusive evidence in the prosecution's case was submitted to the Home Secretary after Chantrelle had been sentenced.

On Friday 10th May the jury, after just over one hour's deliberation, returned a unanimous verdict of "Guilty". After the judge had passed sentence of death, Chantrelle disputed the evidence with him. He no longer adhered to his original submission that his wife had died accidentally from gas poisoning but rather asserted that a third party had placed the opium stains on the bedclothes in order to incriminate him. He gave notice that he would appeal to the Home Secretary. The judge having confirmed the sentence of death by hanging, the date of execution was fixed as May 31st 1878.

In prison Chantrelle remained cool and indifferent. A visit from Dr William Smith, the priest in charge of the Roman Catholic St Mary's Cathedral in Broughton Street, was rejected, the prisoner asserting his Huguenot upbringing. Dr Smith therefore recommended that the Reverend George Wilson of the Tolbooth Parish Church should visit Chantrelle. The latter was greatly impressed by Mr Wilson, who began to visit him several times a day. The prisoner's request to see his children was not granted. The day before his execution the Reverend Wilson spent much time with Chantrelle and indeed was permitted to remain with him overnight. Talking late into the night, the Frenchman's whole manner changed from his original callousness and bravado to an acceptance of Mr Wilson's spiritual guidance. He confessed to a life of constant struggle of conscience and expressed a desire to reject his atheistic beliefs and to return to the simple Christian faith of his boyhood. In a long statement prepared for Mr Wilson he wrote that, faced with the reality of death, philosophy and science brought him no peace of mind. He proclaimed his gratitude to Mr Wilson and wrote that anyone who was aware of the deep love he had for his children would understand that he could not have murdered their mother. He wished his children to be told emphatically that this was so and that he was innocent.

On May 31st 1878, as morning broke over Edinburgh, a great crowd gathered on Calton Hill, looking towards the buildings of the jail and hoping for a glimpse of something happening. At 7 a.m. Chantrelle had a light breakfast which he apparently enjoyed and then was allowed to smoke. At 7.45 a.m. he bade Mr Wilson farewell and the witnesses who were required to be present during Chantrelle's last minutes were greatly impressed by his attitude of calm. He was dressed in a morning suit. There were several Bible readings, which he listened to attentively. Mr Wilson then appealed to Chantrelle to make any final statement which he might wish. Witnesses eagerly awaited a confession of guilt. But this was not made, nor was it so in a long written statement he had given to Mr Wilson. Eugene Chantrelle unflinchingly entered the scaffold. During the recital of the Lord's Prayer there was the click of the trap-door opening and within one minute Chantrelle was pronounced dead. A plaster cast of his head was taken for study and placing in the Phrenological Museum. The first person to have been executed in the Calton Jail, Eugene Marie Chantrelle, was buried within its precincts. Mrs Dyer, Chantrelle's mother-in-law, eventually moved to a house in South Gray Street and his son for many years was manager of a tobacconist's shop in Edinburgh, under an assumed name.

WILLIAM BLACKWOOD

IN 1942, W. Forbes Gray, an authority on the historical development of South Edinburgh, contributed a most valuable article in *The*

Book of the Old Edinburgh Club. Vol. 24, entitled: "The Lands of Newington and their Owners". In this he stated that, initially at any rate, Newington became the residential area associated with "the merchant class... pre-eminently the habitation of the prosperous business man. It has had relatively few notable residents, by which is meant those who have made distinctive reputations in literature, science and art, or any of the public services... Professional people having chosen to dwell either north or west of Princes Street". However true this description may have been, perhaps in the district's earliest days, certainly by the beginning of the 19th century, an increasing number of professional people were coming to reside in the area and indeed before long their number was quite remarkable, each contributing to the literary, artistic or public life of the city and beyond. Certainly a quite notable example of such was William Blackwood, founder of the famous publishing firm of that name, who came to reside in Salisbury Road from 1805 until 1830.

William Blackwood was born in Edinburgh in November 1776, of parents of quite modest background who nevertheless ensured his sound education. At the age of fourteen he became apprenticed to Bell and Bradfute, well-known publishers. Six years later Mundell & Co., booksellers, appointed him to take charge of their Glasgow branch. William Blackwood then spent some time in London, increasing his experience in bookselling, and, having acquired a little capital, returned to Edinburgh in 1804 and opened a shop in the South Bridge, specialising in second-hand and antiquarian books. Soon he became most prominent in the second-hand book trade in Scotland. In 1812 he issued his celebrated catalogue of more than 15,000 books in various languages and the first such classified catalogue in Scotland.

William Blackwood

By 1810 Blackwood had already become involved in publishing, and with Sir David Brewster he pioneered the foundation of *The Edinburgh Encyclopædia*. His most successful early publication was the *Life of John Knox,* issued in 1811, and destined to become a minor classic among standard works. It was written by a Newington resident who lived nearby, one Dr Thomas McCrie. Through Blackwood's influence, it was said, McCrie was awarded a Doctorate of Divinity by Edinburgh University. This was a most unusual distinction, since the recipient was not a minister of the established Church of Scotland.

As the Edinburgh agent of John Murray, the London publisher, Blackwood published Sir Walter Scott's first series of *Tales of My Landlord.* With some support from Murray's literary adviser, Gifford, Blackwood proposed an alteration to Scott's *The Black Dwarf,* which the author indignantly rejected.

In 1816, Blackwood's long-standing ambition to concentrate entirely on publishing led him to leave his South Bridge shop for new premises in the New Town. There he began to build what became a historic and famous publishing house. Edinburgh in the early 19th century was noted for its plethora of newspapers and magazines, *The Edinburgh Review* being especially influential. Blackwood and some of his friends decided to publish yet another review with a different literary and political standpoint. Blackwood's *The Edinburgh Monthly Magazine* first appeared in April 1817. The initial editorial policy, however, was not successful and the new magazine ceased publication. In October of the same year it reappeared as *Blackwood's Edinburgh Magazine* under the publisher's own editorship and this time it met with great success. Thus the famous *Blackwood's Magazine* or "The Maga", as it was familiarly known, was born. It soon earned a high reputation throughout the United Kingdom, and survived more than a century and a half.

Many new and important writers were discovered and became established through their first appearance in *Blackwood's Magazine*, and work initially published in the magazine duly appeared in book form. An important group of Edinburgh writers developed around Blackwood, of which Professor John Wilson ("Christopher North") and John Gibson Lockhart were the leaders. It was Blackwood who first published John Galt's work. In 1818 he took the risk of bringing to light the talent of an Edinburgh lady novelist — hailed as "Scotland's Jane Austen" — who had been working on the manuscript of a novel in the oak-panelled study of the then remote South Edinburgh mansion-house, East Morningside House. This was Susan Ferrier, whose first novel *Marriage* was initially published anonymously and became widely acclaimed. Blackwood's original meagre offer to Miss Ferrier of £150 for the copyright had been readily accepted. As regards her second work, *The Inheritance*, published in 1824, however, some more astute bargaining took place and the publisher had to pay £1,500. Ironically this second novel was less well received than her first.

Despite his extremely busy literary life, William Blackwood still found time to devote much valuable service to Edinburgh Town Council. Lockhart described the highly successful Edinburgh publisher in his heyday amongst "the literary loungers" patronising his Princes Street shop as "nimble, active-looking, with a most sanguine complexion — the grey eyes and eyebrows full of locomotion. Nothing can be more sagacious than the expression of his whole physiognomy".

William Blackwood died on 16th September 1834, aged fifty eight. During a long illness he was constantly and faithfully visited by Dr D. M. Moir, physician, poet and contributor to his magazine, and his great friend and long-standing supporter "Christopher North". Blackwood was buried in Old Calton cemetery.

ROBERT KIRKWOOD

THE Edinburgh student of local history, or, in case such a phrase should seem rather pretentious or off-putting, anyone who is simply curious about or interested in the bygone days of their surrounding district — will find much of the information he seeks through many sources, but especially relevant are old maps, and indeed reference to these will frequently be found essential. In this respect Edinburgh is particularly well provided for. There are quite famous names associated with certain maps, as any member of staff in Edinburgh's Central Public Library Edinburgh Room will readily confirm, and these particular maps are frequently referred to and requests are often placed to have copies made. These include John Adair's *Map of Midlothian* of 1735, which shows so many of the districts that still bear the same names today, and Richard Cooper's *Plan of Edinburgh,* 1861, showing the early appearance of so many of today's street names. Also essential, of course, are the Ordnance Survey maps, especially that of 1852, the first to deal with South Edinburgh in fascinating detail.

Another early map which always seems to prove of very special interest in relation to the beginning of the 19th century is Robert Kirkwood's *Map of Edinburgh of 1817*. Special attention is given to it here not only on account of its own inherent interest and relevance to South Edinburgh, but also in appreciation of the privilege which the present writer enjoyed in meeting the current two generations of Kirkwoods, Mr Alisdair and his son Mr David Kirkwood, who maintain two centuries of skilled engraving, beginning with the first James Kirkwood of Perth. Also I am deeply grateful for their very special kindness and trust in permitting me to borrow the print reproduced herewith of Robert Kirkwood, the famous Edinburgh engraver and map-maker, from a miniature treasured in the family archives, along with a similar reproduction of a portrait of his wife.

Robert Kirkwood

By courtesy of the present partners Messrs. A. C. and
D. W. Kirkwood

The very important Kirkwood family business, Alexander Kirkwood and Son, goldsmiths, silversmiths and engravers, now situated in Albany Street, had its earliest origins two centuries ago with James Kirkwood who was born in Perth in 1745 and duly became a watchmaker and engraver in the Fair City. Perhaps his earliest venture into map-making was his engraving of plans of Perth in 1785 and 1792. No doubt considerable future success and prosperity might well have come to James Kirkwood had he remained in Perth and developed his business there. But in 1790 this highly skilled craftsman took what was something of a risk and set out for Edinburgh. In those days, uprooting one's home and family and moving a considerable distance away to another town was unusual, generally motivated either by deprivation and the need to find a livelihood further afield, or some sinister reason such as scandal. James Kirkwood, however was being attracted by a quite novel and exciting prospect. His setting up in Edinburgh might have gone either way: failure, alas, with no return, his boats having been burned, — or boundless opportunity and success. Happily for James Kirkwood and his descendants it proved to be the latter.

In fact, his move to Edinburgh was not entirely into the unknown. He had gone there at the strong invitation and encouragement of a prominent and shrewd Edinburgh business man of the time who very much desired to make use of his rare skills and had every confidence in them. This was Sir William Forbes, principal of a private banking house, in partnership with J. Hunter & Co. The task which Sir William Forbes had in mind for James Kirkwood, involving his special art, was the engraving of plates to be used in printing the bank notes, not only for

42

his own bank but also for other banks which were subsequently to merge into the Union Bank of Scotland in 1830. In Edinburgh, Kirkwood's premises were in the President's Stairs in Parliament Square.

While James Kirkwood therefore was mainly employed in the engraving processes required for the bank notes, his son Robert, born in 1774, became his partner in 1799, and in 1801 they together engraved Forrest's large map of Hadding-ton. In 1804 they published a *Travelling Map of Scotland* and then from 1815 to 1829, several plans of Edinburgh, the most interesting, perhaps, being their *Plan and Elevation of the New Town of Edinburgh.* Robert Kirkwood was especially noted for his *Map of Edinburgh* of 1817. In Edinburgh's collection of old maps Kirkwood's has become something of a classic and a "household name", frequently used as a reference and checking source for early 19th century local studies. Robert Kirkwood died at aged 44 years, leaving his widow and seven children. The miniature paintings of Robert Kirkwood and his wife, Janet Mitchell, were produced in 1801 and on the back of the painting of Mrs Kirkwood is the handwritten note: "By Mr Saunders, the celebrated miniature painter".

The firm of Kirkwood, built up through so many generations, from which was handed down a constantly evolving skill of engraving and other crafts, still possesses an obvious sense of the oneness of past and present. The demand for its work with its almost limitless variety and range has been described in detail in brochures. Such may illustrate the "everyday" suitably engraved trophies ordered by recreation clubs and then, on the next page, indicate the highly precise and artistic workmanship executed on the stall plates produced for the Knights of the Thistle Chapel in St Giles. Fine skill readily bridges past and present and applies itself to whatever subject. This Robert Kirkwood exemplified, whose engraving of Edinburgh in 1817 remains invaluable today.

GILBERT ELLIOT FIRST EARL OF MINTO

WHILE from ancient times Dalkeith Road, simply known as the "Easter Hiegait", had formed the principal highway southwards on this side of the Burgh Muir, when the lands of Blacket and Newington came to be feued and laid out by Dr Benjamin Bell and subsequently his son George in the early 19th century, the original plans (one in fact dated 1795) showed "the intended new road to the south", which would rival and super-sede Dalkeith Road. By 1817 it appeared in Kirkwood's map of Edinburgh, named "Minto Street". A spacious and elegant new road it certainly was and perhaps one of its most important features was that it lay in direct line with, and was a continuation of, the road which crossed the South Bridge, built in 1788. Kirkwood's map shows a number of villas already built and in the *Edinburgh Directory* for 1827 many residents are listed in Minto Street.

What was therefore to become a most important and extremely busy thoroughfare to the south derives its name from Sir Gilbert Elliot who was

Gilbert Elliot, First Earl of Minto

Painting by George Chinnery, 1813
By courtesy of The National Galleries of Scotland,
Edinburgh, and Roxburgh District Council

governor of Bengal from 1806 to 1814 and who for his many and distinguished public services in India and elsewhere was created the first Earl of Minto in 1814. Sir Gilbert Elliot was born in Edinburgh in April 1751, eldest son of Gilbert Elliot, third baronet of Minto in Roxburghshire. He was educated privately and then from 1764 to 1766 at the Pension Militaire, Fontainebleau. There, the famous David Hume, then in Paris, acted as his guardian. During the following two years he returned to Edinburgh, studying civil law, moral philosophy and history at the University. In 1768 he entered Christ Church College, Oxford, where, it

was said, his studies took second place to sport and social life. In May 1774 he was called to the English bar. Two years later he became the Member of Parliament for Morpeth and in 1786, the Member for Berwick. Following various political and legal assignments here and in Europe, Elliot returned to England in 1798. Soon afterwards he was created Baron Minto. Again he was given various Diplomatic Corps appointments, in Florence, Corsica and Vienna.

In 1806 Lord Minto was appointed Governor-General of India and assumed office in Calcutta in 1807. He had a great respect for the traditions and religious beliefs of the Indians and at one period he was criticised by the Church of England authorities for appearing to suppress Christian missionary work in India, but this accusation was not substantiated. After another period of involvement in various enterprises of British foreign policy in the Far East, he returned to England in May 1814 and was created Viscount Melgund and the Earl of Minto. During his career in India, concluded by 1814, it was noted that he had done much greatly to improve the material conditions of the Indians. He had also done much for native educational development by the setting up of colleges which always respected national traditions and culture.

A most strenuous period as Governor-General of India and a great deal of travel in difficult conditions, particularly to Java, on diplomatic missions, appeared to undermine his health and on June 21st 1814 the Earl of Minto died at Stevenage while travelling North to

44

his Scottish estate. He was buried in Westminster Abbey. In 1777 Lord Minto had married Anna Maria, eldest daughter of Sir George Amyand, by whom he had three sons and three daughters. The tradition of the Minto family holding high office in India continued.

Sir Robert Keith Dick, one of the traditional line of the Dick family owners of Prestonfield House and estate, entered the Civil Service of the Honourable East India Company in 1794, serving for twenty years, latterly in his career as a judge of Sylhet in Eastern Bengal, under the Governor-Generalship of Lord Minto. However, due to the death of his brother in 1814, Sir Robert Keith Dick returned from India to Edinburgh to take possession of the Prestonfield estate. It would seem that when "the new road to the south" was being completed, Dick arranged for the authorities concerned to name the new street on the verge of his Prestonfield lands in honour of his great friend the Earl of Minto who had died in 1814, the same year in which Dick took up residence at Prestonfield.

DAVID OCTAVIUS HILL

MANY of the professional and artistic people who were duly to succeed the merchants in choosing to reside in the pleasant environment of the relatively new 19th-century suburb of Newington, were not only distinguished in their own sphere but some indeed were pioneers in their chosen art or craft. With the passage of time their names have become almost legendary, not only in Scotland but across the world.

David Octavius Hill. Wax medallion by his wife Amelia Robertson Paton Hill

Certainly one of these was David Octavius Hill, R.S.A., who having spent the last few years of his life there, died in Newington Lodge, 38 Mayfield Terrace, described as "an outstandingly fine house behind its curtain of ash trees" and one of the very earliest built in this area.

Although a painter of some note, Hill was to earn an important place in the history of art through his pioneering of the use of early calotype photographs as an aid to portraiture and, in particular, the use of this technique in the production, over a period of twenty-three years, of his world-famous masterpiece, the signing of the Act of Separation and Deed of Demission during the historic Disruption of 1843 which led to the foundation of the Free Church of Scotland.

45

David Octavius Hill, of whom so much has been written and so much of whose early calotype work has been reproduced, was born in Perth in 1802, the eighth child, (as his middle name indicates). His father was a bookseller. David Hill was educated at Perth Academy, a school of very high reputation, and there he revealed early artistic ability, leading to his coming to Edinburgh to be trained at the School of Design in Picardy Place. Hill showed much talent as a landscape painter of romantic approach. His earliest work included *Dunkeld at Sunset* and two views of the Tay which he exhibited when aged 21. He specialised in book illustrations and was commissioned in the publication of Scott's *Red Gauntlet, The Abbot* and *The Fair Maid of Perth.* He was also commissioned by Allan Cunningham to provide fourteen landscapes for an 8-volume edition of *The Works of Robert Burns.* His work also appeared in a 2-volume book on *The Land of Burns* which had a commentary by Christopher North. Much of his book illustration brought enormous praise and popular success.

Hill, in company with many Scottish artists, was dissatisfied with the attention their work received from the Royal Institution, and with Lord Cockburn's strong support, he undertook the secretaryship of the Society of Artists of Edinburgh, which in 1838 became the Royal Scottish Academy, of which Hill remained the active secretary and organiser until shortly before his death in May 1870. At first Hill received no salary for his services to the Royal Scottish Academy, but when at last he did so, he was able to marry Miss Ann MacDonald, a lady of great musical talent, and the Hill household at Moray Place became widely known for its entertaining gatherings of so many notable personalities of the artistic world.

While David Octavius Hill was perhaps earning distinction enough through his landscape painting and widely sought and much acclaimed book illustration, as so often has been the case in the lives of famous people, it was the occurrence of an event outwith his control, and indeed the professional world of art, which was to lead him "to achieve results which have never been surpassed" and to bestow upon him a certain immortality. This was a historic event in Scotland's religious life known as the Disruption, which in 1843 was to tear the established Church of Scotland apart. It was Hill's unique and his last prodigious work; and it was in portraying this event or at least the principal people involved in it, drawing upon the pioneering work carried out by others in early calotype photography, especially in collaboration with Robert Adamson of St Andrews, that Hill achieved fame.

The sequence of events, including the technicalities involved in producing the famous picture may be traced thus. Hill, along with so many other prominent Scots, was a supporter of the Disruption led by Dr Thomas Chalmers and other ministers who stood firmly for freedom from state or any other interference in the appointment of Church of Scotland ministers to their charges. The issue at stake was known as "Patronage". It came to a head during the General Assembly of the Church of Scotland in May

1843, in St Andrew's Church, George Street. At the outset of the Assembly's proceedings, four hundred ministers, led by Dr David Welsh, the Moderator, and Dr Thomas Chalmers, had left the gathering and marched in procession down Hanover Street to Tanfield Hall at Canonmills, and there constituted the first assembly of the newly established Free Church of Scotland. It was a momentous event in Scottish Church history.

David Octavius Hill, present at this Free Church assembly on account of his religious beliefs, also reacted to the occasion with the imagination of an artist. Such a scene deserved, indeed cried out, to be recorded visually. A few days after the event, therefore, Hill approached Dr Robert Gordon of the High Church, Edinburgh, and showed him a small sketch he had prepared for a proposed painting of the Tanfield Hall assembly. Perhaps, it has been suggested, Hill had been influenced by a painting by Sir George Hayter of the scene in the House of Commons during the debate on the Great Reform Bill of 1832—portraying 400 Members of Parliament from life. At any rate, Hill showed Gordon his sketch. While much impressed, Dr Gordon suggested to the artist that it might be more significant to produce a painting of the more solemn subsequent signing of the Act of Separation and Deed of Demission by 450 clergymen specially assembled on May 23rd 1843. Hill immediately agreed to modify his plan. His original sketch of the Tanfield Hall assembly was eventually acquired by the Free Church· authorities and is treasured in their premises at the top of The Mound.

Hill was now confronted by a formidable task—the compilation of a picture containing the individual portraits of around 455 ministers and others who had attended the signing of the Disruption Deed of Demission. The picture was to be commemorative rather than factual.

David Octavius Hill (centre) with James Ballantyne (left) and Dr George Bell (right)

The problems were not just artistic ones. The passage of time involved was an important factor. By the time Hill was to put brush to canvas his subjects had long since dispersed, back to their parishes throughout Scotland. Furthermore, again, by the time the artist did get around to painting them, the subjects would have aged and changed considerably. And not least, Hill was not by training a portrait painter. The solution to so many problems was to be proposed by a man whose distinction lay not in art but in physics. This was Dr David Brewster, Principal of Edinburgh University, himself an ordained minister and a supporter of the Disruption.

Brewster suggested to Hill that the very large scene to be reproduced might be compiled from life portraits where possible but because of the difficulties involved, and especially the time factor, the picture might be built up from the use of a new invention, still in its experimental stage, the calotype photograph, (Calotype came from the word *Kalos* meaning beautiful), or "Talbot type" as they were otherwise known from the name of the inventor of the process Henry Fox Talbot. Following Talbot's instructions, Sir David Brewster had experimented with a group of scientists at St Andrews University and had transmitted the method to Dr John Adamson there, who became most adept in the application of the process. In 1841-42 John Adamson had trained his brother Robert, who was something of an invalid, in the photographic process and it was he who became the great friend and collaborator of David Octavius Hill, through an introduction by Dr David Brewster in 1843.

The great Hill-Adamson partnership began, in their studio at Rock House on the Calton Hill. Each with his different talents, technical and artistic, complemented the other most effectively. Adamson used an early wax negative technique enabling repeat prints to be made, unlike early processes which could produce only "one off" photographs. Indeed, so effective were the wax negatives that even today, so long after the innovation, remarkably good prints can be obtained from them. From their studio on Calton Hill, Hill and Adamson embarked on a most demanding schedule of work. Groups of ministers who had attended the 1843 ceremony were visited, or individuals called at the studio, and steadily the whole scene was reconstructed. The complete work took twenty-three years. Since it was felt by some of the Free Church leaders that certain possible purchasers overseas might be eager to acquire the masterpiece, particularly Americans, a special appeal was made throughout the Church and Hill's work was secured at a cost of £1,500. The canvas measures 11 feet 4 inches by 5 feet and the total weight of the picture is about five hundredweight, set in a magnificent frame. There is a "key" to all those portrayed. David Octavius Hill himself is to be seen, sketch-book in hand. There are also other notable personages who were not in Edinburgh at the time of the Disruption ceremony, but they have been included because of their importance relative to the events.

Despite Hill's concentration on the Disruption picture, he still found time at his Calton Hill studio to produce calotypes of very many other notable Edinburgh people and other subjects, *viz,* various views of the city, ranging from the Scott Monument then nearing completion, everyday street scenes, the Newhaven fishwives in their characteristic striped skirts, and so much else. Unfortunately Robert Adamson died suddenly and Hill had to continue alone using different processes.

While Hill received the highest praise of his lifetime for this work, Sam Bough, the landscape painter, was one of the few to criticise his Disruption picture. However, it must be said that there seemed to be a certain degree of personal pique towards Hill by Bough and others. Yet Hill received remarkably few notable obituary notices or reviews at his death. A feature of his life and character was his very pleasant personality and courtesy.

Those—and they were virtually innumerable, who were his subjects of portraiture by brush or by calotype—found in sitting for him the greatest of pleasure. Hill's second marriage, to Noel Paton's sister, Amelia Noel Paton, was a very happy one. Towards the end of the artist's life they moved house to Mayfield Terrace, where he died on May 17th 1870. It was Amelia Paton, herself a sculptress of some note, who executed a bronze bust of David Octavius Hill which crowns his gravestone in Dean Cemetery, facing towards his favourite view of Edinburgh whose people he portrayed so well. Hill, by his use of early calotype photography in portraiture, most notably in his Disruption masterpiece, "achieved results which have never been surpassed". After his death Hill's calotypes and their negatives were collected by many individuals and institutions and found their way to various parts of the world, but the greatest collection is preserved by the Scottish National Portrait Gallery in Edinburgh.

JOHN ALEXANDER LONGMORE

In November 1880, when the Committee of Management of the Edinburgh Hospital for Incurables met to make the final arrangements for the opening of their new and much larger hospital in Salisbury Place, it was proposed, and agreed unanimously, that "In view of Mr John Longmore's great generosity, the new building will be known as "The Longmore Hospital for Incurables". Although the hospital perhaps bore rather sad connotations, it became well known in Edinburgh and beyond and Mr Longmore earned a place in the city's great roll of generous public benefactors.

Although much remains on record concerning the Edinburgh Royal Association for Incurables, and access to private papers revealed in great detail how carefully Longmore's trustees considered how best and most in accordance with his expressed wishes they might dispose of the sum of just over £10,000, the residue of his estate, unfortunately little is on record concerning Longmore himself. The Longmore family appears to have originated in Elgin and many of the early family lived at Huntly. Adam Longmore, grandfather of John Alexander, and Adam Longmore, father, were both of His Majesty's Exchequer Office in Parliament Square. The grandfather resided in Salisbury Road. John Alexander was a Writer to the Signet and is referred to as "of Deanhaugh". This was a little district beside the Water of Leith at Dean Village. Longmore was unmarried and his home was at 56 Melville Street.

John Longmore died at his home on 16th April 1875 (not 18th April as given in certain books) and was buried in the family enclosure in the west division of Greyfriars Churchyard. From his quite lengthy and detailed will it is possible to glean something of his personal interests and hobbies. He appears to have been a keen yachtsman and was for some time secretary of the Royal Eastern Yacht Club of Edinburgh. To William Scott Hill he bequeathed

49

a yachting cup won by the "Ruby" and to another friend, a hot water jug won by the same yacht at a Largs regatta. To the Royal Eastern Yacht Club he left a painting by a noted seascape painter, William Crawford, of a regatta held at Granton, which had hung in Mr Longmore's dining-room. It is believed that these paintings, and possibly other trophies left by Longmore, are now in the possession of a Clyde yachting club. After other bequests Longmore requested his trustees to donate the remainder of his pictures, books and ornaments to "any building which may come into existence from the residue of my estate, so as in some measure to give the rooms a less bare and more cheerful appearance." Certainly a building did come into being but it is not known if Mr Longmore's items were used as he had suggested. A member of St George's Church in Charlotte Square, Longmore bequeathed a sum of money to the Poor Fund.

Longmore's will concluded: "I direct my trustees to employ the residue of my said estate, means and effects, in instituting and carrying on a scheme for the relief of persons suffering from incurable disease, or of aiding any scheme which now exists or may be instituted by others for that purpose". It was further and quite emphatically proposed that somehere in any scheme which might be set up from his legacy, provision be made for "persons of the better classes of society whose own means or whose friends may not be able to afford them. The comforts or even luxuries which would help alleviate their sore condition should be provided". At the same time, however, Longmore made the comment that he was well satisfied that "when such unfortunates have kind and suitable friends willing to receive them, they are better with them than gathered together in numbers". His trustees were given full powers of discretion with regard to how his legacy might be used and also the right to stipulate criteria governing the type of patients qualifying as beneficiaries.

Soon after Longmore's death, his trustees began consultations with the directors and managers of the then existing associations and institutions concerned with the relief of incurables, with a view to assisting their work financially, and that they might have been given the whole of the residue of the estate, ie. about £10,000, without any requirement of associating his name with their title or his financial support, is quite clear.

The first consultation of the trustees was with the Edinburgh Association for Incurables, founded in 1874, a year before Mr Long-more's death and which received a Royal Charter from Edward VII in 1903. Its committee of management included the notable Edinburgh

Princess May at opening of extension to Longmore Hospital, 1893

By courtesy of the Longmore Hospital

medicals Dr Joseph Bell, Dr James Affleck and Sir John Sibbald. Some of the committee were friends of Mr Longmore. Through certain individual and public financial support plus £5,000 raised by a bazaar, a villa had been purchased in December 1874 for £1,800 at No. 8 Salisbury Place, the former home of Dr Thomas McCrie, the eminent Seceder minister whose *Life of John Knox,* published by Blackwood, had earned him a high literary reputation and an honorary degree from the University. Here the first little "hospital" for incurables had been opened in February 1875, two months before Longmore's death. It provided accommodation for twenty-two patients.

Mr Longmore's trustees also consulted with the managers of a small hospital in Leith known as the "Thomas Gladstone Hospital". This was a small building situated in Mill Lane (but with no connection with Leith Hospital), rather like an eventide home of today, which had been built by Sir Thomas Gladstone of Fasque, a relation of the Prime Minister, Mr. W. E. Gladstone, who in fact for some time was associated with the hospital. Sir Thomas had endowed it for sixteen years. After his death and the end of the endowment period the little hospital was closed. At the instigation of the Longmore trustees an estimate of the cost of rebuilding the hospital had been obtained. This was approximately £2,000, but a specially called meeting of Leith residents, organised by the Reverend Dr. Smith of North Leith Parish Church, decided that there were insufficient known incurable patients in Leith to justify financial assistance from the Longmore trustees or in the latter taking over and re-opening the hospital. In February 1877 it was decided that the residue of Mr Longmore's estate should be given to the Association for the purpose of building a much-needed larger hospital on the Salisbury Place site. It was also hoped that the Longmore trustees would provide £300 p.a. for maintenance of the new building. Two of the trustees were appointed to the Hospital Management Committee. In the early summer of 1877, the houses of Nos. 9 and 10 Salisbury Place were purchased for the total sum of £4,180 and possession obtained at Whitsun 1878. Later that year the lower half of a tenement to the east, with ground entered from Causewayside, was purchased. In 1879 the patients from the original hospital—about 20 in number—were transferred to a house in the High Street, Fisherrow, while the new hospital was being built. On 10th December 1880 the new hospital, named "The Longmore Hospital for Incurables" was opened by Lord Provost Sir Thomas J Boyd. The cost had been £7,487, and the architect was Mr C. G. H. Kinnear. Up to 46 patients could now be accommodated. In accordance with the Longmore bequest, four small private rooms were available for patients able to pay the required sum of £52 per annum.

The building of the new hospital had been made possible not only by the Longmore legacy but also augmented by the funds of the Edinburgh Association for Incurables largely derived from subscriptions and donations. Other sources of money were the weekly halfpenny donations from the female employees of T. and J. Blackwood, Silk Merchants, who owned property near the hospital and after whom Blackwood Crescent was named. A group of farm workers at Linton were also regular contributors. The records of the Longmore trustees give details of the many people suffering from incurable conditions who applied either for financial assistance or, later, admission to the hospital.

Further extensions to the hospital were completed in successive years through the purchase of more adjacent property incuding a boys' school known as Wilson's Academy. On 5th November 1886 Queen Victoria visited the hospital and became a patron. On 3rd October 1893 a new east wing was opened by the Duke and Duchess of York. Mr Longmore in his will had strongly recommended the value of opening a small cottage hospital also for incurable patients and in 1906, through a legacy of £21,000 from Miss Brown of Lanfine, Liberton Cottage Hospital was purchased and opened for the care of patients suffering from tuberculosis, then regarded as virtually incurable. Longmore Hospital, while retaining its commemorative name, has for long been a general hospital, the concept of incurable diseases having changed and with it, of course, relevant treatment.

JAMES C. H. BALMAIN

WHILE David Octavius Hill, famous in the early era of calotype photography, spent the last few years of his most artistically productive life in Newington, another photographer shortly afterwards had come to reside there and over a period of sixty years was to gain a very high reputation as one of Edinburgh's most interesting and celebrated photographers of a later and different era. This was James C. H. Balmain, a pioneer in the old "wet plate" negative technique and whose work and

James C. H. Balmain
By courtesy of Mrs C. Jamieson

subjects were unique, leaving a collection which has provided an invaluable visual documentation of life in the city as the 19th century was reaching its close.

James C. H. Balmain was born in Philadelphia in November 1853 of Scottish parents and came to Edinburgh at the age of twenty. For nearly ten years he worked with a prominent Edinburgh photographer of the time, J. G. Tunney, at George

IV Bridge. During 1897-98, Balmain set up his own business in Maitland Street and many who trained under him became successful photographers in Edinburgh and abroad. He also opened a branch studio in North Berwick in 1914. In the course of sixty years, Balmain accumulated a vast collection of negatives and prints and it was the present writer's privilege to have been shown by the late Mrs Balmain many of her husband's unique original prints. The collection was eventually acquired by the distinguished Edinburgh photographers, Yerbury, who had taken over Balmain's business.

Many of the classical "characters" and quite famous street scenes of Edinburgh at the close of last century were Balmain's special interest. These ranged widely. There was, for instance, "Coconut Tam", one of the celebrated "worthies" known to countless passers-by on the North and South Bridges. He was a little hunchback man who stood beside his ramshackle stall at the pavement's edge, in summer and winter, wearing a large black overcoat. Edinburgh has had many colourful "street cries" over the centuries. Tam's distinctive one was: "Cocky-nit, cocky-nit, a ha'penny the bit, bit, bit". He died in 1894, and this little man whom the Edinburgh folk of the day had known and loved, Balmain's camera has recorded for posterity. Then there were the picturesquely-attired fish-wives from Newhaven or Fisherrow selling their saucers of cockles and mussels at well-known street corners, or selling their different wares they would cry "Caller herrin', three a pennee! ee! ee!" Or again, the eye would be caught by the women who had plodded into the old town with their salt from the salt factories on the shores of the Forth. "Sa—at—wha'll buy my sa—at" was their cry. A unique sight was the lady in a shawl who stood in St Giles Street, with a bird-cage and the propped up showcard: "Charming birds, ladies and gentlemen, for the small sum of one penny these innocent birds will select from this box a planet telling your past or future life.". To all these should be added the "Hokey Pokey" man with his barrow, at the corner of Cockburn Street and the High Street; or the horse-drawn buses; circus parades on the North Bridge; and innumerable scenes not labelled and now difficult to identify. Of Balmain's more general views of Edinburgh, perhaps the genius of his work is seen best in "Auld Reekie", an evening study taken from Salisbury Crags and certainly illustrating its title and capturing the whole atmosphere and profile of the city of which his innumerable individual photographs were but details.

While Balmain's work may not now be readily seen, a typical selection of prints was reproduced in the *S.M.T. Magazine* for December 1952, entitled "Putting the Clock Back", kept on file in certain large public libraries. A man of wide-ranging interests and hobbies, Balmain was a member of the Scottish Arts Club, and as a keen curler was much involved in the activities of Haymarket Ice Rink from its formation. He was a member of several golf clubs in Edinburgh and East Lothian and was a prominent member of Mayfield Bowling Club. Latterly he resided in the little house on the east corner of Salisbury Place and Upper Gray Street, which is now No. 21 Salisbury Place. There he had a studio and there he died on June 23rd 1937, aged 84. During his 64 years as a particularly observant photographer in Edinburgh he created unique and precious portraits of the city in all its characters and moods.

JOHN GEORGE BARTHOLOMEW

A FEATURE of Causewayside in the early 19th century was its numerous fine mansion-houses, each with spacious and pleasant gardens extending westwards into the adjacent Grange estate or eastwards as far as Dalkeith Road, the original "easter hiegait" skirting the ancient Burgh Muir. By the end of the century many of these houses had gone and on their garden land had arisen important factories or other premises of the many thriving industrial and manufacturing enterprises which brought a bustling new life and employment to the district.

Practically all of these firms have long since closed. Reference has already been made to Middlemass, and the many others which once existed but are now to be found only in old maps or street directories. One great commercial establishment remains, which, being situated in Duncan Street, is strictly outwith the former Causewayside manufacturing complex and also of a relatively more modern era: nevertheless perhaps the district may still rejoice in its continuing existence, prosperity and world-wide fame. This is, of course,

John George Bartholomew
By courtesy of John Bartholomew & Son Ltd

the long-established family business of John Bartholomew & Son, carto-graphers, printers and publishers, which a few years ago celebrated both its modest origins and its steady development over one and a half centuries.

Although the John Bartholomew dynasty extends back over several generations to its humble beginnings, from which, through each successive owner new and important and often quite revolutionary developments continued to follow each other in ingenuity and practical application, the one member of the family who has received so much tribute and attention, John George Bartholo-mew (1860-1920) is also the man who on other grounds most appropriately merits a place amongst the biographies of notable people of South Edinburgh. John George

Bartholomew was born in Edinburgh in March 1860. By the time he had completed his education at the Royal High School and the University, the firm's premises, after occupying a succession of sites, beginning humbly at 4a North Bridge and adjacent Carrubber's Close, had in 1879 moved to 31 Chambers Street. In less than ten years John George at the early age of twenty-eight had succeeded his father in the complete management of the growing business and in 1889 he himself moved the firm yet again, this time to Park Road, a name which he coined to replace the street's original and quite ancient name of Gibbet Loan, for long the site of the gallows used for the execution of Edinburgh criminals. Here, in what he called the Parkside Works, he named the premises the Edinburgh Geographical Institute.

In 1888 John George Bartholomew formed a partnership with another famous Edinburgh family in the printing and publishing world, Thomas Nelson. The latter partner however died in 1892 and from 1893 until 1919, John George was in partnership with Andrew E. Scott. While until 1919 the firm's title was John Bartholomew and Co., in the same year it became registered as a private company under the name to become so well and so widely known, John Bartholomew and Son Ltd. In 1911, signifying the end of a long pilgrimage through successive premises, the fine building in Duncan Street was opened, with its impressive pillared façade which had been the Palladian frontage carefully transferred from Falcon Hall in Morningside, the residence of John George Bartholomew from 1878 until its demolition in 1909 and his acquisition of Newington House in Blacket Avenue, very near to the new Duncan Street premises.

Above the new building was inscribed: "The Edinburgh Geographical Institute". The words were certainly most appropriate and significant. They surmounted the entrance to what was very much more than simply a commercial enterprise. It was a firm whose work had recorded more and more new information as regards the extent and nature of the world. During half a century of its existence, very largely under the direction of John George Bartholomew's father, there had been witnessed the growth of the British Empire; the introduction and subsequent proliferation of railways; the discovery of new territories from the heart of Africa to the Polar ice-caps; the changing frontiers of nations; the replacement of sailing ships by steam navigation, and indeed it was John George's father who, under instructions from Robert Louis Stevenson had drawn the famous map of *Treasure Island* as a frontispiece to the first edition of the immortal adventure story. The worn old engraved copper plate remains one of the great and rare items in the firm's fascinating archives, which also include the artist's impression of the Forth Railway Bridge — but "the bridge which never was" since the design of this particular version was never used. Thus with so much material and knowledge centred in it and its staff, the Edinburgh Geographical Institute became the much sought-after resort of scholars and scientists, with its lecture rooms, laboratories and, above all, its stimulating atmosphere of learning and incentive towards further geographical exploration. John George Bartholomew in fact was the friend of such famous explorers as Shackleton, Cecil Rhodes (whom he had met in Africa), H. M. Stanley, a close friend, and A. L. Bruce, son-in-law of Dr David Livingstone.

Many of the fine 19th-century mansion-houses built in the Canaan district in Morningside were far from being simply well-appointed, secluded retreats or ivory towers whose owners at that time were living well away from the city's lively bustle and commerce, or serious preoccupation with learning or the law. On the contrary, it was from such houses to the south of the city that so very many men, and some ladies, rode in by carriage or early horse-drawn tram to make their important impact on the life of Scotland's capital. John George Bartholomew was no exception. During his residence in stately Falcon Hall, he was making very many historic contributions towards the advancement of his field of work.

And perhaps in the calm air of the sunny evenings in Canaan, he found some relief from the suffering which he heroically endured during an adult life plagued by tuberculosis which so often laid him low but never deterred him.

Although the firm already enjoyed a high reputation for map production in the supply of millions of atlases for schools, for example, John George Bartholomew's pre-dominant interest lay in the introduction of relief by contours and layer colouring. Such techniques earned him special distinction, and the process which he pioneered soon became widely applied. He believed maps could be an important civilising influence. He was fascinated by producing maps illustrating various aspects of society, national or worldwide, *e.g.* showing health statistics and the distribution throughout the world of diseases; of religious faiths; economic features; comets and meteors; medicinal plants; distribution of fish; world poverty; mental illness. These have

Bartholomew's Edinburgh Geographical Institute
By Courtesy of Messrs John G. Bartholomew & Son Ltd.

remained a special feature of Bartholomew's publications. Even as this is written they have produced an *Atlas of the Moon.*

The honours bestowed upon "J. G." were virtually countless and world-wide. In addition to his prodigious labours in the firm itself, his fertile brain and enthusiasm triumphed over ill-health to enable him to launch historically important events. He founded the Royal Scottish Geographical Society in 1884, not without many obstacles to his attempts to do so. He was the Society's first honorary secretary, and until his death in 1920 undertook active office. The Edinburgh Geographical Institute having become such a focal point for the documentation of geographical data and constant developments — indeed, being just what it implied, it was natural that John George Bartholomew, the mind and inspiration behind it all, should seek to have Edinburgh University found a Chair of Geography. For the authorities the time was not yet ripe.

Disappointing as this must have been to John George, he was happy to see a lectureship in the subject established and he was a generous benefactor of this post and in the equipping of departmental facilities.

There appear to have been no limits to John George Bartholomew's dreams and schemes. Even his system of industrial relations in his firm and co-partnership and profit-sharing for his employees represent thinking and practice well in advance of his time. He was appointed Geographer and Cartographer to King George V. In 1909, when Edinburgh University awarded him an honorary doctorate, all his achievements, within his firm and in the advancement of geography for the benefit of the world, were simply, yet could not have been more profoundly nor truly, epitomised in the words of the Dean of the Faculty of Law who was his sponsor. When presenting John George Bartholomew to the vast gathering in the McEwan Hall, he was, he said, "A very prince of cartographers".

4 · THE GRANGE

PRINCIPAL WILLIAM ROBERTSON

WHEN Sir Andrew Lauder-Dick inherited Grange House in 1769, and very soon afterwards the baronetcy of Fountainhall, he chose to reside at the latter and not in Grange House. Although this was half a century before the transformation of the house into a most elegant castle-like mansion by Sir Thomas Dick Lauder in 1831, and it may not have been particularly attractive interiorly, nevertheless it was remote from the city and set in pleasant rural surroundings, proving attractive to scholars and writers seeking seclusion; and a succession of tenants chose to reside there. Undoubtedly the most distinguished of these was Principal William Robertson who had been appointed to this position by the University in 1762. When he took up residence at the Grange in 1792, he was already aged 71 years and nearing the close of a life " laden with honours " from many countries and was destined to enjoy the pleasant environment of the mansion house for less than two years before his death in 1793.

In view of his quite brief residence at Grange House and on account of the wealth of biographical material already extant on this most distinguished scholar, it would be rather pretentious and irrelevant to attempt any additional material here. Principal William Robertson, a "son of the manse", of the parish of Borthwick in Midlothian, while honoured for so many distinctions, was pre-eminently a historian. He became a student at Edinburgh University in 1733, qualified as a preacher and minister of the Church of Scotland and was appointed to Gladsmuir church in 1753. It was in Gladsmuir manse that he began writing his famous *History of Scotland*. This was published in 1759, and, it was said, "took by storm both the literary and political world". Horace Walpole, whom Robertson had met the previous year in London, was astounded that a humble Scottish minister, whose English he could hardly understand, could write " what all the world now considers to be the best modern history". Not only that but Robertson's subsequent important publications included a *History of the Emperor Charles the Fifth* and his *History of America.* It has been said however, that subsequent historical research tended to detract from some of Robertson's historical writing.

In 1761 William Robertson was appointed minister of old Greyfriars Church. The following year he was elected Principal of the University, and the next year was appointed Moderator of the General Assembly for Scotland. Having served as Principal of the University for twenty-seven years, he had the honour of laying the foundation stone of the Old College in South Bridge. His name is commemorated in the carved inscription above the main entrance in South Bridge. Robertson was a man of strong individual mind. During the 1745 Jacobite Rebellion he volunteered his

Principal Sir William Robertson by
Sir Henry Raeburn R.A.

Reproduced by kind permission of the University of
Edinburgh

services to Sir John Cope, the English commander, but was not accepted, fortunately perhaps for his future survival and career in view of Cope's disastrous defeat by Prince Charles Edward's troops at the Battle of Prestonpans. Unlike many of his clerical colleagues, he supported the principle of patronage and therefore would not have supported Dr Thomas Chalmers and the others who during the Disruption of 1843 seceded from the Established Church and founded the Free Church of Scotland. Robertson also supported his friend, the Reverend John Home, the minister author of the celebrated play *Douglas* which earned for Home the kirk's severe censure, the theatre then being seen by the church authorities as the "instrument of the Devil".

In Edinburgh's "Golden Age" Principal Robertson was one of that coterie of writers, philosophers, lawyers, artists and others who met in the famous Edinburgh clubs for dinner or over a chopin of wine. In 1754 Allan Ramsay, the painter, founded the "Select Society" which met on a Friday evening when the law courts were in session. Robertson was one of the original founder members who included Adam Smith, David Hume, Adam Ferguson and Lord Monboddo, among others. This society founded the *Edinburgh Review*.

Many of Edinburgh's literary giants, and especially his close friend, Dugald Stewart, were Principal Robertson's regular guests during his short residence at Grange House. Lord Cockburn was another frequent visitor and wrote of the learned Principal's sense of fun and special pleasure in meeting with young people. Robertson died at Grange House on June 11th 1793, and was buried in Greyfriars Churchyard, near the entrance gate to the Covenanters' Prison, and with a large and rather ornate mausoleum. Portraits of this especially famous University Principal were painted by Sir Henry Raeburn and Sir Joshua Reynolds and are in the Edinburgh University collection.

SIR THOMAS DICK LAUDER

In a preface which Dr John Brown of *Rab and His Friends* fame very willingly wrote to Sir Thomas Dick Lauder's *Scottish Rivers,* he remarked that to give even a few

Sir Thomas Dick Lauder 5th Baronet of Grange

By courtesy of the late Sir George Dick-Lauder

60

prefatorial details of the author and his other books was more a matter of form than actual requirement, so well was Sir Thomas Dick Lauder known in the field of Scottish literature. *Scottish Rivers* was a collection of essays published posthumously in book form in 1874, and a work of rather special interest and not without amusement for South Edinburgh residents since its first quite substantial chapter dealt with the district's own " river ", the Jordan Burn, for long the city's southern boundary. Perhaps my introductory remarks, made a century after Dr Brown's praise of Thomas Dick Lauder's work, now seem meaningless. To write nowadays of Dr John Brown " of *Rab and His Friends* fame " and of Dick Lauder as two of the great names in Scottish literature is perhaps rather presumptuous. Is *Rab and His Friends* now widely read or indeed known at all save by a small minority? Likewise the works of Sir Thomas Dick Lauder? Are both their works and the authors practically forgotten? Perhaps so, but I believe that both nevertheless merit a place among the interesting people of South Edinburgh, and if for no other reason than Dr John Brown's relationship with the famous Professor James Syme, and because, in certain respects, Sir Thomas Dick Lauder and the historic district of the Grange are almost synonymously linked.

"Sanct Gelie's Grange " — the Grange of St Giles — was a rather primitive keep or tower which stood out in an area of land on the Burgh Muir on the south of the city and gifted to the monks of St Giles when it was a monastic foundation by David I, some time in the 12th century. The Grange or monastic farmhouse was undoubtedly the earliest place of habitation out on the otherwise forbidding Muir, and around it in the course of time the monks would have brought some part of this wasteland under cultivation. So far back extends the history of the Grange, and, following the departure of the monks, so numerous were the successive owners or tenants of the lands and the gradually enlarged farmhouse residence, that the many strands of history, especially its early ownership by the famous and wealthy Scottish families, the Lauders of the Bass and Dick of Braid, seem to reach their peak and become personified in the man who became the 5th baronet of Grange in 1820 and who integrated the past into a new era and future for a house which already had such a rich and unique heritage.

Sir Thomas Dick Lauder was the 7th Baronet of Fountainhall and 5th of Grange. His father, Sir Andrew Lauder, 6th Baronet of Fountainhall, had married his cousin, Isabel Dick, heiress of the Grange Estate. He eventually inherited Grange also and adopted the title Lauder Dick. When Sir Thomas eventually succeeded his father in Fountainhall and in Grange in 1820, he chose to be known as Dick Lauder. After holding a brief commission in the Cameron Highlanders and following his marriage to Miss Charlotte Cumin, heiress to the large estate of Relugas in Elginshire, he took up residence in that most pleasant northern district where the scenery and legends of the area inspired much of his earliest literary work around 1815; and later he wrote of its natural history and geography. Some of his earliest contributions to *Blackwood's Magazine* in Edinburgh were thought by some reviewers to be the work of Sir Walter Scott. Sir Thomas Dick Lauder's *The Wolf of Badenoch* (1827), set in Morayshire, gained wide popularity, and was translated into several languages. In 1830 his account of the great Morayshire floods was greatly praised and perhaps remains his most important work.

About 1827 Sir Thomas decided to move south to Edinburgh, and in anticipation of taking up residence at Grange House — the ancient "Grange of St Giles" — he engaged the famous architect W. H. Playfair, who by 1831 had transformed the house into a most elegant castle-like mansion. With Sir Thomas and Lady Lauder and their large family now settled in at the Grange the house became a Mecca for many notable figures of the Edinburgh literary scene, as it had been, prior to its architectural restoration, when the famous University Principal William Robertson had been tenant of the house. Sir Walter Scott was a close friend of Sir Thomas Dick Lauder and a frequent guest at the Grange, and indeed it was Sir Thomas who wrote the principal account of Sir Walter's last days at Abbotsford and his funeral ceremony at Dryburgh Abbey, published in *Tait's Magazine.* Lord Cockburn, Dr John Brown and the Reverend John Thomson, minister of Duddingston kirk and celebrated artist, were also frequent visitors to the Grange. With members of his large family (he had two sons and ten daughters), ensuring an adequate cast, Sir Thomas founded the Grange House Salon Theatre.

While with its fairy-tale castle-like appearance it might well have resembled one, Grange House was no remote "ivory tower" cut off from the city's, and indeed the country's, everyday affairs and problems. On the contrary, the literary and philosophical and political speculation which were a feature of the Grange's well-appointed dining-room conversations did not remain matters of mere academic interest. Sir Thomas Dick Lauder, and so many of his after-dinner debating companions, were deeply immersed in the political and social issues of the day. Sir Thomas Dick Lauder was a zealous Liberal. He was closely involved in the passing of the Reform Bill of 1832, and many important meetings to

*Grange House
towers on
the right*

*By
Jane Stewart Smith,
1865*

discuss the Bill were held at Grange House. He presided over a mass meeting of thirty thousand at St Ann's Yards, a field east of Holyrood Palace and he also recorded his impressions of another large rally—probably held in the natural amphitheatre of "Tumblers' Hollow" at Bruntsfield Links—to celebrate the Bill's successful passage through Parliament. Many other campaigns for social reforms in Edinburgh received his strong support.

In 1839 Sir Thomas was appointed secretary to the Board of Scottish Manufacturers, a body which soon afterwards was combined with the Board of White Herring Fisheries, for which he was also responsible. Another appointment was as secretary to the Royal Institute for the Encouragement of the Fine Arts. These various commitments proved very congenial to him, enabling him to undertake much travel around Scotland on various surveys and to meet people involved. One such venture was *A Tour Round the Coast of Scotland* to study the fishing industry. This he undertook in collaboration with his close friend James Wilson, the famous naturalist of "Woodville" in Canaan Lane. The report was published jointly.

Sir Thomas Dick Lauder's *Scottish Rivers,* to which in book form Dr John Brown wrote the preface, has a great deal of interest in relation to South Edinburgh as it was when this work was first contributed as a series of articles to *Tait's Magazine* in 1847 and the following year. It was Sir Thomas's last major work. He was then already beginning to suffer a long and painful illness but, characteristic of his intellectual drive,

he dictated the articles to his daughter Susan.

In the midst of so many commitments Lauder, perhaps finding constant and detailed management of his Grange estate too demanding, and perhaps, too, for economic reasons, in 1825 had negotiated parliamentary approval for the first feuing out plan of the Grange, since it was Crown Land, and in 1845, the building of the first of the fine villas was begun, and the development of the most pleasant and congenial Grange residential district was under way.

Sir Thomas Dick Lauder died on May 29th 1848, aged 64. The vast attendance of mourners at the family vaults on the extreme east side of Grange Cemetery, not far from the mansion house itself, testified to Edinburgh's, and indeed Scotland's deep respect and affection for the man of so many interests and champion of so many good causes. Not least among the mourners were the great many beggars and city "down-and-outs" who almost daily used to wait around the gates of Grange House, walking out from the town, to benefit from Sir Thomas's generosity. His great friend Lord Cockburn described Sir Thomas Dick Lauder as "a tall gentleman-like Quixotic figure with a general picturesqueness of appearance, who could have made his way in the world as a player (actor), ballad singer, street fiddler, geologist, civil engineer, or artist or lawyer or ...." Anyway it is significant that in the course of time a street near to where the great and long-since demolished mansion-house once stood was named to commemorate its owner as St Thomas Road.

DAVID BRYCE

As with so many of the notable residents of South Edinburgh, or others associated with the district, their achievements and distinctions have been recognised far beyond the city. The man described in the catalogue of an exhibition held in 1976 to mark the centenary of his death as "in a certain sense Scotland's greatest Victorian architect" was strikingly a case in point. This was David Bryce, who, while he did not reside in the southern part of the city, did have several close associations with its development.

When Sir George Warrender in the early 1860's began to consider feuing out large areas of his Bruntsfield estate, it was David Bryce whom he engaged to produce the initial plan. This he did in 1869. Bryce apparently envisaged a layout for Sir George Warrender's lands and the building of houses in the style and fashion of the Grange district which had been planned by Grainger and Miller in 1825, and which of course provided for many large detached villas of marked individuality of architecture along with streets composed primarily of terraced villas of high quality. In fact Bryce's original plans for the Bruntsfield area were never to materialise. Only a few terraced villas which he had designed were built in what was at first named Marchmont Terrace, later changed to Alvanley Terrace.

In the Grange district David Bryce was commissioned to lay out the spacious Edinburgh Southern Cemetery, later simply to become known as Grange Cemetery, and opened in 1847. Bryce designed the superintendent's house at the main entrance, but the gabled wing on the west side was built later. The original prospectus for the cemetery stressed its relative remoteness from the centre of the city and thus its atmosphere of seclusion and peace. A little chapel once stood in the centre above a row of tombs.

David Bryce was born in Buccleuch Place, in rented rooms, on 3rd April 1803, the son of a builder. He was educated at the High School and then joined his father's business. Seeing that he showed an early aptitude for the drawing of plans, his father arranged for his proper training, and Bryce served under the famous William Burn, eventually becoming his partner. Burn had a profound influence on Bryce and when the former moved to London in 1844 Bryce acquired his large and lucrative business. His office was at 131 George Street. He began to move away from being simply a "builder" and adopted the more prestigious profession of architect. Bryce indeed "lived for architecture" and at the time of his death in 1876, aged 73 years, he had risen from a very modest background to become the unchallenged leader of his profession in Edinburgh and with a high reputation in Scotland and beyond.

While William Burn undoubtedly had a very great and formative influence on Bryce, nevertheless it has been claimed that in becoming the leading exponent and perhaps indeed the creator of the Scottish baronial style in building, this was very much Bryce's own achievement. Just as he owed so much to Burn, Bryce in turn had considerable influence on many young architects whom he trained and who duly achieved their own distinction. This was especially so as regards Charles Kinnear and the ultimately famous Sir Robert Rowand Anderson, who for a short time had been Bryce's partner. To serve under Bryce, it was for long said, was the key to future success.

Bryce's architectural career in independent practice covered almost exactly the first forty years of Queen Victoria's reign. His work was prolific and exceeded 200 buildings, many of them of very considerable note, especially, and perhaps best known in Edinburgh, the then new Royal Infirmary in Lauriston Place, whch he designed and began in 1870, though he died three years before its completion in 1879. There was a romanticism in the building's silhouette, and also in the incorporation of certain ideas proposed by Florence Nightingale. Fettes College, the commission for which passed to Bryce after W. H. Playfair's death, was the work of eight years and by wide consent constitutes one of Edinburgh's finest buildings. In addition, as one critic has remarked, it provides a masterly addition to the city's rather dull northern skyline. Elsewhere in Edinburgh, Bryce's work may be seen, most notably in the design of the Assembly Hall at the top of The Mound, and nearby, the dominant premises on the Bank of Scotland; at the George Hotel (later added to by Mac Gibbon and Ross); St George's West Church in Shandwick Place; and, as one of the finest pieces of interior design in Edinburgh, the Royal College of Physicians' library in Queen Street. While these do not by any means complete the list of his Edinburgh creations, there remain also and quite apart, the large number of country houses in

Scotland which emanated from his drawing-board, much of this work arising from his close friendship with influential and wealthy aristocrats and political figures in Scotland. In South Edinburgh, it is believed, Bryce designed several of the impressive baronial villas in Clinton Road, such as the Elms, Avallon, Clinton House and certainly the stately Woodcroft, built specially for Lt. Colonel David Davidson in about 1870 from a fine pink sandstone quarried on the site. Woodcroft was demolished to make way for the modern towering STD telephone exchange in 1964.

There is an interesting and striking difference between the chalk drawing by an unknown artist of Bryce as a young man, an alert sharp-featured

David Bryce

Chalk drawing by an unknown artist
By courtesy of the National Galleries of Scotland,
Edinburgh

65

young Scot, and the other portraits of him as the rather heavy, thick-set mid-Victorian man of business. Early portraits presented him as what seemed to be a rather retiring personality, with sandy red hair, left-handed (as the position of an inkwell indicates in one drawing), tending to conceal a character of great determination and vigorous forthrightness. These traits were indeed expressed in his relations with colleagues and customers, and likewise showed forth in his architecture. Later illustrations, while they still clearly revealed all these qualities nevertheless presented a man of very positive achievements. Bryce was elected a Fellow of the Royal Scottish Academy in 1856 and also of the Royal Society of Edinburgh in the same year. He was latterly very wealthy but always remained unmarried and in fact made financial provision for the children of his brothers who had died relatively young. He himself died on May 7th 1876 and was buried in new Calton Cemetery.

ROBERT M. BALLANTYNE

IN 1968 St Catherine's-in-Grange Church at the corner of Palmerston Road and Grange Road united with Argyle Place Church and was renamed St Catherine's — Argyle. Two years earlier the late Reverend Thomas Maxwell, minister of St Catherine's-in-Grange had written a most interesting and scholarly centenary history of this church, tracing it back to its foundation in 1866 as the Chalmers Memorial Free Church, one of the very many churches throughout Scotland named in tribute to Dr Thomas Chalmers who had led the Disruption in 1843 and had been the first Moderator of the Free Church of Scotland. It was certainly most fitting that the little church in Grange Road should be so named since Dr Chalmers had been buried just twenty years before in Grange Cemetery, the first burial in fact in the new cemetery opened in 1847, the year of Chalmers' death.

At the Disruption, a very large number of people left, or as it was said "seceded" from the established Church of Scotland and joined the Free Church, and among those were very many men prominent in public life, the academic world, literature, the arts and sciences. Mr Maxwell in his history of St Catherine's refers to the many interesting and distinguished people who had been members of the original Grange Free Church. One of these was Robert M. Ballantyne, the famous author of adventure stories for boys, based upon his own wide and exciting travels.

R. M. Ballantyne was born in Edinburgh in Ann Street, on April 24th 1825. His father was Alexander Ballantyne whose older brother, James, was Sir Walter Scott's publisher.

Unfortunately, Ballantyne's *Personal Reminiscences* give no details of his early boyhood days and begin in 1841 when he was sixteen. However, in his earlier years Robert must have shown a strong desire for travel and adventure, since when he was still only sixteen his father suggested that he apply for a clerk's job with the Hudson Bay Company. This he did, and on May 31st 1841 was accepted as an apprentice and soon afterwards set sail from Gravesend on the *Prince Rupert,* one of the Hudson Bay Company's ships. At York Factory, the company's head office in Hudson Bay, young Robert Ballantyne had to put in a rather boring six months' training as a clerk before any opportunity for adventure arose. At last, however, he began five and a half years of service with the company which took him to lonely outposts, allowed him to sail on long trips with the Indians in their canoes and to take part in trading expeditions "far north of Canadian civilisation".

Ballantyne returned to Edinburgh in 1848, and soon afterwards published his *Everyday Life in the Hudson Bay Company.* Through his friendship with the Cowan family, the prosperous Edinburgh paper makers, Ballantyne obtained a generous loan which enabled him to become a junior partner in the famous Edinburgh publishers Thomas Constable. Perhaps he would have remained quite content simply to work as a publisher, but a friend suggested that he should attempt an adventure story for boys based on his Canadian experiences. Thus he wrote *Snowflakes and Sunbeams, or the Young Fur Traders.* With the title shortened simply to *The Young Fur Traders,* this book was accepted and published by Thomas Nelson and became an immediate success. Thus, yet another famous Edinburgh writer's career had begun. Ballantyne dedicated himself to it unstintingly, producing on average two books a year for forty years, plus many short stories for Boys' Annuals. While in his books based on his Canadian adventures he was writing from factual experience, in much of his other work he carefully checked the feasibility of what he would write. Thus before completing *Fighting the Flames* he spent some time accompanying units of the London Fire Brigade on actual fire-fighting trips. On another occasion he spent three weeks living with the men who manned the Bell Rock lighthouse.

Undoubtedly the best known and most successful of Ballantyne's vast output of stories is *Coral Island (A Tale of the Pacific),* published in 1857, and translated into almost every European language. This book still remains in print although it is a slow seller in the bookshops and rather infrequently borrowed from public libraries. While *Coral Island* was a tremendous success in itself, unknown to its author it was destined to influence profoundly another writer from Edinburgh, none other than Robert Louis Stevenson. Alison Cunningham, R.L.S.' childhood nurse, in her reminiscences recorded by her great friend, Lord Guthrie, in his little book *Cummy,* relates how during so many of the long, weary, sleepless nights which young Louis suffered at 17 Heriot Row, and she would read to him to pass the hours, when it began to get light he would say: "We'll take Ballantyne now, Cummy, and then we would take *Coral Island*". But this early influence of Ballantyne on R.L.S. did not end there. Eric Quayle in his detailed and fascinating biography *Ballantyne the Brave* strongly suggests that young Stevenson's fascination for the Pacific Islands, which never left him (indeed it was in Samoa that he spent his last days) and which in particular inspired *Treasure Island,* was almost certainly

Robert M. Ballantyne

first awakened by his reading, or having read to him, *Coral Island.* Indeed, Stevenson in his introduction to the first edition of *Treasure Island* includes two verses "To the Hesitant Purchaser" in which he expresses the hope that the youth of that time, (1883) may still share his own youthful pleasure in reading *Kingston, Ballantyne the Brave,* or *Cooper of the Wood and Wave,* and therefore will enjoy *Treasure Island.* if they don't, then "let them be buried with these earlier writers and all their characters".

A fascinating account is given by Quayle of the only known recorded meeting between R.L.S. and his "hero" Ballantyne whom he worshipped. This was after morning service in St Cuthbert's Church at the West End of Princes Street, in 1866.

Ballantyne, then aged 41, was there with his fiancée, Jane Dickson Grant, whose father had been minister of a church at Cavers in Roxburghshire, and who now lived with her widowed mother in Edinburgh's West End. As the couple were leaving St Cuthbert's churchyard, they were approached by a youth aged sixteen, who courteously raised his cap and introduced himself, eagerly telling Mr Ballantyne how much he enjoyed his books. Then he boldly went further. He had received permission from his family, he said, and they would consider it an honour if Mr Ballantyne and his lady would take dinner that evening in Colinton manse where the Stevensons were residing. Ballantyne introduced his fiancée and then explained that they had only recently become engaged and there was an "at home" arranged for that evening at his fiancée's house which they must attend. One can imagine Stevenson's disappointment. It is not thought they ever met again.

After his marriage on July 31st 1866 Ballantyne and his wife took up residence at 6 Millerfield Place, on the south side of the Meadows, the cost of the house, it would appear, having been met by Mrs Grant as part of the dowry given to her daughter. Ballantyne was a staunch member of the Free Church founded by Dr Chalmers and it was most appropriate that he should have been a regular attender at the relatively nearby Chalmers Memorial Church in Grange Road and of which he was elected an elder. Certain literary critics have commented on the very strong Free Church influence they believed was evident in much of his writing, resulting in his themes and his characters conforming to "high moral tone", which they believed narrowed his scope compared with other "more liberal" writers of adventure stories. If this were so, it certainly did not lessen his appeal or diminish his almost uniquely high reputation as a writer for boys. Certainly the many portraits of him are essentially of the bearded, manly figure, dressed as a hunter, complete with gun, spears and other trappings of the adventures.

In 1878 Ballantyne moved with his family to Harrow-on-the-Hill. For a considerable time he had suffered from vertigo and acute nausea, and today would have been diagnosed as having Menière's disease, involving the delicate mechanism which affects balance and related to the ears. In 1893 he decided to go for treatment to a nature-cure clinic run by an English couple at Tivoli, near Rome, whose prospectus and claims attracted him and offered hope. His daughter Jane accompanied him. On arrival at Tivoli, they were quickly disillusioned. The clinic was completely at variance with the advert which had attracted them. It was a cold, dismal, depressing part of an old disused monastery. Ballantyne's condition was now quite advanced and the "cure" which he began to undertake was positively harmful. Father and daughter decided to return to London. *En route*, they spent a few days in Rome, sightseeing and trying to forget the ordeal of the clinic. During the night of February 8th 1894, in a small pensione at 7 Via Corso, Ballantyne suddenly became seriously ill and died.

The famous adventurer and author of so many captivating stories for boys was buried in the beautiful Protestant cemetery in Rome, near the graves of Shelley and Keats. When the news of his death reached England, thousands of boys, who had been their great hero's avid readers, were deeply saddened. A movement immediately began, led by the boys of Harrow school, to raise a great monument to his memory. It has been said that such a spontaneous reaction by so many boys of little or no financial means remains without precedent until the present day and is a quite remarkable tribute to Ballantyne's reputation.

In a very short time, over six hundred pounds had been raised, much of this from pennies and sixpences sent in to the fund from boys all over Britain. But, amidst the enthusiasm to commemorate fittingly the writer by some impressive monument, one voice intervened—that of a now famous author who, perhaps more than any other, owed so much inspiration to Ballantyne It was the voice of one who had first heard the words of *Coral Island* on his childhood sick-bed in Heriot Row— Robert Louis Stevenson, now famous and residing at Vailima in Samoa. Stevenson wrote to many British newspapers, in no way opposing the erection of some monument to Ballantyne but pointing out that since the author had not left a very large sum as future provision for his widow and family (Ballantyne, in fact, had generously provided financially for the families of his various relations who had encountered hardship), of the money raised for a monument only a small part should be devoted to this end and the balance given to Ballantyne's widow and family. Stevenson's characteristically considerate view was widely accepted. Consequently, only forty guineas were spent on a simple grave-stone, and the balance of the fund subscribed given to Ballantyne's family.

On the grave in the cemetery in Rome there is a white marble tombstone, with these words inscribed:

IN LOVING MEMORY OF
ROBERT MICHAEL
BALLANTYNE
THE BOYS' STORY WRITER
Born at Edinburgh, April 24th 1825
Died at Rome, February 8th 1894
This stone is erected by four
generations
of grateful friends in Scotland
and England

DR HORATIUS BONAR

ONE of the most striking features of the large number of distinguished people who have resided in South Edinburgh has been the very wide variety of their involvements and achievements. This has been no less true of the Grange district. While reference has been made elsewhere to the interesting people who became members of the original Chalmers Memorial Free Church in Grange Road, none was to achieve greater fame in his own special field than this church's first minister, Dr Horatius Bonar, who has been described as the "Prince of Scottish Hymn Writers", and whose compositions became known and sung world-wide and by many denominations. Yet there was just a little touch of irony in that of his prolific writing of hymns which were to be sung all over the English-

speaking world, the one place where for long they were not sung was in his own church in the Grange, since in the Free Church which Dr Bonar had chosen to join during the Disruption of 1843, hymns as such were not sung, only "the pure psalms of David".

Dr Horatius Bonar

Portrait by John Davidson in St Catherine's Session House
From "St Catherine's in Grange" by Rev. Thomas Maxwell

Horatius Bonar was born in Edinburgh at Old Broughton on December 19th 1808. His father was a solicitor in the Excise Department and his name in fact occurs in the records of the arrest of Deacon Brodie whose robbery of the Excise Office led to his execution. Educated at the High School and Edinburgh University, Horatius Bonar was ordained for the ministry, and his first appointment was at St John's

70

Church, Leith, under the Reverend James Lewis. Soon afterwards he obtained his first charge as minister of the North Parish Church in Kelso, spending twenty-nine years there. He had an important influence as a preacher, but more especially as the author of religious tracts and pamphlets, one of these achieving a sale of 285,000 copies throughout the country. Another tract which apparently greatly impressed Queen Victoria sold a million copies. One book of his hymns had 150,000 copies published.

At the Disruption of 1843, being a staunch supporter of Dr Thomas Chalmers, Dr Bonar resigned his Kelso North charge to become minister of the town's newly established Free Church. For his hymn writing and authorship, which had begun during his many years at Kelso's established church, he was awarded the degree of Doctor of Divinity by Aberdeen University in 1853. In 1866 he was appointed minister of the Chalmers Memorial Free Church in the Grange and was elected Moderator of the Free Church Assembly in 1883. A contemporary writer during Dr Bonar's Edinburgh ministry drew attention to the unobtrusive but powerful influence he had in the city. "He preferred the study to the platform, and the quiet duty of pastoral labour to the excitement of the church courts. His writings are voluminous. His public appearances are few".

Dr Bonar, if unobtrusive, was nevertheless frequently involved in public controversy. One of his special studies, which did not win him much approval or popularity, was his intense interest in Biblical prophecy, first inspired by the famous and

rather dramatic divine, Edward Irving. Bonar eventually gave up prophesying in terms of exact dates and places but he was especially convinced about the imminence of the "Second Coming of Christ". The other principal controversy, already referred to above, was his advocacy of hymn singing in his own Grange Free Church. This led to bitter feeling within the congregation. However, eventually the approved Free Church Hymnal was introduced into Grange Free Church in 1883, amidst considerable opposition and indeed several prominent members of the congregation resigned. When the singing of psalms at the Grange church was led by a precentor, the first of these was James Colston, who was a leading city councillor and author of an important history of Edinburgh's first and subsequent drinking water supply – another of this congregation's "interesting members".

Dr Horatius Bonar married Jane, daughter of the Reverend Robert Lundie, minister of Kelso, and had one son and three daughters. His son Horatius N. became minister of the Free Church at Saltoun. Dr Bonar died on July 31st 1889, in the 52nd year of his ministry, and was buried in Canongate Churchyard. Among his literary works a book entitled *My Old Letters* had a wide and deep impact. The author presents the work as if he were in fact looking over old letters received from a wide variety of people on a broad range of topics. His replies to these and his comments permitted him to deal with them in many ways, sometimes in poetry, in philosophical and scientific discourse, or in theological terms, together revealing an incredibly far-reaching knowledge of the current issues and problems of his day.

It has been suggested that the Bonar family, with the possible exception of the McLeods, gave more members to the ministry of the church in Scotland than any other. Dr Horatius Bonar's earliest clerical forbear was John Bonar, minister of Torphichen in 1693, and other members of the family served as ministers of the Established or Free Church for over 350 years. His many hymns, still widely known and sung today, provide perhaps the greatest and most perennial memorial to Dr Horatius Bonar.

JAMES BUCHANAN

ONE of the most dramatic and indeed historic events in the proud chronicles of Edinburgh's Medical School during its 19th-century heyday of world renown was that which occurred on November 8th 1847, in the house of Professor James Young Simpson, Professor of Midwifery, at 52 Queen Street. Many accounts and indeed illustrations, some of the latter of quite a humorous nature, tell of the after-dinner experiment carried out on themselves by Simpson and his two medical colleagues, Dr James Matthews Duncan and Dr Thomas Keith to ascertain the anaesthetic properties of chloroform.

For some considerable time prior to 1847, anaesthesia had been administered during surgical operations by the use of either nitrous oxide or ether. The latter indeed had been widely used and certainly had a strong anaesthetic effect but could give rise to unfortunate side effects and the search therefore continued

for substances of greater purity and a safer effectiveness. None was more anxious to find an ideal chemical reagent – what he called a "drowsy syrup" – than Professor James Simpson who had in fact been promised a sample of such a "syrup" – "a perchloride of formyle" – by a friend, a Linlithgow surgeon, chemist and bookseller, Dr David Waldie, whose premises were in Linlithgow High Street. Simpson waited eagerly for the promised sample of purified chloroform. Waldie had moved to Liverpool to become a chemist to the Apothecaries Company there but continued working on the preparation for Simpson. Then disaster struck. Waldie's Liverpool laboratory and its highly inflammable contents were destroyed by fire.

Simpson conveyed his sympathy to Waldie, and indeed, in a paper, later paid tribute to his work, but he also indicated that since he was anxious to press on with his proposed trials of chloroform and having been offered a purified sample by another friend Mr J. Duncan of the then quite famous and pioneering Edinburgh pharmacists, Duncan Flockhart and Co., he intended to go ahead. The first samples supplied by Duncan Flockhart failed to impress Simpson, and then on the evening of November 8th 1847, the doorbell at 52 Queen Street rang and a young apprentice chemist delivered the historic bottle of purified chloroform. This sample Simpson decided to use.

Dinner being over, Simpson and his two young medical colleagues, in place of liqueurs perhaps, each had a small glass of chloroform from which they proceeded to sniff, cautiously at first, and then more boldly. "The seductive, sickly aroma of the drowsy syrup", one account relates, "enchanted them, producing a reckless, magical sense of forgetfulness and relaxation". And then the three experimenters passed out. Simpson, apparently, was first to awaken, his two friends still prostrate on the floor. When they "came round", Simpson expressed their common experience in a few simple words: "This is much better than ether". Four days later Simpson used chloroform in one of his midwifery cases with quite remarkable results. The further systematic purification and development of chloroform proceeded. Soon it was in widespread use – but much more rapidly by surgeons in Britain than in the United States where for some time ether still remained in wider use. The fame achieved by Simpson through his experimental work in the introduction of chloroform forms an important chapter in the history of world medicine and brought him numerous honours.

At the time of writing this an elderly lady resident in the Grange district of Edinburgh still speaks with legitimate pride of Duncan Flockhart's young apprentice pharmacist who on that historic evening in November 1847 had been sent on the errand from the firm's shop at 52 North Bridge across the New Town to Queen Street to deliver the precious bottle. The apprentice with the humble part in the important event was her father, Mr James Buchanan. James Buchanan was born in Corstorphine on January 1st 1831. He attended school at Corstorphine and later at Liberton. His father had been an orra-man and general factotum to one of the Duncans of the pharmaceutical firm

James Buchanan

By courtesy of his daughter Miss Margaret Buchanan

and it was as a result of this that young James Buchanan was taken on as the firm's first indentured apprentice. In those early days prior to systematic courses, college training and degrees, the road to qualification and promotion was through daily experience – the old apprenticeship system. Long before the advent of neatly packaged proprietary medicines and antibiotics, Duncan Flockhart had their own "physic garden" at Warriston where the plants used in their pharmaceutical preparations were grown. A knowledge of botany was then essential for a chemist and James Buchanan became so expert in this subject and its medical or therapeutic applications that he was appointed a teacher and examiner to the University medical students who were then required to serve a short apprenticeship in pharmacy. Buchanan eventually became a senior partner in the thriving and expanding pharmaceutical firm and was responsible for the later Princes Street shop, serving there for just over fifty years. The North Bridge and Princes Street shops have long since closed.

James Buchanan was one of the very many Edinburgh people with positions of heavy responsibility who found respite from the pressures of city life by residing in the peace and seclusion of ·the Grange district. Brother-in-law of Robert Morham, a notable City Architect of his day, it was the latter who designed for James Buchanan and his large family the very fine villa which came to be known as Oswald House in South Oswald Road. Here Buchanan, already an expert botanist in his profession, still found the subject a rewarding hobby in his spacious gardens and large greenhouses which were a feature of Oswald House, and in which he grew orchids, palms, vines and peaches. James Buchanan, friend of many of the notable and interesting Edinburgh men of his day, died in 1909.

5 WHITEHOUSE/ BRUNTSFIELD

JOHN HOME

"WHAUR'S yer Willie Shakespeare noo!" The wildly enthusiastic and perhaps provocatively aggressive words rang out from one captivated member of the audience in Edinburgh's Canongate Theatre in the Old Playhouse Close on December 14th 1756 as the curtain fell on the apparently highly successful "first night" production of *Douglas*, a Scottish drama by playwright John Home. Playwright, yes, but also a man with a prior commitment to another calling – the ministry of the Kirk. The successful author was in fact the Reverend John Home, and while the man in the audience had been so carried away as to assert Home's defiant challenge to England's William Shakespeare, the Kirk authorities were not so (or indeed at all) impressed. On the contrary the Reverend John Home by his very theatrical success had in the eyes of the church authorities struck a blow for "Satan and all his works" – not on account of the play's content, which was inoffensive enough: no, the iniquity was in the theatre itself and especially that the play had been written by a minister, a circumstance seen as furthering the influence of the Devil in their very midst. Certainly any minister so involved was deserving of the strictest censure: hence the reputation and the fate of John Home in the Edinburgh of 1756 were in the melting-pot or the fiery furnace.

There is a traditional belief that Home was for some time a tenant of the Whitehouse, the early 16th century mansion house which was eventually to become part of St Margaret's Convent in Whitehouse Loan in 1834, and that he wrote part of *Douglas* while residing there. After a succession of owners of the Whitehouse estate from around 1505 onwards, from the early 18th century the house, then situated well out from the city in pleasant rural surroundings, seems not to have been resided in by its owners but proved desirable and conducive to tenancy by a sequence of Edinburgh literary

John Home
By an unknown artist
By courtesy of the National Galleries of Scotland, Edinburgh

figures, amongst these being the Reverend Hugh Blair, the Reverend

December 14th 1756 and the play sustained a long and successful run — that is to say successful perhaps for its author, but leading churchmen were outraged, not only because a minister had written the play but also that many other ministers had attended and praised it. A great public controversy ensued, with many pamphlets published either defending or condemning Home. In February 1757 *Douglas* was staged in London, and certain critics hailed the author as introducing "a great revival of the true language of the stage". Home was fêted in London literary and theatrical society circles.

If not all London drama critics were at one about Home's success, certainly the Church authorities in Edinburgh were unanimous: Home must go! However, before the church could officially censure him, he resigned his ministry on June 7th 1757, preaching his farewell sermon at Athelstaneford two days previously "to a sorrowing congregation". Latterly, Home resided in a farmhouse, which he purchased at Kilduff in East Lothian. He still had plays performed successfully in London and continued to enjoy a high reputation for his generous hospitality in Edinburgh circles, being particularly friendly with Walter Scott and David Hume. It was said that Home and Hume differed in only one subject — their taste in wine. While Home preferred claret, the philosopher greatly favoured port, which Home described as "poison". David Hume kept up their amicably tacit "agreement to differ" until the end, even introducing a personally written codicil in his will leaving Home a consignment of port by way of a last

John Home and Principal Robertson of the University, although the last is usually associated most closely with tenancy of the then nearby Grange House.

John Home was born at Quality Street, near Bernard Street, Leith, on September 21st 1722, his father being Town Clerk of the port and a distant relation of the Earl of Home. Educated at "the Grammar School of Leith" and then the University, Home was licensed to preach in 1745. Strongly anti-Jacobite, he offered his services to the English forces under Sir John Cope. Indeed he subsequently wrote an account of the '45 Rebellion which was considered remarkably pro-English, biased and distorted. In 1747, he was appointed minister of Athelstaneford in East Lothian, but did not live at the manse there, spending an active social life in Edinburgh with his close friends, among whom was the future University Principal Robertson, and David Hume, to whom he was related.

Much of Home's early dramatic writing which he took to London in the hope of performance there was rejected, as also was *Douglas*, which he had hoped Garrick would perform. He therefore felt impelled to stage a first production of *Douglas* in the Canongate Theatre. It is said that a number of his friends, prominent Edinburgh literary men, took part in the first rehearsal — including David Hume, Professor Adam Ferguson, and the future Principal Robertson, along with Home himself in the role of Douglas, but this account may well be apocryphal. However, at any rate, the first public performance took place in the Canongate Theatre on humorous gesture of "reconciliation".

John Home, centre of so much controversy, friend of so many Edinburgh writers, well known in London theatrical circles and London high society, where friendship with influential people such as the Marquis of Bute brought considerable financial advantage, but above all (for some at least) "Scotland's ane Wullie Shakespear", died in Edinburgh "at Merchiston" (although the precise place of residence is not stated) on September 5th 1808, in his 86th year.

BISHOP JAMES GILLIS

THE convent of St Catherine of Sienna in Sciennes, built in 1517, and giving its name to the district, was the last religious house to be built in Scotland before the Reformation of 1560. Not very far away, on the lands of Whitehouse, the convent, dedicated to St Margaret of Scotland and established in 1834, had the distinction of being the first religious house to be built in Scotland after the Reformation. The latter convent was the long-desired creation of one of the most distinguished Roman Catholic bishops of that period, the early 19th century, when, following the Catholic Emancipation Act of 1829, the Catholic Church in Scotland was beginning to emerge from its "underground" situation and striving to re-establish itself during an era hailed as "the second spring". The bishop concerned, whose name is synonymous with St Margaret's Convent in Whitehouse Loan, and who certainly merits inclusion in the biographical annals of South Edinburgh, was James Gillis, a man of wide-ranging and very appreciable talents.

James Gillis was born at Montreal on April 7th 1802. His father had emigrated thence from Banffshire in his youth and had eventually become a successful and quite wealthy businessman. He had married a Miss Langley, a native of Kent and an Episcopalian, although she became a Roman Catholic shortly before her death. James Gillis was their only child. He began his education at Montreal in a college run by the priests of the French Congregation of Saint Sulpice. Much of the teaching was in French, and young James Gillis became fluent in that language, a fact which was to provide a valuable asset later in his career.

The future bishop's parents came to Scotland in the summer of 1816, residing in Fochabers in Morayshire, where they spent their retirement. A year later, James Gillis, then aged 15, entered the small Catholic seminary of Aquhorties in Aberdeenshire as an ecclesiastical student. Shortly afterwards he was sent with other students to the seminary of Saint Nicolas in Paris. Here he specialised in the classics and rhetoric. His philosophical and theological studies were pursued at a college just outside Paris. In 1826 recurring ill-health forced James Gillis to return to Scotland, and it was a year later that he was ordained.

Towards the end of 1827, Father Gillis was residing at Blairs, the large Aberdeenshire country home of Mr J. Menzies of Pitfodels, a man of very considerable wealth, whom he had already met in Paris. In 1828 Gillis came south to Edinburgh to serve as a "missionary priest" under Bishop Paterson, the Vicar Apostolic of the

Eastern District of Scotland. On account of the stringency of the Reformation in Scotland and the resultant great reduction in the Catholic population and diminution of its social status, Rome still regarded the country as missionary territory and this situation and the division of the country into districts under Vicars Apostolic obtained until the restoration of the Catholic hierarchy in 1878. Ill health prevented Father Gillis undertaking the heavy responsibilities of the few priests on the Edinburgh "mission" and, on account of his great pulpit oratory and his fluency in French, he was sent in 1829 to France to make a series of appeals from the pulpit for funds required for the repair of St Mary's Chapel (later Cathedral) in Broughton Street. His French financial appeals were highly successful, although while he was there the Revolution of 1830 broke out and he was fortunate to make his escape back to Scotland. When the exiled French royal family subsequently came to reside at Holyrood, Father Gillis was of great service to them there and a close bond of friendship developed.

In 1831 Mr Menzies of Pitfodels took up residence in Edinburgh, at first at 24 York Place, where Bishop Paterson accepted his offer of accommodation in the proximity of St Mary's Chapel. Bishop Paterson also appointed Father Gillis to be his secretary at that time, and he began to reside at York Place, where his friendship with Mr Menzies deepened further. One of Father Gillis's major concerns was for the better religious education of Catholic young people and he believed that this could best be achieved by the establishment of a religious community in Edinburgh, a teaching order, even though this might be opposed by the civic authorities and indeed by the Catholic community itself, considering such a step premature. However, Bishop Paterson was persuaded to allow Father Gillis to undertake another "begging mission" in Europe and this he did, going to France with a letter of introduction and support from the exiled French royal family. Although his pulpit appeals for funds were not too well received everywhere in France, Italy and Spain where the churches had their own financial problems, nevertheless he did acquire quite a considerable sum, such was his eloquent oratory and mastery of the language.

While Father Gillis was abroad, Bishop Paterson died, and among his papers were found letters in which he intended to petition Rome that Father Gillis be appointed his successor. This petition was not supported by the other Catholic episcopal authorities in Scotland, who considered Father Gillis too young to take on the burden of a bishop's responsibilities. Bishop Carruthers was appointed, in 1833, and enjoyed Father Gillis's complete allegiance and support. The new bishop in turn encouraged Father Gillis in his plan to see a religious order established in Edinburgh, and Mr Menzies of Pitfodels promised substantial financial support for the building required. The lands of Whitehouse, including its 16th-century mansion-house, were duly purchased from the then owner, Mrs Anne Grant of Kilgraston in Perthshire, for £3,000 in February 1834. At the same time, Mr Menzies purchased

Greenhill Cottage, a short distance north-west of the Whitehouse and there took up residence with Father Gillis. This house in later years was to become the home of Dr Sophia Jex-Blake and the embryonic Bruntsfield Hospital.

After negotiations with the superiors of the Ursulines of Jesus, a French teaching order of nuns, it was agreed that a number of sisters would come from France to form the nucleus of the new community at Whitehouse Loan, to be dedicated to St Margaret, Queen of Scotland. They would join the two Scottish foundresses, Miss Anne Trail and Miss Margaret Clapperton, who had entered the Ursuline Order and were completing their novitiate at Chevagnes in France. The convent was ready for occupation on December 26th 1834. The magnificent chapel, designed by the celebrated architect, Gillespie Graham, was opened six months later, on June 16th 1835. Soon after their coming to Whitehouse Loan, any misgivings which may have been in the minds of Edinburgh's non-Catholic (and indeed Catholic) population were soon dispelled as the valuable religious educational work of the nuns became obvious, and their visiting of the poor and sick in their own homes or Edinburgh institutions and hospitals was greatly appreciated.

In July 1838 Father Gillis, who had seen his dream realised with St Margaret's established, and who had done so much besides for the development of the Catholic community in Edinburgh, was appointed assistant bishop to Bishop Carruthers of the Eastern District. After his consecration and despite continuing and deteriorating ill-health, he set out on yet another visit to Paris, his preaching there being in great demand, while he also sought further financial support for the needs of the church in Scotland. In 1843, while Bishop Gillis was visiting the Scottish Benedictine abbey at Ratisbon in Germany, news reached him of the death of his great friend and generous benefactor, Mr Menzies of Pitfodels. He immediately returned to Edinburgh to preside over his friend's funeral service. Mr Menzies was interred in the crypt of St Margaret's Convent. In his will Mr Menzies made further generous bequests to the church, including his house and lands at Greenhill. Bishop Gillis, never without new ideas for developments, had for some time

Bishop James Gillis

Artist unknown
From Journal and Appendix to Scotichronicon and
Monasticon. Ed. J. F. S. Gordon. John Tweed, Glasgow
1867

planned to build a new Catholic cathedral of St Margaret and a college at Greenhill. Plans drawn up for these by the famous architect Welby Pugin were publicly exhibited with an accompanying appeal for funds, but by the time the latter seemed sufficient, much building of fine villas in the desirable district of Greenhill had begun and the plans for the cathedral and college were abandoned.

Amongst the many developments which were a feature of Bishop Gillis' episcopate was the introduction of sung liturgy, especially High Mass, with orchestral accompaniment, by eminent composers, in St Mary's Cathedral in Broughton Street, which attracted very large congregations, including many non-Catholics, as did his own pulpit oratory.

Few portraits of Bishop Gillis exist. That reproduced here is by an unknown artist and appears in the *Journal and Appendix to the Scotichronicon and Monasticon*. In St Margaret's Convent is a large portrait in oils of the bishop by a celebrated artist who for some time resided in South Edinburgh, Sam Bough, R.S.A. Although a non-Catholic and self-styled "Bohemian" who seemed to delight in defying convention, Bough was a great friend and admirer of Bishop Gillis, often slipping in to one of the back-row seats in St Mary's Cathedral to hear him preach and to enjoy the fine music.

Bishop Gillis, responsible for most impressive and varied developments during his service as an ordinary priest and as a bishop, died on February 24th 1864. A few days later his remains were interred in the crypt of St Margaret's Convent, which survives as perhaps his most fitting memorial.

ANNE AGNES TRAIL

THE foundation of St Margaret's Convent in Whitehouse Loan evokes predominantly the names of three people: Bishop James Gillis, Miss Anne Trail and Miss Margaret Clapperton. While Bishop Gillis was essentially responsible for planning and establishing the convent, and finding much of the funding required, the two ladies, having joined the Ursulines of Jesus, were the foundresses of the convent and its first entrants. Much is known concerning Miss Trail, who wrote a short account of her conversion from Presbyterianism to Catholicism, published in 1897 as a series of letters, and who became the first Mother Superior of St Margaret's. Little is on record concerning the other co-foundress, Miss Margaret Clapperton, who was a native of Fochabers. She was aged only twenty-one and very much younger than Miss Trail, when they together entered the Ursuline Order. Margaret Clapperton, born of a Catholic family, a member of which in later times was to become a prominent member of the Scottish clergy, nevertheless became a nun very much against her father's wishes. He was simply concerned and a little doubtful that her decision was the right one. There is some evidence from the history of folk songs in the north that in her teens Margaret Clapperton ("Bonnie Peggy Clapperton") was a girl of rare beauty and the subject of at least one such song.

Miss Anne Trail was born in

Panbridge, Forfarshire, on February 2nd 1798, one of the large family of the parish minister. When she was aged fourteen and had undergone some years of education, she was "appointed" tutor to her younger brothers and sisters whom she taught at home, in her own words "taking up eight hours a day". Her home was one of strict religious observance, and from an early age Anne Trail appears to have adopted a severe Calvinistic outlook on life which gave rise to much mental conflict and torment. She imposed a strict rule upon herself, "refraining from reading novels and plays, even poetry, and avoiding amusements".

In her early twenties Miss Trail went to reside with some relations in Ireland and then proceeded to London to study art, for which she apparently had considerable talent, especially in pencil drawing and sketching. In London she stayed with wealthy relatives, but deliberately avoided parties, the theatre, and "the social round". Her London artistic tuition must have proved effective, since on her return to Edinburgh she spent two years busily engaged on various commissions – "one of these for one of the greatest connoisseurs of art in the Scottish Capital".

At the age of twenty-eight Miss Trail went to Italy for further studies in art, arriving in Rome in November 1826. She spent some time in Venice with the Reverend Mr Middleton and his wife, friends of her father; then went for some time to Parma before returning to Rome via Florence and Milan. In the course of her Italian travels and especially of her art studies, she had visited very many famous churches. Initially and for a considerable time, as a spectator at

Catholic services, she was confirmed in her belief that "Catholicism was essentially superstition and idolatory" and was strengthened in her adherence to Presbyterianism for "its simplicity of worship and republican nature of its government – so different from Catholicism".

Sister Agnes Traill
From "History of St Margaret's Convent, Edinburgh" 1886

However, inevitably, in her visits to churches and famous buildings and through the friendships she made in Rome, and discussions in which she took part, she was forced to look behind the external aspects of Catholicism and to learn more of its basic doctrines and claims. These she resisted strongly in her own mind and in discussions with priests and others, but she did agree to read Catholic literature, simply to demonstrate her openness of mind. Eventually she began to have doubts about her own traditional Presbyterian beliefs, and the conflict which began to arise in her thinking she has set out in her published letters.

When Miss Trail's friends had first heard of her projected visit to Italy to study art they had jocularly referred to her as "The lady who has gone to Rome to convert the Pope". On June 16th 1828, the lady became a convert to the Catholic Church. She returned to Scotland in the summer of 1829 and visited her family. When she had written to her father from Rome, indicating her intention of becoming a Catholic he had begged her to postpone such a step and to come home and discuss it fully. She did not accede to this appeal so, with a deep awareness and acute sensitivity as regards the inevitable effect upon her father, she must have found the confrontation which took place when she did come home agonisingly painful. She would be made to feel she had brought disgrace upon her family.

Miss Trail returned to London and there was invited by the Abbess of the Benedictine convent at Hammersmith to visit her there. While she was residing at the convent Bishop Gillis arrived, *en route* for France, and they were introduced. She heard him outline his plans for the establishment of St Margaret's Convent at Whitehouse Loan. After the bishop had returned to Scotland she wrote to him offering herself as a member of the proposed new community. Her offer was readily accepted, and, with Miss Margaret Clapperton, she duly set out for the Ursuline convent at Chevagnes in France and entered the novitiate. When she took her final vows Miss Trail chose the name of Sister Agnes Xavier. As the first Mother Superior of St Margaret's she served there for forty years, and died on December 3rd 1872.

DR SOPHIA JEX-BLAKE

THE founder of Bruntsfield Hospital, Dr Sophia Jex-Blake, was amongst those pre-Suffragette ladies who heralded a new era in national life. She was born in Hastings on January 21st 1840, when it was still rare for women to seek or achieve a career in the professions or public life. Dr Jex-Blake's parents were comfortably off, of professional background, some of the male members having been doctors. The strong determination of character she showed in early childhood continued at boarding school in Brighton and subsequently at Queen's College, London, where she qualified as a teacher. Various friendships awakened her interest in medicine, and on coming to Edinburgh in 1869 she found that while certain fringe medical studies were open to women, graduation in medicine was not. She was compelled to qualify in Berne and then as a practitioner in Ireland. In 1874 she opened a small medical school for women in London.

Returning to Edinburgh, Dr Jex-Blake began campaigning fearlessly and vigorously for the admission of female students to complete medical training. The opposition led by Professor Robert Christison and other prominent medicals was fierce. The struggle was exhausting: constant meetings, continual correspondence, dramatic confrontations, and even rioting. But Dr Jex-Blake persevered with unflinching tenacity. She was not without influential male

Dr Sophia Jex-Blake

conditions, often requiring facilities not yet available in the city. After moving her home to Bruntsfield Lodge, formerly Greenhill Cottage, and still to be seen in Greenhill Terrace, she received many more patients there. Her constant supporter and adviser was Dr Henry Littlejohn, Edinburgh's first and long-serving Medical Officer of Health.

In 1898, after nearly thirty years of demanding and pioneering struggle, Dr Jex-Blake retired and settled in Mark Cross, in Sussex. There she died on January 7th 1912. She was buried in Rotherfield Churchyard. There is a memorial to her in St Giles Cathedral in Edinburgh, and a special bronze medallion mounted on marble is treasured in Bruntsfield Hospital for Women and Children in Whitehouse Loan, built around her home at Bruntsfield Lodge. At the time of writing the future of Bruntsfield Hospital is in the balance.

supporters, notably Professors Masson and Charteris, Mr Alexander Russell, editor of the *Scotsman*, and Mr Duncan McLaren, M.P. Victory came at last, in 1889, with the Universities (Scotland) Act granting women full admission to medical graduation, although Edinburgh did not implement this in full until 1894.

Dr Jex-Blake opened her own small medical school for female students in 1888 in Surgeons Square. Acting on her other great conviction, that women patients should have the right to treatment by doctors of their own sex, she first accepted women and children at her home at 4 Manor Place. She opened a small dispensary with a few beds for women at 6 Grove Street in 1885, and later at No 73. She attempted to treat a wide range of

SIR GEORGE WARRENDER

TWO other names are intimately associated with Bruntsfield. Towards the end of the 14th century Richard Broune was the King's Sergeant responsible for law and order in this part of the Burgh Muir, which from even earlier times was Crown Land. Broune was granted a small portion of land here and probably built himself some primitive type of dwelling, the forerunner of Bruntsfield House. It is from this fact that the name "Broune's field" originally arose, eventually becoming corrupted to the name we know today. Sir George

Warrender, 6th Baronet of Lochend, near Dunbar, and also owner of the lands and castle-like mansion-house of Bruntsfield from 1867, was so closely associated with the district that for long many people referred to the 16th century mansion-house as Warrender House. Today many local street names bear the name Warrender or are named after persons or estates linked with the Warrender family by intermarriage.

While little is known about Richard Broune, much more is on record concerning his 19th-century successor at Bruntsfield, Sir George Warrender. Malcolm Cant in his most informative work *Marchmont in Edinburgh* provides considerable detail as regards Sir George's business acumen and foresight in his having drawn up a great feuing and building plan for his Bruntsfield estate, originally by the celebrated architect David Bryce in 1869, to be superseded by Watherston's scheme of 1876. But this building enterprise, while perhaps constituting his principal Edinburgh business activity, was only one of Sir George's many schemes. While no doubt extremely lucrative, it was not the main source of his considerable wealth.

Sir George Warrender was born in October 1825, only son of the 5th Baronet of Lochend in East Lothian. The Bruntsfield estate was acquired by the Warrender family in 1695 and the baronetcy was originally conferred on another Sir George Warrender, Member of Parliament and Lord Provost of Edinburgh from 1713 to 1715. He was strongly opposed to the 1715 Jacobite Rebellion and the attempt by the Stuarts to regain their rightful claim to the British throne. It was this stand, no doubt, that resulted in his being rewarded by conferral of a baronetcy.

Sir George Warrender, 6th Baronet, was an only son. His mother was a daughter of the 8th Earl of Lauderdale, hence one of the street names in Sir George's building plan. After retiring from service in the Coldstream Guards, he commanded the 1st Haddington Rifle Volunteers. Upon his succession to the Lochend baronetcy in 1867, he concentrated on the development of his estates, especially at Bruntsfield, and after the completion of the developments there, he became one of the most extensive owners of feus in Edinburgh. Sir George always resided for a few months every year with his family ar Bruntsfield House. He was a good neighbour to the community of the adjacent St Margaret's Convent in Whitehouse Loan, making certain arrangements of his lands which were to their benefit.

Six years before feuing out his Bruntsfield estate, Sir George Warrender accepted an appointment which was to become the principal source of his wealth. In 1873 he was appointed Chairman of the newly formed Scottish American Investment Company, founded by Mr William Menzies, Professor of Conveyancing at Edinburgh University. Among Sir George Warrender's other colleagues on the board of this company, which was to make available much-needed capital for the rapidly expanding Americas, were Thomas Nelson, head of the famous Edinburgh publishers, and John Cowan head of the prosperous paper-making firm. Sir George's chairmanship of the new trust was of key importance in view of his other business associations, such as directorship of the Royal Bank of Scotland and the Caledonian Insurance Company, as also his interests in the Arizona Copper Company, the London Scottish American Trust and the Anglo-American Debenture Company. In addition, Sir George was a Deputy-Lieutenant of Edinburgh and of Haddington. Certainly an experienced businessman. An ardent Conservative in politics, he did much to build up the party at a period when it was certainly far from strong in many Scottish constituencies.

A member of the Scottish American Investment Company described Sir George Warrender as "a shrewd, keen man of business, inclined to be purse-proud but just in his ways and methods. At a board meeting, was expeditious and clear-headed . . . if a shareholder proved unruly or was unduly prosy, Sir George could snuff him out in a very polite yet decided way". Thomas Nelson was "the richest and most influential of those who gathered round the board. Small in stature, physically rather weak, he was mentally a giant, with a great bump of kindness in his nature. He was keen after money, but it was not his god". Edward Blyth, "a big handsome man who had made a fortune as a civil engineer [he constructed the Caledonian Railway], was almost as well known in Edinburgh as Sir Walter Scott's monument". Of the many American enterprises which these Edinburgh businessmen combined to support financially under the shrewd chairmanship and steadying advice of Sir George Warrender, perhaps the most lucrative for all of

them was the building of the Canadian Pacific Railway.

Sir George married a daughter of Sir Hugh Campbell of Marchmont in 1854 (another reason for the subsequent street names) and they had three sons and three daughters. Lady Warrender died in 1875. The eldest son, a lieutenant in the Grenadier Guards, died unmarried in 1894. The second son, George John Scott, had a most distinguished naval career. Enlisting in 1873, he saw service as a midshipman in the Zulu War of 1879. His advancement was rapid. He became a competent interpreter in French, a rare and valuable ability at that time. During the Boxer Rising of

Sir George Warrender

1900 he was captain of *HMS Barfleur.* By 1908 he had been created admiral. He was much concerned about transitions in naval warfare, especially the use of torpedoes. In May 1914 he attended the Kaiser's birthday celebrations at Kiel, when there was as yet no realisation of the imminence of the First World War. He greatly impressed the German naval leaders, who were so soon to become his enemies. In August 1914 Admiral Warrender was a leading figure in a most remarkable episode of the war, when the German navy threatened to attack Britain's east coast. With a small fleet, he turned back the German battleships although they had already bombarded Scarborough, Whitby and Hartlepool. By the end of 1915 Admiral Warrender was Commander-in-Chief at Plymouth. Ill-health forced his retirement a year later and he died in London in 1917. He had married a daughter of the 8th Earl of Shaftesbury and they had two sons and one daughter.

Sir George Warrender of Lochend and Bruntsfield died at his London home in Eaton Square on June 13th 1901, after a long illness. He had remained chairman of the Scottish American Investment Company and was involved in other business activities until his death. His body was brought to Bruntsfield House and then taken in a hearse drawn by six horses with two postillions, to St John the Evangelist's Church at the end of Princes Street, of which Sir George had been a member. After the funeral service his body was taken for burial to Grange cemetery. Sir George's successor, his second son, George John Scott Warrender, was not present, being in command of *HMS Barfleur* in Chinese waters, but George John's wife, Lady Maud Warrender, was among the chief mourners, together with Sir George's youngest son, Hugh Valdave Warrender, and his three daughters, Margaret, Eleanor and Alice. Also present were the Earl of Haddington, the Earl of Rosslyn, Lord Binning, Lord Arran and the directors of the Scottish American Investment Company.

The present head of the Warrender family is Lord Bruntisfield of Boroughmuir, the 8th Baronet, who resides in Switzerland. He was named Victor since Queen Victoria was his godmother and it is believed that he is her last surviving godson. Continuing the family's military traditions, Lord Bruntisfield served in the Grenadier Guards during the First World War and was awarded the Military Cross. He served as Member of Parliament for Grantham from 1923 until 1942 and was created a Peer in that year, choosing to adopt the ancient spelling of Bruntisfield in his title. In his parliamentary career he held many government posts, being Vice-Chamberlain to the Household 1932-1935, Financial Secretary to the Admiralty in 1935 and likewise to the War Office 1935-1940. From 1940-1945 he was Parliamentary Secretary to the Admiralty. Lord Bruntisfield's eldest son, Colonel the Hon. John Warrender, O.B.E., M.C., who resides in Edinburgh, also saw distinguished military service in the Royal Scots Greys.

MARGARET WARRENDER

SIR George Warrender, 6th Baronet of Lochend, whose name is closely associated with the development of the Marchmont district, had three sons and three daughters. The former have already been referred to, and while less is on record concerning the daughters, Margaret, Eleanor and Alice, two of them have literary associations which merit attention.

Margaret Warrender is known to many lovers of Edinburgh as the authoress of a most fascinating little book *Walks near Edinburgh*, published by David Douglas in 1890 and illustrated with black and white sketches by the writer, who was a gifted water-colour artist. In a prefatory note she acknowledges her indebtedness for much of the book's material to her great-aunt, Lady John Scott, and indeed dedicates it to her. Margaret Warrender also published two other works of considerable scholarship. In 1889 *Illustrations of Scottish History in the 16th Century* was published by James Stillie, "being letters and documents of Queen Mary, Queen Elizabeth, James IV and Bothwell, from originals in the possession of Sir George Warrender, Bart., of Lochend". This work contained "secret and confidential letters of Queen Elizabeth and James VI". The papers in this book were part of the important Warrender Collection to which Patrick Fraser Tytler acknowledged his indebtedness in compiling his *History of Scotland*. Miss Warrender was particularly anxious that the Warrender Papers should be carefully collected and safeguarded, since Lochend House at Dunbar, the family seat, had been virtually burned to the ground in 1859. In 1894 William Blackwood & Sons published Miss Warrender's *Marchmont and the Humes of Polwarth*,

which contains interesting illustrations. This work, she wrote, was "Affectionately dedicated to Sir Hugh Hume Campbell, Bt., of Marchmont by his grand-daughter".

Margaret Warrender (Julian Margaret Maitland Warrender) was born in 1855 and resided for a great part of her life in Bruntsfield House for which she had an obviously deep affection, and in 1901, after her father's death, took up residence in London where she remained for nearly half a century. Unlike her ancestor, Sir George Warrender, who in 1715 did so much to resist the Jacobite Rebellion of that year and to save Edinburgh from capture, Margaret was an ardent admirer of Prince Charles Edward Stuart. She had a wide circle of friends, many of them of Polish nationality, whom she valued especially, on account of the Young Pretender's Polish connections. She took an active interest in philosophical and religious matters and in fact became a convert to the Roman Catholic Church. In her will, drawn up in 1943, she described herself as a "domiciled Scotchwoman", and included in a very long catalogue of possessions bequeathed to relatives and friends were details of what was to be known as "The Margaret Warrender Bequest". This consisted of a most interesting collection of holograph letters relating to Prince Charles Edward Stuart, Marie Antoinette, Cardinal Richelieu and other famous personages, along with 37 Jacobite medals and a considerable collection of miniature paintings of the Stuart family and their close supporters. Her bequest was earmarked for the National Library of Scotland, the Scottish National Museum of Antiquities and Portrait

Gallery. The items of the bequest are now in the possession of the last-

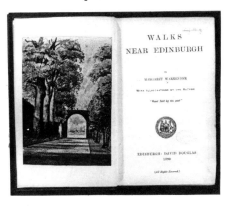

Title page of Miss Margaret Warrender's book, with her own sketch of entrance to Bruntsfield House

By courtesy of the National Library of Scotland, Edinburgh

named institution. Miss Warrender died on April 5th 1950, aged 95, in her London home at 50 Wilton Crescent. Her body was brought for burial to the tiny cemetery at Polwarth in Berwickshire. No portrait of Miss Warrender could be traced.

Miss Alice Helen Warrender, another of Sir George Warrender's three daughters, who was born in 1857, was also to have an association with the literary world, which still continues. In 1919, she founded the prestigious and indeed the oldest of British literary awards, the Hawthornden Prize. It consists of £100 awarded annually to a British writer under forty-one years of age for "the best work of imaginative literature". The award is especially designed to encourage young authors but the word "imaginative" is

broadly interpreted. Biographies are accepted and the work need not be published in book form. It is not a competitive award and a panel of judges decides upon the winner. Since its inception nearly seventy years ago some of the Hawthornden Prize winners have included such famous authors as Sean O'Casey, Siegfried Sassoon, Victoria Sackville-West, James Hilton, Robert Graves, Evelyn Waugh and Graham Greene. Miss Alice Warrender died in 1947 in Cheshire.

JAMES GILLESPIE

IF the Warrender family was to become so closely associated with Bruntsfield House that the mansion-house was referred to by many people as Warrender House, the other name that was to become woven into the annals of Bruntsfield Links and the adjacent village and famous "castle" of Wrychtishousis was James Gillespie, although as a matter of fact he resided far from the district. Sir George Warrender, "the Laird of Bruntsfield", who was responsible for the feuing out and building of so much of the Marchmont area in the late 19th century, and James Gillespie, were both very wealthy men. While a large district commemorates Sir George's planning and business acumen, the present-day high school built around the one-time Warrender family home perpetuates the name of the man who "made his fortune" from the sale of snuff and tobacco and who became known as "the Laird of Colinton".

James Gillespie was born in Edinburgh in 1726. He had one sister and a younger brother, John. Having opened a tobacconist shop in the High Street, at No 231, a little east of the original Mercat Cross, in 1759, the Gillespie brothers purchased a snuff mill, with land attached, at Spylaw in Colinton. By 1786 James Gillespie had acquired the whole of the lands of Spylaw, and five years later became the owner of the nearby estates of Bonaly and Fernielaw. James also profited from property transactions in Leith and from a very successful enterprise in tobacco speculation during the American Civil War. While the younger brother, John, managed the High Street shop (its site is still commemorated by a plaque) James supervised the Spylaw mill where he himself regularly worked late into the night. The business greatly prospered.

Despite his wealth, in his fine mansion at Spylaw, under the high bridge spanning the Water of Leith, James Gillespie treated his domestic staff with great kindness and indulgence. He frequently dined with them, enjoyed their conversation and good humour, and since he himself seldom left Colinton, listened eagerly to their news of the city. The tenants on his estates he also treated most generously. The "Laird of Colinton" permitted himself only one luxury. It was a horse-drawn carriage, of very plain style, simply displaying his coat of arms and the initials J.G., but he very seldom used it, preferring to walk even quite considerable distances, until he found this impossible. Nevertheless, as regards the carriage, Lord Erskine facetiously suggested a motto for the wealthy snuff merchant of Colinton:

"Wha wad hae thocht it
That noses had bocht it".

Kay in his famous portraits quotes these lines and also has a caricature of the Gillespie brothers, portraying James with a large nose.

James survived his brother John by two years, and actively carried on his business until his death at Spylaw on April 8th 1797, aged 71. He was buried beside his brother in a large vault in Colinton parish churchyard and an inscription commemorates his generosity and benefactions. While the brothers had worshipped at Colinton parish church, they were adherents, as had been their parents, of the Cameronians, an early secession sect which had supported the Solemn League and Covenant, and they had regularly attended the annual tent meetings of that body held at Rullion Green near Flotterstone.

Apparently it had been James Gillespie's intention to bequeath a great deal of his wealth to "a youth whom he had conditionally promised to make a man". It is not on record who this young person was, although Lord Cockburn refers to him in his *Memorials*. It would appear that he had offended Gillespie in some way and was excluded from his will. The wealthy "Laird of Colinton" directed that his estate, plus £12,000, should be devoted to the foundation of a hospital for the maintenance of elderly men and women. Additionally, £2,700 was left for the establishment of a school "within the City of Edinburgh or suburbs thereof for the education of 100 poor boys, to be taught reading, writing and arithmetic".

The site chosen for the erection of "James Gillespie's Hospital and Free School" was that on which from early centuries had stood that most impressive and castle-like mansion of Wrychtishousis, to the west of Bruntsfield Links and in what was to be commemoratively named Gillespie Crescent. This most interesting building, dating perhaps from the 14th century, was the early seat of the Napier family (a branch unrelated to the Napiers of Merchiston) and its sudden and over-hasty demolition and the razing of its walls adorned with carved stones of considerable antiquity, many of which bore interesting inscriptions, gave rise to much public controversy and widespread condemnation. Lord Cockburn was particularly outraged. In its place, James Gillespie's hospital was completed in 1802. It was described by one critic as "a tasteless edifice in carpenter's Gothic". The small free school was separate from the main building.

At first, old people eligible for admission to the hospital were required to have been James Gillespie's former servants or tenants, then persons named Gillespie aged 55 and over from any part of Scotland, with those residing in Edinburgh, Leith, Newhaven and Midlothian receiving priority. No-one already in receipt of a pension was eligible. The building could accommodate 66 pensioners but seldom were more than 50 in residence. The governors included twelve members of the Merchant Company of Edinburgh, of which Gillespie himself had been a member; five nominees of Edinburgh Town Council, and two ministers. Eventually, with changes in poor law legislation, residence for pensioners ceased to be provided and pensions were paid instead. In 1887, 167 females and 42 males were beneficiaries. With the ending of provision

of residence for pensioners the school facilities were greatly increased in the main building. From 63 "poor boys" enrolled when the school opened in 1803, by 1887 numbers had risen to an attendance of 1,450 boys and girls.

James Gillespie

Bust in Merchants' Hall, Edinburgh
By courtesy of the Merchant Company of Edinburgh
Photograph by A. C. Robson

The development of the school from its original free admission of poor children to its becoming a fee-paying school has been related elsewhere, as also its transfer to Bruntsfield Links and to its purpose-built premises beside Bruntsfield House as a High School for Girls until it became a comprehensive co-educational school in 1972. Just as the famous mansion of Wrychtishousis was rapidly demolished to make way for the building of James Gillespie's Hospital, which became a subject for artists, so too this building, which for long had been part of the Royal Blind Asylum at Gillespie Crescent was very hastily demolished to make way for a sheltered housing scheme. As for the commemoration of James Gillespie himself, this remains in the streets bearing his name under the towering Barclay Church steeple, in the High School centred on Bruntsfield House, and at the annual Founder's Day ceremony held in the school when tribute is paid to his memory. The specially chosen guest speaker on this occasion was for long presented with a silver snuff-box, but nowadays the memento takes some other form.

SIR JOHN USHER

THE Usher Institute in Warrender Park Road not only commemorates the generosity of its benefactor and founder, Sir John Usher of Norton and Wells, but also in its historical context as a gift to Edinburgh University it highlights a milestone and marks an important era in the development of concern for public health in Edinburgh, traceable in origin to the tercentenary celebrations of the University held in April 1884 and the assembly then in the city of what must have been the most distinguished and international gathering of learned men it had ever welcomed; it has remained unequalled since. The establishment of the Usher Institute marked the triumph of a small group of Edinburgh men, medical and non-medical, and their association with one of the world's greatest scientists

and benefactors, Louis Pasteur. As Sir John Usher remarked in his speech during the opening ceremony of the Institute, it was his recognition of the idealism of these men and the possibility of its receiving practical expression which prompted his financial support.

The special feature of the University's tercentenary celebrations a century ago was the attendance at its proceedings, especially at the honorary degree awarding ceremony and the banquet, of delegations from learned bodies from many countries, which included very eminent men. In the French delegation representing the French Academy of Sciences was the great Louis Pasteur. While Pasteur's official engagements and speeches during the occasion are on record, of great importance for the future of the health of Edinburgh, in the light of the distinguished French bacteriologist's discovery of the bacterial origin of so many epidemic diseases, were the informal meetings between Pasteur and Dr Henry Littlejohn, Edinburgh's first Medical Officer of Health, whose famous report of 1865 had drawn attention to the appalling health conditions and social environment in Edinburgh and the need for radical reforms and improvements in the prevention and treatment of infectious disease. Of crucial consequence also, especially as regards the health of the city, was the establishment of a University Chair of Public Health with suitable laboratories and teaching facilities, and the eventual recognition of these needs may be attributed to Pasteur's meetings and discussions with Mr Alexander Low Bruce (son-in-law of David Livingstone, the famous explorer) who was a director of

Younger's Brewery in Holyrood Road and regarding whose problems in beer fermentation processes, Bruce had persuaded Pasteur to visit the brewery and provide practical advice.

Apart from its application to brewing and the financial importance of this, Bruce was also greatly interested in the new science of bacteriology, of which Louis Pasteur and Robert Koch were the pioneers, and its practical relevance to the health problems of Edinburgh. Indeed, such was Pasteur's influence on Bruce that when the latter suddenly became seriously ill, he introduced a codicil to his will, providing for the sum of approximately £5,000 to be set aside for the establishment of a Chair of Public Health in the University. When Bruce died, his bequest, with added contributions from other members of his family and Sir John Usher, was readily accepted by the University and the Bruce and John Usher Chair of Public Health, the first of its kind in Britain, was created in 1898. While the establishment of the chair and the importance which it now attributed to the subject of public health in medical education represented an important step forward, as Sir John Usher remarked in his speech when he handed over the Usher Institute to the University that someone had commented to him, "a chair without an institute is not much good". "There was an old saying," Sir John continued, "In for a penny, in for a pound," and when I was asked if I would build the institute also, I said that I would".

The John Usher Institute of Public Health was officially opened by University Principal and Vice-

Sir John Usher

From "A History of the Usher family in Scotland"

Chancellor, Sir William Muir, on June 11th 1902. In response to the University's expression of gratitude, especially by the student representatives, for his munificence, Sir John Usher stressed that it was really the late Mr Alexander Bruce who, through Pasteur's visit, had first thought of the creation of the Chair. He himself saw great importance in the provision of the laboratories and classrooms. The building and its facilities were also to be made available to the Public Health Administration of the City of Edinburgh.

Sir John Usher, commemorated by the building in Warrender Park Road, was born in 1828, the fourth son and twelfth child of Andrew Usher and his wife Margaret Balmer. In 1853 he married Mary Ann, daughter of Thomas Balmer of Ettrick Braes. They had five sons and two daughters. As a young man John Usher was a Liberal in politics and an ardent admirer of Gladstone. When the Liberal Party split up over the Irish Home Rule issue, John Usher joined the Liberal Unionist Party. In 1892, while Gladstone was campaigning in Midlothian, John Usher attended one of his meetings and heckled his former friend and hero. Gladstone was quite furious. In 1899 John Usher was created a baronet and in 1903, in recognition of his generous gift of the Usher Institute, the University awarded him the honorary degree of Ll.D. In 1896 Usher had purchased the estate of Wells and Bedrule near Hawick, formerly the property of the Earls of Traquair. He had also acquired the estate and mansion of Norton, near Edinburgh. Both estates and houses have passed from this branch of the Usher family. Sir John Usher who was a member of the Free Church of Scotland and a generous benefactor of that body died suddenly in Cairo in 1904.

Dr Hunter Stewart was appointed the first Professor of Public Health. He had been a close academic colleague of Dr Henry Littlejohn and indeed during the opening ceremony of the Usher Institute and Professor Stewart taking up office, no-one in the whole distinguished assembly must have been more deeply satisfied at this historic event than Dr Littlejohn, the city's first Medical Officer of Health, appointed in 1862, who served in that capacity for nearly fifty years. Since the publication of his famous report on the health of the city in 1865, he had struggled ceaselessly for innumerable reforms and improvements in public health administration. The opening of "the

Usher" was the crowning of all his labours and signified a new era, and the course now inaugurated would lead on to the degree of the Diploma in Public Health, which soon and for long would become the pre-requisite for all doctors who wished to specialise in public health and to become Medical Officers of Health in various towns and cities. The degree is now no longer awarded, and what used to be called "public health" is now referred to as "community medicine".

ALEXANDER McKELLAR

BRUNTSFIELD Links remains a largely unbuilt-upon reminder of the ancient Burgh Muir, sloping gently upwards from the former Borough or South Loch, now the Meadows. It occupies a proud place in the city's history as its earliest course for the pursuit of the Royal and Ancient game of "gowf". This claim is sometimes disputed and the point made that Leith Links, in fact, first witnessed the game at a much earlier date; this is undoubtedly true but in the 15th century and for long afterwards Leith was a separate burgh and thus Bruntsfield Links constituted Edinburgh's earliest course.

Apart from the several famous golfing societies which originated at Bruntsfield Links, such as the Royal Burgess and the Bruntsfield Links Golfing Societies, both long since possessed of their own private courses far from Bruntsfield, notable individuals have also earned an honoured place in the records. Most celebrated of these must surely be Alexander McKellar who enjoyed the proud title of "Cock o' the Green".

If amongst today's golfing enthusiasts there are some for whom the game has become an obsession, it is unlikely that their "condition" is as acute as was that of McKellar. After his retiral from the post of butler with a wealthy family, whose name is not on record, McKellar became the owner of a tavern in Edinburgh's New Town. The management of this he left to his wife, for his interest lay elsewhere. Immediately after breakfast he set off for Bruntsfield Links, regardless of the weather. Frequently he would play for the whole day and even after early darkness in winter, would continue by the light of a lantern held by a friend. Having taken to golf late in life it was as if he was anxious to make up for lost time.

On occasion McKellar's wife would bring his meals to the links, but frequently he was so engrossed that he left the food uneaten. His wife, perhaps not unnaturally, developed an almost fanatical dislike for golf and indeed any of the game's devotees frequenting the McKellar tavern were made far from welcome when she was behind the bar. On one occasion Mrs McKellar arranged to visit friends in Fife and planned to stay overnight. McKellar seized the opportunity to invite a group of his golfing cronies to his house adjacent to the tavern. Talk of golf and of each other's great achievements would be the order of the night. Alas, disaster struck. The Queensferry passage to Fife had been cancelled due to bad weather and Mrs McKellar returned home unexpectedly to find her husband's golfers' party in full swing. Her reaction to the scene she encountered can well be imagined. McKellar resolved that should his wife plan another trip to Fife, his golfing friends would not assemble until he had knowledge that his wife had duly landed in Fife.

McKellar's only non-golfing day was the Sabbath when he acted as door-keeper of an Episcopalian chapel. On one occasion, Mr Douglas Gourlay, a golf club and ball maker at Bruntsfield, placed a golf ball in the collection plate. This was promptly and gratefully retrieved by McKellar. It was Mr Gourlay and Mr Douglas McEwan, both authorities on the history of golf at Bruntsfield, who proposed to Kay, the author of the famous "Portraits" that he should include "The Cock o' the Green". This Kay did after a special visit to Bruntsfield Links, some time during 1803, when he made the sketch which found a place

Alexander McKellar " Cock o' the Green"

From "Kay's Portraits"

94

in his celebrated book and which is reproduced here. Kay also included with his cartoon McKellar's customary cry on the tee when addressing the ball: "By the la' Harry this shall not go for nothing!". Despite his enthusiasm and long hours spent on the course McKellar apparently never achieved great prowess and was not a member of any of the famous Bruntsfield Golfing Societies. Nevertheless, until his death in 1813 he proudly retained the title of "Cock o' the Green".

CADDIE WILLIE

IF Alexander McKellar enjoyed the undisputed reputation of being Bruntsfield Links' most enthusiastic golfer, it would seem that the most eccentric and mysterious character associated with the course was Caddie Willie. Willie Gunn came to Edinburgh from the Highlands in about 1780. While travelling around Edinburgh selling religious tracts he would pass Bruntsfield Links, where he stopped to watch the golfers. On one very busy day, caddies were in short supply and a player invited Willie Gunn to carry his clubs. He was persuaded to do so and rewarded with payment of one shilling, for an hour's work. This means of income appealed to Willie and he became a regular caddie. In order to be nearer the Links he obtained lodgings in a garret belonging to Mr John Brand, a gardener who had the lease of lands of Leven Lodge and Valleyfield nearby.

Willie Gunn was very honest, paying his rent most regularly. He lived entirely on a diet of baps and

"Caddie Willie"
By courtesy of Mr N. Inglis

milk, never cooking hot food or having a fire in his room even in the coldest of weather. The motive behind his spartan existence was to save enough money for his burial when his time should come, since, like many people at that time, he had a horror of a pauper's grave. On the links Caddie Willie was always happy and cheerful. The strangest feature about him was the way he dressed. All the clothes he possessed he carried with him, summer and winter. He would wear one suit above another, in layers. To enable him to wear three or four jackets or coats, he would cut off the sleeves of all save the top one. Outermost was an old red coat, the official uniform of the Bruntsfield caddies. He wore several pairs of trousers at once and two or three bonnets all sewn within each other and wore numerous vests under the several layers of other garments.

When not engaged in caddying, Willie, who was a keen sportsman, regularly visited the many village fairs in and around the city, hoping to earn a few pence by performing various conjuring tricks. These were so designed that Willie never failed to win any money at stake. The fairs which Willie found profitable were frequently organised by carters and featured horses and carts in procession, all colourfully decorated with ribbons and flowers. Such a fair was a regular annual event in Morningside village in the early 19th century.

Every autumn Willie Gunn returned to his home in the Highlands, selling his tracts *en route*. He remained away for about six weeks but always returned to Bruntsfield Links to earn his shillings. During the autumn, in about 1820, he set out for the north, telling his friend Mr Douglas McEwan, golf-club maker at the Links, that he now had enough money saved to ensure a respectable funeral. From this journey to his home Willie never returned to Bruntsfield and no one was ever able to discover what had happened to him.

MARY BARCLAY

WHILE the well-known Barclay Church – re-named in more recent times the Barclay Bruntsfield Church – with its 200-foot high rapier-like steeple is a most prominent landmark on the city's south-western skyline, and indeed is visible from Fife and perhaps beyond, unfortunately much less prominent are any details of the lady whose generous bequest led to the building of the church which bears her name. Likewise little biographical detail remains of its architect, Frederick T. Pilkington, of whom one writer has said that had he built nothing else, the creation of "the Barclay" would have established him as a man of genius.

Miss Mary Barclay, of 7 Carlton Terrace, Edinburgh, died in 1858, fifteen years after the Disruption. Just ten years after that far-reaching event she had willed a trust for the erection of a Free Church of Scotland building. The terms of Miss Barclay's Trust Disposition and Deed Settlement conveyed her whole estate to certain trustees and one of the specified purposes of her Trust was that part of her estate be used "to purchase, feu or acquire on such terms and conditions as they might think reasonable in one of the public streets of the New Town of Edinburgh, either a vacant building, stance or such property, as when taken down should afford a suitable site for a church, and should cause to be expended upon, a sum of Ten Thousand Pounds Sterling in building thereon a suitable church or

Barclay Church

96

place of public worship to be called Barclay's Church". Miss Barclay's will repeatedly specified that her bequest was for the spread of the Free Church, created at the Disruption in 1843.

In her will Miss Barclay also made provision that the remainder of her estate, after defraying the cost of building the church, should be invested and that "all moneys accruing thereof be paid to and divided annually amongst such a number of the ministers in Scotland of the said Free Church, and amongst the sons of such ministers or sons of deceased Free Church ministers to assist in educating them for the ministry of the Gospel in connection with the said Free Church. . ." The sums to be thus disposed of should not exceed Ten Pounds Sterling in any one year to any one individual. In 1856, Miss Barclay revoked the clause requiring that the church bearing her name be built in the New Town and authorised her trustees to acquire a site "in any portion of the town, new or old or in the suburbs".

After Miss Barclay's death in 1858, her trustees considered the purchase of sites at Warriston, St Leonards and the Grange. Eventually the present site at what was Wright's Houses was acquired. Discussions were then held with Fountainbridge Free Church concerning the possibility of that congregation eventually moving to the new church to be built on the verge of Bruntsfield Links. Such a transfer was agreed upon. A competition was held for the design of the church, limited to six chosen architects, and conditions specified that the stone to be used must be from the Binny or Redhall quarries and also that "the

doors were to be sheltered as far as possible from the winds". The commission to build was awarded to Frederick Thomas Pilkington in October 1861 and a preliminary fee paid.

Pilkington's design has been described variously as "Medieval combined with Victorian Romanticism", and in a recent authoritative architectural publication as "Powerful Ruskinian Gothic". Pilkington's completed work also drew criticism to the effect that exteriorly it was unfinished, being devoid of further decoration. Such critics were unaware that the minister appointed to the new church was, in the Free Kirk tradition, against undue ornamentation. There were certain carvings executed by Pearce. The interior of the church with its heart-shaped auditorium and two-tier galleries was eminently suitable for the Free Church liturgy. One of the church's slated lucarnes blew down in a gale in 1969 and along with the other three was replaced in grey fibreglass.

The Barclay Church was opened in 1864, two years after Pilkington had commenced work, and in 1865 the Reverend James Hood Wilson, the first minister, and his congregation at Fountainbridge, transferred to the new building. A manse was acquired at 1 East Castle Road at Merchiston. The cost of the building exceeded the £10,000 allocated in Miss Barclay's bequest and the balance was provided by the congregation. Unfortunately, apart from the fact that she resided at 7 Carlton Terrace, and the details of her generous bequest, no further personal biographical details of Miss Barclay or any portraits of her could be traced.

FREDERICK THOMAS PILKINGTON

WHILE Pilkington's work, much of it noteworthy and of considerable interest, is to be seen in many other parts of Edinburgh and beyond, it is in the context of his striking creation of Barclay Church that these notes are primarily concerned. As with the benefactress whose legacy provided Pilkington with the opportunity of creating the church, little is on record concerning him either. Frederick Thomas Pilkington was born in Lincolnshire in 1832 and died in 1899. His father, Thomas Pilkington, was architect to the Marquis of Exeter and it is said that he destroyed his family pedigree since it revealed a worldliness in his forebears which offended his devout Methodist beliefs. Young Frederick Pilkington began his training as an architect in London, then subsequently attended Edinburgh University, graduating in mathematics and also being awarded the Hamilton Prize for Logic. He served in his father's Edinburgh office for a few years, then began in practice for himself in 1860. The contract to design Barclay Church must have been one of his earliest commissions.

A great deal of Pilkington's work exhibits a wide range of styles and yet frequently his own characteristics are immediately recognisable. In the Grange area he built Grange Park (1866-70), at 38 Dick Place as his own residence, originally named "Egrimont House" after his second wife's home. Numbers 48 and 50 Dick Place, completed in 1865, are the only pair of semi-detached houses which he built. A very fine mansion-house, "Craigmount", at No. 52 Dick Place, for some time a private school, was also Pilkington's work, but was demolished in 1956. Numbers 129 and 131 Grange Loan completed his Grange design. Elsewhere in the city, Dean Park House in Queensferry Road, which Pilkington built originally for a noted geologist, S. J. Jolly, actually became a boarding house for pupils of the adjacent Daniel Stewart's College. Next to this house, another fine villa, built as the college headmaster's residence and now a hotel, represents some of Pilkington's finest work, especially interiorly. The Kingston Clinic, in French Gothic, in Kingston Avenue near Liberton, has a bold confidence. Tenements which he built at West Fountainbridge and Stockbridge bear his characteristic stamp. Not far from his undoubted masterpiece, Barclay Church, Pilkington built another Free Church, Viewforth St. David's and St. Oswald's at the corner of Gilmore Place and St. Peter's Place, designed in Gothic style in 1871. Both his churches in due course, after the various stages of re-union became places of worship within the established Church of Scotland.

6 · GREENHILL

AMONG the earliest owners of the lands of Greenhill were the Aitkenhead family, one of whom, David, from 1601 until his death in 1637 was a member of Edinburgh Town Council and served as Lord Provost for various periods, selling the estate to the ill-fated John Livingstone, who fell a victim to the most severe epidemic of plague 1645 and was interred on his own land in the private burial-ground, still to be seen in Chamberlain Road. After feuing began in 1840, and when the northern section of Greenhill Gardens was completed, in 1852, the district soon began to attract a most diversified and interesting number of distinguished residents occupying the seventeen villas, which also differed widely, each being of divergent architectural design.

Indeed such was the distinction and interest of Greenhill's first residents in the mid-19th century that John Smith, a Fellow of the Society of Antiquaries, who himself lived in the district, was prompted to produce two hand-written "sixpenny" note-books in 1930: *Greenhill Gardens, Bruntsfield Links with notes on some of its Early Residenters* and *Notes on the Lands of Greenhill, Bruntsfield Links and their Owners.*

SIR WILLIAM FORBES OF PITSLIGO

FOLLOWING the successive early ownership of Greenhill by the Aitkenheads, the Livingstones, the Fairholmes, one of whom became City Treasurer, a title later changed to City Chamberlain (hence the origin of Chamberlain Road), in 1806 Thomas Wright sold Greenhill, including its fine mansion-house, to Sir William Forbes, who in the same year succeeded his father, the famous Scottish banker of the same name, as 7th Baronet of Pitsligo in Aberdeenshire. Unfortunately, little personal information is on record concerning William Forbes himself, who seems to merit the attention of writers largely because of the fame of his father, or on account of his marriage, and even in this only in so far as it involved Sir Walter Scott. In the annals of South Edinburgh he takes his place in his own right as "Laird of Greenhill".

Sir William Forbes of Pitsligo

Portrait in private collection
Photographed by G. A. Shakerley

Sir William Forbes, who was born in Edinburgh in 1773, was the eldest son of Sir William Forbes of Pitsligo whose northern estate and title had

99

been purchased back in 1781 following its forfeiture by the Jacobite Lord Forbes after the 1745 Rebellion. This Sir William's banking house in Parliament Square achieved great prominence in Edinburgh's commercial life in the late 18th century. The bank, which in 1838 eventually became the Union Bank of Scotland, has been described in great detail in Sir William Forbes' *Memoirs of a Banking House*, which he wrote in 1803, dedicating it to his son, who was to acquire the lands of Greenhill, and who permitted publication many years after his father's death. Sir William, 7th Baronet of Pitsligo and of Greenhill, continued in the family banking business, taking over the directorship in collaboration with his father's former partner and great friend, Sir James Hunter Blair.

When, it is to be presumed, Sir William Forbes took up residence in Greenhill House, which stood on his land, shortly after 1806, he had already been a widower for sixteen years. It is in this context that Sir Walter Scott enters the story. Apparently young Walter was much attracted to Miss Williamina Stuart, daughter of Sir John Stuart of Fettercairn in Aberdeenshire, whose Edinburgh house was in George Square close to Walter's family home at No. 25. According to Lockhart, Scott's biographer, one Sunday morning when rain greeted the congregation as they came out from Greyfriars Church, young Walter Scott gallantly offered Miss Stuart the shelter of his umbrella and to escort her back to George Square. Although no doubt greatly appreciating this courteous act, nevertheless the young lady gave

Scott little further encouragement. Young Walter, however, hopefully persevered, taking every opportunity of making his admiration for Miss Williamina very clear. Alas, it was to no avail. The man who won Miss Stuart's hand was one of Walter's great friends, William Forbes. They were married in 1797.

Walter Scott was deeply affected, for "the scar of his loss", it was said, "remained till his dying day". It was suggested that in *The Lady of the Lake* he makes a character experience the kind of sadness which he himself had undergone in failing to win Miss Stuart. In *Rokeby*, written in 1812, he draws a portrait of "La Chere adorable" who had inspired and saddened his youth. Miss Stuart's marriage to William Forbes was very happy, though short-lived. She died in December 1810, at about the age of only 35. The estate of Fettercairn in the north was eventually to pass to the Forbes family of Pitsligo.

Scott's friendship with William Forbes was profound and rose above their early rivalry in romance. When Scott was in the midst of the financial crisis which overtook him, Forbes was among the first to come to his assistance. "At a meeting of my creditors", Scott wrote, "Sir William took the chair and behaved as he had always done, with the generosity of ancient faith and early friendship". When one of Scott's creditors was threatening and most insistent on urgent payment Forbes, unknown to Scott, paid the two thousand pounds due from his own pocket. He continued to offer Scott further assistance until his crisis had passed and he was beginning to achieve the eminence which, in fact,

Lady Forbes in earlier days had often prophesied for him.

Sir William and Lady Forbes had four sons and two daughters. The youngest son became Principal of St Andrews University. Sir William, who had not enjoyed good health since his wife's untimely death, died on October 20th 1828, at Colinton House, the Forbes country seat. The family tomb is in Greyfriars Churchyard. It has been remarked that the one-time rivals both have prominent landmarks in Princes Street as their memorials — Sir Walter's famous monument at the east end, and St John the Evangelist's Episcopal Church at the west end which Sir William Forbes' efforts and generosity greatly helped to build.

Sir John Stuart-Forbes, 8th Baronet of Pitsligo and Fettercairn (1804-66), who succeeded Sir William, resided in Greenhill House. He was a generous benefactor in the Morningside district. In 1838 he presented the site for the building of Morningside Parish church at the north-west corner of Newbattle Terrace. The latter street owes its name to the marriage of a member of the Stuart-Forbes family with one of the Kerrs of Newbattle Abbey, then the property of the Marquis of Lothian. Sir John Stuart-Forbes would not grant a site for a Free Church. For some time the southern and later section of Greenhill Gardens with its spaciousness and pleasant green grass plantation was commemoratively known as Stuart's Green. Forbes Road and Pitsligo Road also take their names from a similar association, while Clinton Road commemorates the fact that the Greenhill estate eventually passed from Stuart-Forbes of Greenhill who, in 1852, arranged for the Bore Stone to be brought from a nearby field at Churchill and placed on the wall of Morningside Parish Church, with the inscribed tablet beneath.

Seven years after Sir John Stuart-Forbes' death in 1866, Greenhill House was purchased from his trustees by the Right Reverend James R. A. Chinnery-Haldane, Scottish Episcopalian Bishop of Argyll and the Isles, who in 1882 sold it to Beattie & Co., builders. Demolition took place soon afterwards. Three quarries in the grounds of the old mansion-house supplied stone for much of the building of the adjacent Bruntsfield Place flats. For Greenhill and the nearby vicinity a new era was beginning.

DAVID COUSIN

WHEN No 7 Greenhill Gardens was built in 1849 by an architect as his own residence, certainly he should have taken pleasure and found it a very minor undertaking compared with many of his prolific other creations in the city and beyond. The architect was David Cousin and a list of his works seems almost incredible in extent and in diversity of function and style. Well might the writer of a historical review of the City Architect's Department, issued in 1937, make the comment: "Mr David Cousin left his mark on the city".

David Cousin was born in north Leith in 1809. His father was a joiner, and after quite an ordinary education David became apprenticed to him. While he acquired competence in his trade he was also intensely interested in science and frequently carried out various experiments in his workshop. He undertook special studies in mathematics under Mr Edward Sang. While still young David Cousin left his father's business to be trained by the famous William Henry Playfair, an experience which evidently greatly influenced his future, especially his preference for classical architecture. He was involved with Playfair in the planning of Donaldson's Hospital, the New College at The Mound, the National Gallery and other important commissions.

In his early twenties Cousin set up his own business and soon was awarded various building contracts in open competition. His early work included churches in Glasgow, Greenock and Cambuslang, and the restoration of Maybole Castle. The Disruption of 1843, which led to the establishment of the Free Church of Scotland, provided and influenced much of Cousin's future work. He had been a supporter of the Disruption and had seceded from the Established Church. He became the new church's consultative architect and was soon engaged in the somewhat hurried building of many new and necessarily inexpensive churches all over Scotland for the Free Church congregations which had temporarily to meet in all kinds of improvised premises. Some of this work of Cousin's came in for criticism. During 1860-62, Cousin built the Free Church Offices and College on The Mound for the donor, Mr John Maitland, and the adjacent Commisssary Court building was also his work. Within the Free Church premises, Presbytery Hall is a very fine spacious room,

Free Church College, The Mound, Edinburgh

Designed by David Cousin
By courtesy of The Free Church of Scotland

"reproduced in 17th-century Victorian revival Jacobean style", with very fine carved woodwork, and adjacent to it are beautiful stained glass windows donated by Cousin himself; also the Moncrieff Memorial Window, all executed by Ballantyne and Sons of Leith. Within the Presbytery Hall is David Octavius Hill's famous painting of the Disruption and among the many ministers and other officials depicted David Cousin may be seen, holding his plan for the offices on the Mound.

In 1847 Cousin was appointed the city's Superintendent of Works, at a salary of £300 p.a., but was allowed to carry on his own work from an office in the City Chambers. The title of Cousin's post had long been the subject of controversy. In medieval times, his predecessor was called "The Maister of workes for the good toune", then eventually "Superintendent of Public Works" became the form. Whatever may have gone before, Cousin signed himself "City Architect", although this title was not officially introduced until 1919. Regardless of wording, his post was an onerous one and his responsibilities wide and demanding. The list of the city's buildings and other properties which he was bound to maintain reads like a guide book.

As architect to the City Improvement Trustees, he had additional responsibilities. While "City Architect" David Cousin's work included a plan for "the ornamentation of West Princes Street Gardens", when the drained Nor' Loch had become the site of the new railway line from Waverley Station, the landscaping of East Princes Street Gardens also followed. The Corn Exchange in the Grassmarket, the restoration of Old Greyfriars after extensive fire damage, the planning of a new slaughterhouse at Lochrin, the designing of the north side of Chambers Street for the Lord Provost whom the street commemorates, interior restoration and alterations in the City Chambers, the laying out of the Mayfield district for its owner, Duncan McLaren, M.P., former Lord Provost, the planning of Dean, Dalry, Warriston and Newington cemeteries, such prolific commitments fell to David Cousin single-handed. Yet, almost incredibly, he still undertook such private commissions as the building of St Catherine's convent in Lauriston Gardens ("one of his happiest undertakings"), India Buildings in Victoria Street, and the Epworth Halls, these three achievements being most notable. For some time he was also the University's consultant architect and designed the Reid School of Music in Teviot Row. The laying out of several of the city's main streets was another of his undertakings and he was greatly

The Reid School of Music, University of Edinburgh

Designed by David Cousin
By courtesy of the University of Edinburgh
Photograph by Jack Fisher

concerned with supervising the building of suitable "working class" housing.

Little wonder that after some years of single-handedly coping with the functions of "City Architect", Cousin sought assistance, and the appointment of Mr John Lessels led to more sharing of the burden and Lessels indeed did work much on his own initiative. Impressive as Cousin's achievements were, he "didn't win them all". He had been beaten in competition for the prestigious contract to build the New College on The Mound, by his former master, William Playfair; and his plan for the New Medical School in Teviot Place failed to gain precedence over that submitted by Rowand Anderson.

After thirty years' service as "City Architect" David Cousin retired in 1875. He was succeeded by Robert Morham, who had been his principal assistant in private practice, and Morham it was who completed some of Cousin's designed but unfinished work. Having suffered indifferent

*Detail from famous Disruption
painting by David Octavius Hill.
David Cousin is seen (centre) showing
his plan for the New Free Church
College to Mr John Maitland*

muir. A portrait of the notable one-time "City Architect" could not be traced, and it is believed that no descendants of his remain. David Cousin's brother, George, resided and died in the Tower House, originally No 5, now No 8, Bruntsfield Terrace, at the northern entrance to Greenhill Gardens. He was Edinburgh Town Council member for Newington in 1864 and an ardent social reformer.

SIR JOHN STEELL, R.S.A.

NOT only did the Greenhill district attract residents of already diverse professions and achievements but many who were destined to become highly distinguished in their respective fields. This was certainly true of one who in his life-time won wide renown as a sculptor – Sir John Steell, R.S.A., who resided and died at No 24 Greenhill Gardens. Perhaps of his quite prolific work, especially as regards statues in Edinburgh and elsewhere, the two most popularly known were his equestrian monument to Wellington outside Register House in Princes Street, and his marble statue of the seated Sir Walter Scott within the base of George Meikle Kemp's famous monument in East Princes Street Gardens. This creation of Steell's, completed in 1846 at a cost of £2,000, which included Sir Walter's favourite staghound "Maida" at his right foot, is said to have been the first marble statue commissioned in Scotland and earned the sculptor an award. In fact, a marble figure by Steell of Provost James Blaikie of Aberdeen had been completed ten years earlier.

In *Memorials of His Time*, Lord Cockburn described the unveiling of

health for some years, Cousin after retiral spent the winter of 1877 in Mentone; later, on medical advice, he settled in Sans Souci, Louisiana, where he died on August 14th 1878. Cousin was twice married — first to Miss M. Galloway, and, after her death, to Miss A. Lawson of Cairn-

104

the Wellington statue in 1848 before a vast cheering crowd. Later, after a thunderstorm had passed, they stood in silent groups, captivated by the sculptor's genius. Cockburn relates the couplet which was composed at the time:

"Mid lightning's flash and
thunder's peal
Behold the 'Iron Duke', in bronze
by Steell."

Steell's greatest work was perhaps the Scottish memorial to Albert, the Prince Consort, in Charlotte Square, completed in 1876. After its unveiling by Queen Victoria the sculptor was knighted. He was elected a member of the Royal Scottish Academy in 1829 and became Sculptor to the Queen in Scotland in 1838. His large seated statue of Queen Victoria herself, above the Royal Institution, which became the Royal Scottish Academy, is another of his striking Edinburgh creations. There are a number of others including the Allan Ramsay statue in West Princes Street Gardens, and Thomas Chalmers, in bronze, in George Street. Outwith Scotland, Steell completed many commissions, notably a huge statue of Robert Burns in New York and a smaller replica of James Wilson in Calcutta. His subjects varied greatly, from Florence Nightingale to "the opium eater", Thomas de Quincey.

John Steell was born in Aberdeen on September 19th 1804, elder brother of Gourlay Steell who also became a notable artist. His father, who had married Margaret Gourlay of Dundee, was a carver and gilder of great skill. He came to Edinburgh when John was only one year old. In due course the elder son was trained by his father as wood-carver and also given tuition by John Graham in the

Sir John Steell

Trustees Academy. From quite early years, John Steell had shown great artistic ability. After the apprenticeship with his father, he set off for Rome, there to study and breathe the genius of the great masters. He returned to Edinburgh in 1833, when his first commission was the group piece of *Alexander Taming Bucephalus*, erected at the east end of George Street but eventually transferred to the quadrangle of the City Chambers. This work, which he had begun in Rome, earned him considerable recognition and a small award. It was copied many times. It also attracted attention in London artistic circles and he received an offer to open a studio in London where his talents would be greatly appreciated and suitably rewarded. Unlike many of his fellow Scotsmen, before and since, Steell resisted the attractions of going south, desiring to remain in Scotland in order to contribute towards his country's development in sculpture and the other arts. Indeed, having first introduced artistic bronze casting in Scotland, he built at his own expense a foundry in which not only his own work but that of other young sculptors could be reproduced in metal. Undoubtedly his foregoing the lure of English acclaim and prosperity led to his high reputation in Scotland and his great influence on the development of Scottish sculpture and the arts generally.

In 1826 Sir John had married Elizabeth Graham, daughter of an Edinburgh merchant. She died in 1885. A son, Graham, became a professor in medicine in Manchester. Steell's younger brother, Gourlay, became an artist of considerable note, and was appointed animal painter (his speciality) to Queen Victoria in 1872. For some time he was President of the Royal Scottish Academy. He died at No 23 Minto Street in 1894 and was interred in Morningside cemetery. Sir John Steell in his later years suffered much ill-health. He received a civil list pension and retired in 1890. He died on September 15th 1891 and was buried in the Old Calton cemetery. Perhaps his genius was summed up in a simple epitaph:

"In all his creations he imparted life".

PROFESSOR ARCHIBALD HAMILTON CHARTERIS

JOHN SMITH in his booklet on the "Residenters" of Greenhill was especially fascinated by the diversity of their professional backgrounds and commitments: men (and one woman) of the church, architecture, law and other spheres. It was appropriate that within such close proximity to what became known as "Holy Corner", with its four churches of different denominations, there should reside three eminent churchmen: Dr Thomas Chalmers, famous pioneer of the Free Church of Scotland, Dr John Kirk, prominent leader of the Evangelical Union, and Professor Archibald Charteris, a memorable and dynamic figure in the established Church of Scotland. And to widen further the ecclesiastical interest, in 1890 "St Bennets" in Greenhill Gardens became the residence of successive Roman Catholic archbishops of St Andrews and Edinburgh, but this house's "finest hour" was to be in 1982, when Pope John Paul lived for some days here as the guest of Cardinal Gray.

Professor Archibald Charteris, who resided at No 4 Greenhill Gardens, was born at Wamphray in Dumfriesshire in 1835, eldest son of the parish schoolmaster, and was educated first in the local school, then at Edinburgh University, where he graduated Bachelor of Arts in 1853 and Master of Arts a year later, with Honours in Latin, Mathematics, Philosophy and Natural Philosophy. His clear and fluent style of preaching, coupled with a deep interest in and zeal for the practical work of the church, especially directed to meeting contemporary needs, soon led to his promotion. After initial parish work at St Quivox in Ayrshire in 1858, then at New Abbey near Dumfries, he became minister of Park Church in Glasgow in 1863.

Here in Scotland's great industrial city, with its special problems *vis-à-vis* religion and the realities of working life, Dr Charteris saw a real challenge to the church and consequently set up a "Committee on Life and Work", concerned with bringing the Christian message to bear on the problems of industrial life and the community. This committee received the General Assembly's strong support, and its work spread. In 1879, with the same concern for the relationship between the Gospels and everyday life, he founded, and was the first editor of, the Church of Scotland's inportant monthly publication *Life and Work*, still widely read today.

In 1867 Dr Charteris was appointed Chaplain to the Queen in Scotland, and Edinburgh University awarded him the degree of Doctor of Divinity. After a short period abroad for health reasons, in 1868 the University appointed him to the Chair of Biblical Criticism, which he occupied until 1898. Within the church itself, his efforts continued to create responses to challenging needs. He was largely responsible for setting up the Young Men's and Young Women's Guilds. It was from the latter that the most important of Dr Charteris's ideas was to develop and take practical form. Influenced to some extent by his first-hand knowledge of the foundation of an "Order of Deaconesses" by Pastor Fliedner at Kaiserwerth in Germany, and by other similar forms of dedicated service by women within the Protestant churches elsewhere, and rejecting criticism that he was adopting Roman Catholic practices, he founded the "Order of Deaconesses" in Edinburgh, claiming to base them

Professor Archibald H. Charteris

Portrait by William Hole from "Quasi Cursores"
published during University of Edinburgh's Tercentenary
Festival, 1884

on the "deaconesses" who worked with and were praised by St Paul. The first lady to be specially ordained for the order in Edinburgh was the rather remarkable Lady Grizel Baillie who was commissioned in this new form of service by the kirk session of Bowden on December 9th 1888. The plan in Professor Charteris's mind was that from the Women's Guild, which he had founded, the work of the ordinary members would taper upwards, in pyramid fashion, through leaders and associates, towards the special committed service of the deaconesses. The latter would be selected at two levels: ladies who had had seven years' active service in the Guild or those who underwent two years' special probationary training in the

107

Institute of Deaconesses. The founder's scheme received strong General Assembly support, and despite a number of individual critics the Order of Deaconesses soon became well established and developed steadily, their dedicated practical work in congregations, especially among the poor and needy, bringing a new spirit into the church. The Women's Guild, the background support to, and source of, deaconesses also grew rapidly.

The Order of Deaconesses' first house was rented at 33 Mayfield Gardens in 1887. The headquarters for two years was at 41 George Square, then later at No 27. This was to be the Order's "Mother House". Eventually the premises in the Pleasance became the principal centre. In due course the need for these specially dedicated ladies to have some kind of medical training arose and some went to learn nursing at the Royal Infirmaries of Edinburgh and Glasgow. It then became clear that a small hospital under the direction of the order and staffed by trained members would be a great advantage. Apart from caring for patients, the proposed hospital would be a centre of training in nursing for deaconesses engaged primarily in house visitation. Eventually, Edinburgh's famous Deaconess Hospital was opened in the Pleasance in 1894. It was dedicated to the memory of Lady Grizel Baillie, the Order's first member. The hospital was purposely built on a small scale to ensure a more intimate relationship than was practicable with larger institutions. Prominent Edinburgh doctors and surgeons were amongst the original staff. An extension was added in 1897. When opened, Edinburgh's Deaconess Hospital claimed to be the only such hospital of any Protestant church in Christendom with the exception of those run by the Waldensians. The hospital and adjoining church, costing £25,000, were erected entirely from donations, and opened free of any debt. Above the door was the legend observed by Professor Charteris over a Swiss hospital: *Christo in Pauperibus.* (To Christ in His poor). The hospital also had an important role in training deaconesses for medical work in foreign missions.

Professor Charteris was a man of quite unusual idealism and dynamic drive. He contemplated a rest-house for deaconesses, "worn out by house visiting, working with prisoners, *e.g.* in Calton Jail, and other labours", and a house was opened at Dalkeith. He encouraged a friend to introduce a pension scheme for the dedicated ladies in their early retirement. His mind worked ceaselessly. Despite so many practical commitments, Professor Charteris served as Moderator of the Church of Scotland in 1892. On April 24th 1908, this great pioneer and innovator died of a stroke, at 4 Greenhill Gardens, aged 73. His funeral took place from St Cuthbert's Church to the kirkyard of his native Wamphray. On June 1st 1911 the foundation stone was laid of a church adjacent to the Deaconess Hospital, to complete this centre of healing and missionary service. Named the Charteris Memorial Church and situated beside the buildings which had housed the practical realisation of his most idealistic dream, it was a most fitting memorial to "the dreamer who got things done". In recent years a number of Edinburgh's South Side churches, whose buildings have closed, have become united in the Charteris Memorial Church, now bearing the historic name of Kirk o' Field. At the time of writing, the Deaconess Hospital, long since a National Health Service hospital of course, faces an uncertain future.

ELIZA W. KIRK

HALF a century ago and for many years thereafter, whatever might be the traditional wedding gifts that parents might give to their sons and daughters as they embarked on the sea of matrimony, many a mother added her own personal gift to her daughter, something which she herself, from her own wedding day, had found invaluable and the source perhaps of much marital bliss. This was the young Scottish bride's *vade mecum*, a remarkable book entitled *Tried Favourites Cookery Book* – "With household hints and other useful information". The authoress, Mrs Eliza W. Kirk, another of Greenhill's residents of wide-ranging talent, whose published recipes for the kitchen (and, some might say, therefore for domestic happiness) reached the remarkable sales figure of three-quarters of a million copies.

Tried Favourites first appeared in early form around 1900, which was nearly forty years later than the great English classic, Mrs Beeton's *Book of Household Management* of 1861. It was also written for a slightly humbler readership than the book by Mrs Beeton, who offered guidance on how to deal with butlers, footmen and kitchen-maids. The cookery book which emanated from Mrs Kirk's study at Hopefield Cottage, 17 Greenhill Gardens, with its more than 1500 recipes (and among its miscellaneous hints, guidance ranging from the treatment of chest conditions to gout, and from ear-ache to the common cold) became a household name in Scotland. It was said that its friendly, sympathetic style gave confidence to many a nervous young housewife and was a most valuable psychological aid as much as a guide in domestic economy.

Mrs Eliza Kirk
By courtesy of Mr Logan Kirk, grandson

Eliza Walker Kirk was born in Edinburgh in 1855, the only child to survive of prominent city Baillie David Lewis and his first wife, Margaret Mitchell. Lewis, a native of West Linton, was a shoe-maker with a shop in the High Street near the

City Chambers. He became treasurer of the George Heriot Trust and served long on the Town Council, becoming deeply involved in the controversy in 1894 over the decision of the Edinburgh Water Trustees to draw upon the Talla Water rather than St Mary's Loch, a decision which Lewis and certain other councillors strongly favoured. The Baillie was very active in the temperance movement, and strongly opposed to the serving of alcoholic drinks at civic functions. Indeed, it was said that this attitude lost him support in an election for the Lord Provostship.

David Lewis re-married and had other daughters. It is possible that it was at temperance campaign meetings that Eliza met the Reverend John Kirk, son of Professor John Kirk, one of the leaders of the Evangelical Union denomination and a lecturer to its ministry students, who had built Hopefield Cottage in Greenhill Gardens. Professor Kirk, who was a close friend of the famous explorer, Dr David Livingstone, died in 1886. His son and Eliza Lewis, who were then married, took up residence in Hopefield Cottage.

The Reverend John Kirk, junior, was minister of an Evangelical Union Church at the south-east corner of Murieston Road and Dalry Road, which still stands, although now a Scottish Episcopalian church. Popular methods of fund-raising for this church were through the traditional sales of work, and for these Mrs Eliza Kirk produced handwritten copies of recipes, costing a few pence each. They very quickly sold out. A proposal to publish her recipes Mrs Kirk readily accepted. The first edition was extremely successful. Reprints and enlarged new editions followed rapidly. Today *Tried Favourites* is still in print, in its 26th edition, after selling nearly three-quarters of a million copies since first published.

Mrs Kirk and her husband had two daughters and five sons. Three of the sons graduated in medicine, two becoming missionaries in China, one of whom subsequently on returning home became Professor of Anatomy in Middlesex Hospital. The third doctor was a general practitioner in Gullane for most of his long career. One of the daughters married John Hamilton, a notable civil engineer, who eventually was appointed resident engineer to the Forth Road Bridge. For this work he was awarded an honorary Doctorate in Science from Edinburgh University. Mrs Eliza Kirk, authoress of the quite remarkable best seller died in 1917 and her husband five years later. Hopefield Cottage remained in the possession of the Kirk family until 1957. Following the death of her husband, Dr David Livingstone, Mrs Livingstone was kindly received into the Kirk family at Greenhill. In more recent times the house was the residence of the late Professor Robert Cruickshank, one-time Professor of Bacteriology in Edinburgh University Medical School, who was also for long a consultative expert of the World Health Organisation and a close friend and former colleague of Sir Alexander Fleming, famous for his research into the antibiotic effect of penicillin.

ANDREW USHER

SIR John Usher, as has been mentioned, is commemorated by the

Institute in Warrender Park Road which still bears his name, for generously donating that Institute to the University in 1902 for the advancement of studies and training in what was then known as "Public Health". His elder brother Andrew, who resided in Greenhill Gardens from 1851 to 56 and died at 3 Greenhill Park, expressed his public spiritedness in relation to the world of music by bestowing upon Edinburgh in 1896 the magnificent gift of £100,000 for the building of a civic concert hall, appropriately named the Usher Hall, which was not actually opened until March 1914.

Andrew Usher was born at West Nicholson Street in Edinburgh in 1826, the eleventh child and third son of Andrew Usher, founder of the famous brewers and distillers, and his wife Margaret Balmer. With his younger brother John, Andrew, who prior to residing at Greenhill had lived in the Blackford district and at St Abbs, where he met the cost of a new harbour, further developed the prosperity of the family business, buying up smaller firms, specialising in the distilling section as well as blending, and achieving a rich export market. Although of a kindly disposition, Andrew Usher was not without eccentricities, especially while at work, which created something of the image of a martinet. In the firm's office he would avoid verbal communication with his brother, instead sending him quite formal notes in a rather distant tone; then they would lunch quite happily together. On one occasion a note to his brother stated: "Although I have allowed your son, Robert, to lunch with us, I wish it to be understood that he must not speak unless his

opinion is asked. Yesterday he spoke several times when he had no right to do so". In his spare time Andrew Usher was an enthusiastic and capable marksman, hunter and angler. He was a member of Mayfield Free Church.

Andrew Usher

From "A History of the Usher family in Scotland"

In the official history of the family it is related that Andrew Usher once informed his friend, James Aitchison, a Princes Street jeweller and Town Councillor, that "he had more money than he knew what to do with". Aitchison was incredulous but suggested that his wealthy friend might build a hall for the city. This was the birth of the idea of the Usher Hall and the cheque, for £100,000, was written in the shop. One can imagine Aitchison's proud and eager conveyance of the magnificent gift to the appropriate civic official.

Various difficulties apparently arose in enabling the Town Council to decide upon and acquire a suitable site for a new hall of the size made possible by such a large and generous gift, and indeed before agreement was reached Andrew Usher died, in 1896. He was buried in Grange Cemetery. When the Lothian Road site had at last been acquired, plans were invited for a hall to cost £65,000, including all sculptural and architectural embellishments. The balance was earmarked for other furnishings and facilities. The exterior was to be dignified yet simple and the capacity was to be for an audience of 3,000 (actually 2,900 was the figure provided for), with a platform to accommodate 500. One hundred and thirty three sets of plans were submitted and these were publicly exhibited at the New Corn Market, Gorgie. Sir Aston Webb was empowered to choose the most suitable design and the commission to build was awarded to Messrs J. Stockdale Harrison of Leicester. Certain features of E. A. Rickard's unsuccessful submission were eventually incorporated in the final plan. Building took place during 1910-14, and Darney stone was employed.

The city arms over the hall's main entrance were designed by W. Birnie Rhind and other sculpture was by Crossland MacClure, Hubert Paton and H. S. Gamley. The Usher Hall's two memorial stones were laid by George V and Queen Mary in July 1911 during their first state visit to Edinburgh after their coronation. These stones may be seen flanking the Cambridge Street entrance. On March 6th 1914 Andrew Usher's widow performed the opening ceremony; her husband had so much hoped to see the hall completed in his life-time; however, through the inauguration of the Edinburgh International Festival the Usher Hall has echoed to some of the world's greatest orchestras and solo artists, and the name of the donor is known and remembered universally.

HIPPOLYTE JEAN BLANC

A NUMBER of distinguished architects have resided in South Edinburgh, but most of their work has lain outwith the area. Two, however, have particular associations with the Greenhill and Morningside districts, as regards the building of churches and residential property, namely George Washington Browne and Hippolyte Blanc. An evident feature of the latter's work was his variety of style which, unlike that of many other architects, makes it difficult to identify it immediately, except for certain subtle hints.

Hippolyte Jean Blanc was born in Edinburgh in 1844. His father was French and his mother of Irish origin. Following his education at George Heriot's School he was trained as an architect by David Rhind, whose distinguished work included Daniel Stewart's College. In 1865 Blanc was appointed an inspector with the Office of Works for Ancient Buildings under Crown Jurisdiction, and became Chief Assistant in 1877. While still occupying this post he set up in private practice and soon won several commissions. One of the earliest of these was the building of Christ Church (Scottish Episcopalian) at Holy Corner, from 1875-78, of whose congregation he himself was a member. The church is French

Hippolyte Blanc, second from right
with left hand on stone when
foundation stone of St Matthew's
Parish Church, Morningside was laid
in June 1888

By courtesy of the Very Reverend Dr Robert Mathers, D.D.

Gothic in style, with a 130-feet spire, and it has been praised in many architectural journals. While Christ Church was being built, Hippolyte Blanc, again after winning an open competition, commenced work on what has been described as the best of the many Edinburgh churches which he built. This was Mayfield Church, originally built as a Free Church, at the south-west corner of Mayfield Road and West Mayfield. This was in stylish French Gothic and the 150-foot spire, altered later, of Norman type.

Hippolyte Blanc was in demand for the building of churches not only in Edinburgh: at Paisley in 1886 he built the Coates Memorial Church, considered one of the best relatively modern churches in Scotland and which occupied his attention for several years. The design of the Middle Church at Perth is a fine example of Scottish Revivalism, while others at Greenock and Broughty Ferry came from his drawing-board too. Returning to Edinburgh and to a very different sphere of activity, Blanc was engaged in 1888 to restore the Great Hall at Edinburgh Castle and also to work on the Argyle Tower, the Portcullis Gatehouse and St Margaret's Chapel. After the Greenhill estate had been sold in 1882, under the direction of Beattie, the building firm which had bought the land, Hippolyte Blanc built a section of the Bruntsfield tenements, which were rising rapidly, his work being numbers 155-195 Bruntsfield Place. He also built flats at Marchmont Road and other residential property at Colinton Road and Mayfield Gardens. The frontage of Mary Erskine's College at Queen Street was his work, in 1913, as was early property at York Place. No 92 Fountainbridge, which very many Edinburgh people came to know well as the head office of St Cuthbert's Co-operative Wholesale Society, with its turrets and baronial style, was built by Blanc in his early days in 1880.

St Cuthbert's again featured in his long catalogue of work but this time it was the famous Edinburgh church at the West End of Princes Street. Here from 1892 to 95 Blanc had an important commission undertaking a major rebuilding of the church, greatly increasing its size. The late 18th-century steeple of the earlier church was retained. Prior to commencing his work at St Cuthbert's Hippolyte Blanc was engaged in the building of two of Morningside's best known churches: St Matthew's Parish Church at the corner of Cluny Gardens and Braid Road, which became Cluny Parish Church in 1974, and Morningside High Church, the last of Morningside Free Church's places of worship and now the Church Hill Theatre. St Matthew's, an extension from Morningside Parish Church at Newbattle Terrace, was completed in 1890, and with its cruciform design, impressive chancel, choir stalls and sanctuary, has a cathedral-like atmosphere, a fine example of the

architect's best work. Four years after the completion of St Matthew's, Blanc saw the opening of Morningside High Church, which he built to provide for the increasing congregation of the Free Church, whose vacated building became the Baptist Church on the opposite side of Morningside Road. The High Church (so named on account of its site, not liturgy), of fine bold Renaissance style in pink Corsehill sandstone, was later vacated, when after the various stages of church re-union, the congregation returned to its original mother church, Morningside Parish Church, in 1960, over a century after the Disruption had caused its breakaway. In 1965, after its earlier purchase by Edinburgh Corporation and necessary interior alterations, the very well-appointed Church Hill Theatre was opened.

Hippolyte Blanc, although with so many churches to his name, was not primarily or exclusively an ecclesiastical architect. As already noted, his work and his style evinced wide variation. Outwith Edinburgh, his plans for "Bangour Village", which provided for mentally disturbed patients within the aegis of Bangour Hospital, was a highly imaginative concept and considered as perhaps his best contribution to civil architecture. The design of the Carnegie Baths and Gymnasium at Dunfermline and the building of Bernard's Brewery in Edinburgh again demonstrate the versatility of his work. He received many distinctions, awards and medals both here and abroad.

Despite such a demanding work load, Hippolyte Blanc still found time to engage in the city's social life and professional organisations. He served for three different periods as

President of the Edinburgh Architectural Association. He was elected an Associate of the Royal Scottish Academy in 1892, and full membership was awarded him in 1896. Blanc acted as the R.S.A. treasurer for ten years until his death. He was also a Fellow of the Royal Institute of British Architects and of the Society of Antiquaries in Scotland and similar bodies in England. A keen photographer, he was awarded many prizes for his work. Hippolyte Blanc lectured regularly, presenting illustrations of his travels abroad and on archaeological expeditions. He was a member of the Scottish Arts Club and was widely known throughout Edinburgh as a man of warm personality and generous hospitality. Blanc died at his home, 17 Strathearn Place, on March 12th 1917. The House is now the Iona Hotel and the ceiling of an upstairs drawing-room, a work of great delicacy, is a fitting reminder of the house's one-time highly artistic owner.

GEORGE SETON

IN the chronicles of the Sciennes and Greenhill districts of South Edinburgh the name of Mr George Seton, advocate, occurs quite frequently. He resided in "St Bennets", which he so named, i.e. 42 Greenhill Gardens, built for him in 1856 by John Henderson, architect of the nearby Morningside Parish church, and it was his home for thirty-four years. He was an authority, indeed the principal one, on the Convent of St Catherine of Siena (or Sienna), built in Sciennes in 1517 and giving its name, in vulgarised form, to the district. He was largely instrumental in the foundation of the Athenium Club which functioned at Holy Corner in the 1880s. A prolific writer, George Seton was the author of nearly sixty published works. For long, although his name occurred repeatedly in recorded local history, virtually nothing was known about the man himself. Most fortuitously, through the kind and professional interest of Mr George Ballantyne, librarian of Edinburgh's Signet Library, a full obituary of George Seton was found, together with a portrait of him never previously seen by the general public.

George Seton was born at Perth in 1822, the son of Captain George Seton of the Setons of Cariston, a family of very ancient lineage. He was descended from the Earls of Winton and from Mary Seton, one of Mary Queen of Scots' "four Maries". Educated at Edinburgh's High School and at the University, George Seton then entered Exeter College, Oxford, where he graduated Bachelor, then Master, of Arts. In 1846 he was admitted to the Faculty of Advocates in Edinburgh, and practised for eight years in Parliament House. In 1854 he was appointed Secretary in the General Registrar's Office in Edinburgh, holding this post for thirty-five years. He played an important part in the re-organisation of the system for the registration of births, deaths and marriages following the Act of 1854.

Despite a very busy professional life, George Seton's active mind turned to a wide variety of interests. Among his many publications perhaps the two of most importance were: *The Law and Practice of Heraldry in Scotland* (1863) and *A History of the Family of Seton during*

George Seton

From "The Scots Law Times" November 28th, 1908

Eight Centuries (1896). The latter work was, obviously, inspired by deep pride in his Seton ancestry. Likewise this was perhaps the main reason for his most detailed and active interest in the history of the convent at Sciennes, whose founder members included many titled ladies, widowed through the disastrous battle of Flodden in 1513, and including his ancestor Lady Seton. George Seton's paper, read before the Architectural Institute of Scotland on April 11th 1867, and privately printed in 1871, is a uniquely valuable source of information on the subject and includes several interesting illustrations. It was he who was responsible for having the plaque placed in the front garden at 16 St Catherine's Place, off Sciennes Road, which marks the site of the convent and provides a quotation from Scott's *Marmion*. It is said that George Seton salvaged some of the stones from the ruined convent and built these up as a cairn in his garden at "St Bennets", but this cannot now be identified.

When North Morningside Church, originally a United Presbyterian Church, at the north-west corner of Chamberlain Road, moved to its fine new building at the opposite corner of the street, in 1881, the vacated premises were sold to the Morningside Athenium Company for £2,000. Here, with George Seton as the prime mover, a group of local professional men established the Morningside Athenium Club, which provided a library, lecture-room and concert hall. Programmes for the concerts, poetry recitals, lectures etc. organised by the club, with George Seton's name frequently prominent, are preserved in the Edinburgh Room of Edinburgh's Central Library. Mr Seton also found or made time to give support to the Society for Improving the Condition of the Poor in Edinburgh. In his recreational time he was a founder member of the St Andrew Boat Club, based on the Union Canal. He was also a keen shot, hill climber, and no mean golfer. Travel was another of his leisure pursuits and it is on record that he had visited every European capital, as well as Canada, Russia, Algiers, Egypt, South Africa and the Holy Land.

At the Royal Review, of 1881, on account of his height (six feet five inches) he was the member of the Royal Company of Archers chosen to be right-hand man of the Royal Bodyguard and stood next to Queen Victoria. Many years before, he had personally raised a company of forty volunteer grenadier artillery men (Midlothian Coast Artillery), all men over six feet tall. Seton was a Fellow of the Royal Society of Edinburgh. A staunch Conservative in politics, he nevertheless adopted an independent stand on many of the issues of his day. He was a strong Presbyterian, and notwithstanding the Disruption of 1843, one of the liveliest events of his time, he always remained a member of the Established Church. In September 1890, a few years after the death of his wife, Sarah Elizabeth Hunter of a Thurston family, George Seton decided to sell "St Bennets", and the fine villa was purchased at a cost of nearly £4,000 by the Roman Catholic authorities of the Archdiocese of St Andrews and Edinburgh, becoming the official residence of successive archbishops. Mr Seton moved to 3 Melville Crescent, where he died on November 14th 1908, aged eighty-six. His only son, George, entered the tea-planting business in Calcutta; developed various firms there and increased greatly Britain's interest in tea-trading with India. He died in 1929, leaving no children. Two of the three daughters of Mr George Seton of Greenhill pre-deceased him, and the male line died out. A nephew, Mr R. W. Seton Watson of Ayton, became Professor of History in the University of London.

7 · MERCHISTON

JOHN NAPIER

To many people Merchiston immediately suggests Merchiston Tower, and likewise the Tower seems synonymous with its one-time famous owner and occupant, the almost legendary John Napier. Such was Napier's fame, and so much has been written about him by expert biographers, that to attempt to enlarge upon their tributes, or even to summarise his achievements, would be superfluous, pretentious, even absurd. John Napier, therefore, is included in this volume simply in the context of his having resided in South Edinburgh and the connection which this had with various aspects of his life.

While the name Merchiston, in various spellings, first enters the records in 1266, the Napier family – "a race second to none in Scotland" as they claimed for themselves – first acquired ownership in 1438. The Tower was built in the middle of the 15th century either by Andrew Napier, merchant and Provost of Edinburgh, or by his son, Sir Alexander Napier, Vice-Admiral of Scotland and Comptroller of the Royal Household of James II, and twice Provost of Edinburgh, who acquired ownership of the lands in 1454. Until relatively recent times Merchiston Tower stood in isolation out on what had been the rather forbidding ancient Burgh Muir of the city, an object of siege and familiar with the sound of gunfire and the clash of swords. John Napier, who was born in the Tower in 1550, would

be well aware of all this, which was evident in his subsequent interest in military affairs. While his early childhood is not on record, at the age of thirteen he attended St Salvador's College in St Andrews, but left in 1565 without taking a degree.

John Napier of Merchiston

By an unknown artist
Reproduced by kind permission of the University of
Edinburgh

Napier next set out on a tour of Europe, which lasted five years, visiting France, Italy and Germany before returning to Scotland in 1572, marrying and settling down as a Lowland Laird on the family estate of Gartness in Stirlingshire. In 1608, following the death of his father, John Napier inherited Merchiston and took up residence in the Tower.

118

Though he had left St Andrews without a degree, he had nevertheless acquired a taste for scholarship, which was no doubt stimulated by his visits to the European capitals with their famous scholars, universities and libraries. Deeply interested in religion and its relevance to the great issues of his day, in 1593, he published *A Plain Discovery of the Whole Revelation of St John*, which was translated into several languages and won him great acclaim in learned circles in Europe.

In the late 16th century there was a constant fear in Britain of invasion from Europe, and Napier in his study in Merchiston Tower, leaving aside his theological preoccupations, applied his mind to inventions which might be used in war, both in defence and attack. These included the use of large mirrors to magnify and redirect the rays and heat of the sun on to enemy ships. An early version of a tank or armoured car was also described and recommended to the military authorities. Again, a primitive type of submarine was amongst "These inventions . . ., with diverse other devices and stratagems for harrowing of the enemies, by the Grace of God and work of expert craftsmen I hope to perform". (Signed) John Napier of Merchiston.

It was in 1614 that Napier's constantly inventive mind, after much study of astronomy, produced the mathematical system which was to earn him world fame. In that year he published a small book of fifty-seven pages of text and ninety pages of tables under the title *Mirifici Logarithmorum Canonis Descriptio*. The scholars of the world, especially the scientists and mathematicians, were astonished at this revolutionary discovery. Napier's system of logarithms opened up the modern field of mathematical sciences, even presaging the ultimate development of computers. Famous scientists wrote to him from various universities in Europe. Professor Henry Briggs of the Chair of Geology at Gresham College, London, visited Napier at Merchiston Tower in the summer of 1615. In 1620 the famous German astronomer Kepler dedicated a book to Napier, without being aware that the genius of Merchiston had died three years before.

In publishing his celebrated book, compiled in his study at Merchiston Tower, it has been authoritatively said that Napier had made Britain's first significant contribution to the advancement of science, and he thereby took his place alongside Copernicus, Kepler, Tycho Brahe and Galileo. Next to Isaac Newton's *Principia*, Napier's *Mirifici* was the most important work on the development of mathematics ever published in Britain.

As with so many men of genius, the Laird of Merchiston was not without his eccentricities. Local people and his servants called him "The Wizard", perhaps because he wore a long black cloak; or it may have been because of his seemingly magical powers: for example, when pigeons from Merchiston Tower's very large dovecot (on the site of present-day Albert Terrace, for long known as Doo Loan) invaded the grounds below his study and created a distracting noise, he would throw down handfuls of grain soaked in alcohol, which, to the amazement of his servants, quietened down the noisy birds considerably. This merely confirmed the aura that surrounded him of being a dabbler in black magic.

John Napier died in Merchiston Tower on April 4th 1617, aged 67. For long it was falsely believed that he had been buried in the family tomb in St Giles. In 1831, however, Professor William Wallace, a former Professor of Mathematics at the University, after diligent inquiry, produced evidence that Napier was buried in the graveyard of St Cuthbert's Church, of the congregation of which he had been a member. In 1842 a mural memorial in marble was erected in St Cuthbert's to the memory of the famous mathematician. It is suitably inscribed. Napier was twice married and left sons and daughters. His eldest son was raised to the peerage in 1627. An original portrait of Napier, dated 1616, is in the possession of Edinburgh University and there is another in the very fine Board Room of Napier College, situated in the skilfully restored Tower.

CHARLES CHALMERS

IN 1847, the leader of the Disruption, Dr Thomas Chalmers, died at his villa, No 1 Church Hill. However, it is not generally known that his rather less celebrated younger brother, Charles, for some years resided in the relatively nearby Merchiston Tower where he had founded Merchiston Castle School in 1833, becoming the first headmaster. As one researches the life of Charles Chalmers and his relationship with his brother Thomas, one is reminded of that between the famous Charles Kingsley and his similarly less celebrated brother Henry, who for a short period resided in Morningside. These may simply be but two instances among many of the difficulties that beset a young brother living in the shadow cast by a more distinguished elder one.

Charles Chalmers was born in 1792 at Anstruther, where his father was Provost. He was twelve years younger than Thomas. From the parish school Charles went on to St Andrews University where he acquitted himself well in mathematics and science. Unfortunately, he contracted tuberculosis and was forced to leave the university before graduating. On partially recovering his health, he went to Glasgow, perhaps to be near his elder brother, who, after ordination to the ministry and a short period at the parish of Kilmany in Fife, had been called to an important charge at St John's Church in Glasgow. In Glasgow Charles Chalmers took up various occupations, including private tutoring, but none lasted for long. Someone wrote that "he was a strange apparition on the Glasgow scene". Certainly he was a source of worry and embarrassment to his elder brother who was making a successful impact on St John's influential and wealthy congregation of merchants and businessmen. Indeed his influence on the life of Glasgow was immense. Thomas Chalmers had begun to publish his sermons and other writing on social problems, but after encountering difficulties with John Smith, then Glasgow's chief bookseller and a publisher, he persuaded William Collins, a rather remarkable and largely self-educated Glasgow teacher, to set up as publisher.

Collins, in fact, had been in the deputation which had come to hear Chalmers preach at Kilmany and had offered him the St John's charge. Chalmers offered Collins financial support in his publishing venture.

Charles Chalmers

Photograph by David Octavius Hill and Robert Adamson
By courtesy of the National Galleries of Scotland,
Edinburgh

Meantime, Charles Chalmers was still proving a problem. Thomas wrote in his journal: "He is noisy and impetuous and wilful to such a degree that I do not feel myself at liberty to offer him a single direction or request". Opportunities to work with William Blackwood in Edinburgh and at the Court of Session there fell through, as did a post in Whyte's bookshop in the capital. While briefly engaged with the latter, at £36 per annum, Chalmers had married an Australian girl. His health suffered another breakdown and he returned to Glasgow and his brother's support. Then, suddenly,

Thomas Chalmers saw a possible opportunity for the hapless Charles. He could become a partner with William Collins in the new publishing enterprise. This proposal, backed by £800 which Thomas put up as his brother's share, Collins readily accepted, and in 1819 the firm of William Collins and Charles Chalmers was established – the beginning of what was to become the famous Collins publishing house of the present day. Charles Chalmers was most grateful and told Collins that he had been about to take up stone-breaking and road-laying, in desperation. On September 23 1879 *The Glasgow Courier* announced the publication of Thomas Chalmers' first major work: *The Christian and the Civic Economy of Large Towns.* "Published by Chalmers and Collins, booksellers and stationers". The bookshop was in Glasgow's Wilson Street; the printing works in Candleriggs.

In 1827 the Chalmers and Collins partnership suffered in the nation-wide financial crisis. Again Thomas Chalmers helped out with a generous loan. Then, after six and a half years, through various other difficulties and Charles Chalmers' instability, the publishing partnership broke up. Chalmers received quite a substantial sum of money as his share in the winding up, and with his wife, two sons and a daughter, returned to Edinburgh, residing first in Morning-side, then in the Grange district and finally acquiring a substantial house at 3 Park Place, a little street of titled and wealthy residents near the Bristo area and George Square. Here, in March 1827, to Thomas Chalmers' annoyance, Charles used much of his share of the Glasgow split-up to

121

launch *Chalmers' Journal of Useful Knowledge*, a periodical which he used principally as a medium for much of his own writing on scientific theories and inventions. Collins, obviously still friendly, acted as one of several joint publishers and assisted with distribution. Six issues appeared, then funds ran out. Charles desperately sought money from his late father's estate. His future seemed bleak once more. Then, suddenly through an idea of his own, his fortune turned. In greatly improved health he resumed private tutoring, and went even further.

In November 1827, at 3 Park Place, Charles opened a small boarding-school with three boys who were attending other Edinburgh schools in preparation for the University. He charged them seventy guineas per annum for a shared room and eighty guineas for a single. From this income and a further loan from his long-suffering brother, who was doubtful about the scheme, he laid the foundations of what was eventually to become a famous public school, and, it has been suggested, the pioneer of Scottish boarding-schools, Merchiston Castle. In 1833, at a time when the Napier family were temporarily not in possession of Merchiston Tower, Chalmers, finding his Park Place premises increasingly inadequate, obtained a lease of the ancient property and on May 24th 1833, bringing with him about fifteen boys, founded the school which he called "Merchiston Castle Academy". Traditionally referred to as Merchiston Tower, it was Chalmers who helped to popularise "Castle". He himself resided with his family in a villa, "Castlebank", within the precincts of the Tower.

Within a short time the new school's roll had risen to eighty. Boys joined the school at the age of eight and they were "mothered" by Mrs Chalmers, and a Mrs Burton, who looked after all domestic arrangements. Mrs Burton apparently – and somewhat expeditiously – bathed all the smaller boys every Saturday evening! The school curriculum included the classics, French and English, but, on account of Chalmers' own special interest, provided more science and mathematical studies than other comparable schools. In the mid-1800s Merchiston Tower was still well out from the city and "in the country" and was ideal for walks to the Blackford and Braid hills, providing physical recreation, before sports were regularly introduced. When the latter did commence, the playing fields were opposite the school, where Abbotsford Park was eventually built, and then ground was acquired where George Watson's College now stands. Botanical excursions and visits to factories were another of Charles Chalmers' extra-mural projects. On Sundays the boys walked to and from church at Buccleuch Street, but after the opening of Morningside Parish Church in 1838, transferred to this more convenient place of worship. Dr Thomas Chalmers, when he had left Glasgow and become Professor of Theology at Edinburgh University, from 1842, residing at his newly built house at Churchhill, regularly addressed his brother's pupils on Sunday afternoons.

Charles Chalmers eventually drew upon the assistance of his two sons,

John and Thomas, to augment his teaching staff, the latter in 1848 succeeding his father as resident house-master. In 1850, due to indifferent health, Chalmers sold the school to Mr John Gibson, then Government Inspector of Schools for Scotland, but the founder continued to reside at Castlebank, there writing scientific articles and cultivating his roses. In 1860 he suffered a stroke and died at his home.

In 1883 the Jubilee Celebrations of the then long-established Merchiston Castle School were held in the Morningside Athenium Club, in the former North Morningside Church premises at the north corner of Chamberlain Road. Tribute was paid to the school's founder, and his son Thomas replied to the toast. Until 1896 the school remained privately owned, but upon the resignation of the notable headmaster for thirty-three years, Dr Rogerson, a company and governing body was formed. In 1930 the school, with 210 boys, moved from Merchiston Tower to the 90-acre Colinton House Estate, this mansion-house having been built by Sir William Forbes of Pitsligo, father of the Sir William who became owner of Greenhill.

The school now numbers 320 boys, over 300 being boarders. Looking at its many fine buildings today, and considering its impressive record academically and in sport, and the high reputation which it enjoys among Scottish boarding-schools, one feels that Dr Thomas Chalmers would have expressed the utmost admiration, even if with a wry smile and albeit tempered by incredulity, for the initiative and enterprise which his "feckless" problem brother ultimately proved he possessed by having founded such a famous school.

SIR JAMES GOWANS

MERCHISTON seems noted for its eccentrics, and although one simple connotation of the term is 'odd people', certainly that would be an understatement when applied to "the astonishing house" which James Gowans built for himself and his family at Merchiston in 1858. This was "Rockville", originally No 3 Napier Road. Gowans' personality, and his career and achievements as an architect and builder, have been presented in detail in Duncan McAra's authoritative book: *Sir James Gowans – Romantic Rationalist*. Any attempt to add to this would be superfluous.

"Rockville", known variously to many people as "the Pagoda House", "the Chinese House" or "Sugar-Loaf House" was, alas, demolished in 1966. It had ultimately become, temporarily, an expensive private college for boys; for very many years it had been the home of the Harrison family, prominent in the public life of Edinburgh. Finally, there was a succession of private owners or tenants. Only the original low street boundary wall remains. To those who never saw it, some re-collection of what it looked like may be gleaned from the appearance of "Lammerburn", No 10 Napier Road, which Gowans also built a year after his own house, almost directly opposite it, but of less striking style.

Much of the former Dean of Guild's work may still be seen else-

Sir James Gowans

where in the city, some of it with characteristic two-foot-square modules clearly signifying his design. The tall flats at Nos. 25 to 36 Castle Terrace, with their twin crown-capped towers, were by Gowans. So too, were Rosebank Cottages, prototype houses for "working class" people near Gardiner's Crescent and Nos. 23 and 25 Blacket Place. The Synod Hall in Castle Terrace, demolished in 1966 to make way for a prospective opera house, will be remembered by many. Gowans married a daughter of the distinguished sculptor, William Brodie, who made for him a statuary group, "The Genius of Architecture crowning the Theory and Practice of Art." This stood in Gowans' garden at Rockville but was eventually moved to West Princes Street Gardens.

Perhaps Gowans' "finest hour" was his planning of the International Exhibition of Industry, Science and Art, held in the Meadows in 1886, souvenirs of which remain in the form of the Prince Albert Victor sundial in the East Meadows near Melville Drive and Brougham Place, designed by Gowans: the twin pillars at the west entrance to Melville Drive, comprising sections of stone from quarries all over Scotland, a memento of the Master Builders and Operative Masons of Edinburgh and Leith, were also planned by Gowans; and the whale jawbone arch at the Melville Drive entrance to the fittingly named Jawbone Walk, the arch having formed part of the Zetland and Fair Isle knitting stand. The mastermind behind what was a unique exhibition in concept and scale was knighted by Queen Victoria during her visit to the Exhibition in August 1886, and a great gathering took place in the Meadows to honour him and his family. But his great personal triumphant achievement had taken its toll, in both physical and financial strain. His health deteriorated, and, leaving "Rockville", he moved to nearby Blantyre Terrace, where he died in June 1890. He was buried in Grange Cemetery.

THEODORE NAPIER

IF John Napier, "the Wizard of Merchiston", was noted for his eccentricities, two centuries later another Merchiston resident undoubtedly qualified as the district's literally most colourful character. This was Theodore Napier, whose home was at 7 West Castle Road. No relation of the famous family who owned the Tower, Theodore Napier was a well-known figure as he walked the nearby streets and down in Morningside habitually wearing the full tartan costume of a Highland chieftain.

Napier was born in Melbourne, Australia, in March 1845, son of Thomas Napier, J.P., of Marykirk, Kincardineshire and Rosebank, Victoria. His education began in Australia and continued at Edinburgh's High School and the University when his family moved to Scotland. In December 1877 he married Miss Mary Ann Noble, daughter of Thomas Noble of Somerton, Australia, and they had one son and two daughters. His elder daughter, Zoë Alfredo, married Dr J. Malcolm Farquharson of Edinburgh. Napier was a Companion of the Jacobite Order of St Germain and Honorary Secretary for Scotland of the Legitimist Jacobite League of Great Britain and Ireland. He was also an ardent member of the Scottish Home Rule and Scottish Patriotic Associations, as well as of various literary societies.

In 1898 he published *A Plea for the Restoration of the Royal House of Stuart*, a spirited appeal against Hanoverian usurpation of the British Crown and for the return of a Scottish Parliament. Every year, on February 8th, the anniversary of the execution of Mary Queen of Scots at Fotheringay, Theodore Napier, often with a party of relations and friends, travelled to England and placed a floral wreath on what had been the actual site of the executioner's block. The wreath, of golden immortelles, was in the shape of a crown and bore

Theodore Napier

By courtesy of the late Mr E. John D. Cameron, Montrose, and Mr Gilmour Main

a card commemorating Mary's martyrdom at the hands of her English cousin Elizabeth. This annual gesture of loyalty to the ill-fated Queen's memory, in the course of time became provocative to anti-Stuart societies, and on the advice of the local constabulary Napier reluctantly discontinued his visits. He was also a regular visitor to the scene of the Battlefield of Culloden. He died in 1900.

GEORGE WATSON

ONE of Edinburgh's most famous fee-paying schools, George Watson's College, founded in 1723 as a charitable "hospital" for the education of boys in difficult circumstances, after two centuries of its existence in the Lauriston district, was transferred to its fine new premises and spacious playing fields in Colinton Road in 1932. Like so many of Edinburgh's educational foundations, originally of a charitable nature, George Watson's had long since become transformed.

George Watson was born in Edinburgh on November 23rd 1654. His father, John, was a merchant who died relatively young and in impecunious circumstances. On his mother's re-marriage George and his brother were "left to the care of destiny". Their paternal aunt, Elizabeth Davidson, took care of them and arranged their education. George was subsequently apprenticed to an Edinburgh merchant, and then his aunt sent him to Holland to broaden his commercial experience. He seemed to become quite expert in financial matters. Returning to Edinburgh in 1676, George Watson was employed by Sir James Dick of Prestonfield, then Lord Provost of the city and grandson of the ill-fated Sir William Dick of Braid, who, having once been extremely wealthy, on account of his financial support of the Royalist cause ultimately died a pauper's death in a London debtors' prison. Sir James Dick had gradually rebuilt the family estate. He was greatly impressed by George Watson and entrusted him to conduct much of his financial affairs on his own responsibility. It has been said that George Watson was the first professional accountant in Scotland. In 1695 he was appointed the first accountant to the Bank of Scotland.

When he died on April 3rd 1723, Watson had amassed a very considerable fortune and perhaps, recalling well his own experience when his father had died in financial difficulties, he bequeathed the sum of £12,000 to found "a hospital or charitable foundation school for the sons and grandsons of decayed merchants". Fifty years earlier, Mary Erskine, widow of an Edinburgh druggist, had left 100,000 merks for the establishment of a similar foundation for "the daughters of decayed merchants". Both benefactors, along with others, were emulating the original generosity of George Heriot. By the time the first premises were opened in Lauriston Place in 1741, in a building designed by William Adam and to become the site of the Royal Infirmary in later years, Watson's legacy by careful investment had increased to £20,000.

George Watson

From the portrait by William Aikman, painted in
Edinburgh in 1720
By courtesy of the Merchant Company of Edinburgh

At first there were ten resident foundationers; by 1869 there were approximately a hundred. In July 1870 the Edinburgh Merchant Company, the governing body of George Watson's were empowered by Parliament to reform all the "hospitals" under their management and Watson's became a fee-paying school for boys of senior and primary level, retaining a nucleus of foundationers. In this new form, in September 1870, the roll numbered approximately one thousand. A year later the college site had been sold to the governors of Edinburgh Royal Infirmary, who were anxious to move from the old and inadequate hospital in Infirmary Street to David Bryce's extensive new Royal Infirmary at Lauriston Place. Parts of the original college, including the fine chapel, were retained by the Royal Infirmary and still remain today. Fortunately, Watson's were able to move into the vacated fine building at the foot of Archibald Place, which had been the Merchant Maidens' Hospital. This had removed, to become Queen Street Ladies College, in recent times transferred to Ravelston.

In 1871, when the boys' college departed to Archibald Place, the governors founded George Watson's Ladies' College on the north side of George Square, with five hundred girls on the initial roll. In 1929 the former extensive playing fields of Merchiston Castle School in Colinton Road, extending from Tipperlinn Road to Myreside Road, were acquired, and in 1932 George Watson's moved from Archibald Place to the impressive new premises here, designed by James B. Dunn. Above the college's entrance is a galleon wind-vane, symbol of the Merchant Company; this had stood above the previous school. In 1967 the Education Board decided to amalgamate the boys' and girls' schools and the George Square building was made available to the University. George Watson's therefore became co-educational at Colinton Road in 1974 and a year later the combined roll was 2,400. This figure has now been reduced. In 1976 the name of the former, but unconnected, John Watson's School at Belford Road was incorporated with George Watson's College.

8 · CHURCH HILL/ EAST MORNINGSIDE

DR THOMAS CHALMERS

ON the front wall of the fine villa at 1 Church Hill, which came to be named "Westgate", a metal plaque states: "In this house Thomas Chalmers died. 31st May 1847." How great a saga lies behind this brief announcement! When Chalmers had been Professor of Theology in the University for nearly fifteen years, he built this villa in keeping with his status, in 1842, a year before the Disruption and his resigning his University post. He wrote: "Mean to build at Morningside: but let me not forget the end of the World and the Coming of Christ".

There are books enough to relate in detail the events in the life of this widely acknowledged and very famous man who from humble origins in Anstruther in Fife, having become a minister of the established Church of Scotland, was to become an author, preacher, professor and orator without equal and the leader of the Disruption in 1843 which tore the Established Church apart and led to the foundation of the Free Church of Scotland. Chalmers was elected the first Moderator and Principal of the newly established college of the Free Church. When he was buried in Grange Cemetery – the first interment there – on June 4th 1847, it was said that the vast crowd which attended had never been equalled for the funeral of any man in 19th-

Dr Thomas Chalmers

Painted posthumously by Sir John Watson Gordon
By courtesy of the National Galleries of Scotland, Edinburgh

century Scotland. A summary of his life and of the repercussions of the Disruption on Morningside was presented in an earlier volume of this work.

Following his death, memorials to Dr Thomas Chalmers abounded throughout Scotland. Very many then quite recently built Free Churches bore his name, and statues were erected in villages and towns; Edinburgh's principal one, by the famous sculptor, Sir John Steell, is in George Street. So, nearly a century and a half after his death is Chalmers' name recalled only on memorials?

128

Many of the churches once commemorating him, e.g. St Catherine's-in-Grange, in Grange Road, not many yards from his grave immediately beyond the wall of Grange Cemetery, renounced his name following the various reunions which brought certain Free Churches back into the establishment. After all the fluctuations of interest in Chalmers and in his writings and influence over so many years he would now seem to be experiencing something of a revival of interest. In 1979 the Chair of Dogmatics in Edinburgh University's New College was renamed the Thomas Chalmers Chair of Divinity. In the New College Library, which has a very large collection of Chalmers' papers, including a voluminous file of correspondence with his brother Charles, books on the life and writings of the founder of the Free Church are constantly in demand, whose college and offices are close by on the Mound.

One of Chalmers' most interesting and important spheres of work – and they were many – which is attracting attention today and is particularly thought-provoking in this era of the Welfare State, concerned domestic economic hardship and deprivation. So also, at a time when the churches are constantly debating their role as regards social problems, is his "Territorial Mission", which he introduced in the important St John's parish in Glasgow, to which he was specially appointed in 1819 to enable him to try out his experiment. This parish comprised an amalgam of the wealthy and the destitute. Chalmers believed that in a Christian church community the better-off should be responsible for the material welfare of the poorer

members, – almost a practical application of the early Christian principle of "having all things in common". He arranged for the Glasgow Poor Law authorities to cease paying out "dole" and other "social security" payments to the needy of his parish, and guaranteed that his people of means would care for the poorer parishioners. The parish was divided into "Territories" or "Proportions", with elders and others responsible for each of these; "providing material assistance, obtained from collections in the all-important church plate, finding unemployed people jobs and improved housing, and opening schools for children where none existed". This Christian caring and sharing, Chalmers believed and wrote, was better and more dignified and humane than impersonal statutory dole payments which simply reinforced a pauper mentality. The experiment was highly successful and, to the surprise of many, remained so for many years long after Chalmers had left the parish.

In Edinburgh, in 1844, one year after the Disruption, and following the resignation of his University Professorship, Chalmers, now settled in his fine new house at Church Hill, instead of seeking a well-earned rest after a life of almost ceaseless and incredible drive, activity and controversy, turned his attention to his one overriding interest – greater than any further academic ambition or authorship – the establishment of a Territorial Mission in the West Port, one of the city's worst areas of poverty, deprivation, drunkenness and social irresponsibility, the district which twenty years before had been the scene of the notorious

Burke and Hare murders, and where, apart from the labours of a few Catholic priests, the people had been abandoned. Chalmers found men and women from outwith the area, willing to undertake responsibility for a "Territory" *i.e.*, a certain number of stairs and closes, overcrowded with virtually illiterate people with all their problems and near-hopelessness. The slum-dwellers were regularly visited, befriended, encouraged, but also chastened and challenged to overcome their adversities and to change their environment. A school was opened in a tannery in Portsburgh Square and services also held there. A fine church was built on the south side opposite Portsburgh Square, the West Port Territorial Church.

Chalmers, himself a familiar figure in and out of the closes, wrote that despite his failing health and lack of strength to contribute adequately, this West Port mission was the fulfilment of his life's work. But perhaps the demands were too great. On the morning of May 31st 1847 he was found to have died peacefully in his sleep. He was sixty-seven. It was reported that after his interment in Grange Cemetery the vast crowds lingered, reluctant to go away. People just could not believe that a man like Chalmers could ever die. Other people were famous for what they had *done* or *achieved*. Chalmers was famous for what he *was*. People said: "There was something about him. When you met him, even briefly, you could never forget him. You felt a power in him, going from him, drawing you to him..." None would have experienced this charisma more than the people in the West Port Territorial Church, still standing, though for long derelict, perhaps his greatest memorial. Certainly it is the one, which, if any, he would have chosen. As we write, during the restoration of the West Port, the future of the Territorial Church remains conjectural.

JANE WELSH CARLYLE

It is September 1862. At the junction of Doo Loan (now Albert Terrace) with Marmion Terrace (now Morningside Road) a lady waits, rather impatiently, every few moments peering down the slope of Church Hill towards Morningside Village, anxiously watching for the approach of the horse-drawn bus. She is Mrs Jane Welsh Carlyle, who is residing with her two maiden aunts in a large villa just opposite where she is waiting. A letter to Thomas reveals the object of her journey. She is a martyr to insomnia and requires more morphia, to induce sleep. "I am just going in an omnibus to Duncan Flockhart's for it". Duncan Flockhart, for long famous early Edinburgh chemists, were established at No 52 North Bridge.

Jane Welsh Carlyle's published letters and those of her famous husband, Thomas, contain many references to her occasional short visits to her aunts at Morningside. Six years before the above occasion, Thomas Carlyle had written: "My Jeannie has come across to Craigenvilla (fond reminiscences of Craigenputtock), her aunts' new garden residence of their own in the

130

Morningside quarter, some neat little place where the surviving two still live". These were her father's sisters and the Edinburgh and District Post Office Directory for 1856 contained the entry: "The Misses Welsh, Craigenvilla, No 2 Banner Place". Banner Place was the short stretch of road from the south-west corner of what is now Church Hill Place to Newbattle Terrace. The Misses Welsh's house had previously been known as Graftden Villa and Thomas Carlyle's jocular comment linking its new name with Craigenputtock is a reference to what had been his and Jane's home in Dumfriesshire shortly after their marriage.

Jane Welsh Carlyle

Painted by Samuel Laurence in 1849 when she was aged
48
In a private collection

Jane's aunts were very staunch Free Church members – the Disruption had occurred relatively recently and they would have attended the church services in a temporary building almost directly opposite their house in what was then Marmion Terrace. Again, almost opposite their house on the other side of Church Hill, was the villa in which, as they doubtless knew well, had lived and died the great Dr Thomas Chalmers, the Disruption leader, less than ten years before. The fact that Dr Chalmers had resided there would also be of interest to Jane since it was the celebrated Edward Irving, Chalmers' assistant minister in Glasgow, and a friend of Thomas Carlyle, who had first brought the latter to Haddington and introduced him to her. Writing to her husband from Craigenvilla in August 1857, Jane commented: "Certainly it is a devil of a place for keeping the Sunday this". Apart from its religious climate, she also found the district's unsurfaced roads and lack of pavements created much dust, swirled up by the wind. She wrote: "I used to fancy Piccadilly dusty. But oh my! – if you saw Morningside Road".

Jane Welsh Carlyle in her later life seldom left their home in Cheyne Row, Chelsea, and eight years after she had written the above comments Thomas was elected Rector of Edinburgh University in November 1865. When he came to the city to deliver his Rectorial address on April 2nd of the next year, while he actually resided with his friend Thomas Erskine, he may well have visited Jane's aunts. Certainly towards the end of March Jane sent them two tickets for the installation ceremony in the Music Hall in George Street. The demand for tickets had been so great that Jane requested the sisters to return those she had sent without delay if not required. It is not known if they attended. Carlyle, who apparently considered his election as Rector of his old University perhaps the greatest honour bestowed upon him, was nevertheless most apprehensive, and Jane even more so, at the prospect of delivering the traditional Rectorial Address. He had had no real practice in public speaking and hated doing so. She considered the ceremony so great an ordeal that she could not face accompanying her husband to Edinburgh and remained at Chelsea, anxiously awaiting a report of his performance. Her advice to him regarding his speech was: "Keep up your head the first three minutes, and after, it will all be plain sailing". A letter to Thomas just before the ceremony reveals her extreme anxiety and concern for his success.

At Chelsea Jane awaited news in agony. The post brought nothing. Then, at last, a telegram from Carlyle's great friend, Professor Tyndall. It read: "A perfect triumph". The new rector had taken his audience by storm. While Jane now eagerly awaited her husband's return from Edinburgh, after a few days' rest at Scotsbrig in Dumfriesshire, anxious to hear every detail of the ceremony and his triumphant reception, this was not to be. When Thomas received what was Jane's last of so very many letters to him, dated April 21st 1866, he had already received a telegram informing him of her tragic sudden death while riding in her carriage in Hyde Park on the same day as her letter. By her own wish, Jane, aged 64, was buried in the Abbey Churchyard in her native Haddington, in her father's grave. Carlyle composed the words on her headstone, commemorating their remarkable relationship, her unwearied devotion to him and his success, and, "the light of his life as if gone out".

SUSAN FERRIER

PERHAPS not many pedestrians pass along leafy, secluded Clinton Road, just beyond Church Hill at the top of Pitsligo Road. Those who do are more likely than the motorist to observe that since 1982 one of the gate piers to stately East Morningside House displays a simple little wooden plaque which reads quite briefly: "Susan Ferrier (Writer). Born 7th September 1782. Died 5th November 1854." It was a privilege to be present on that evening in 1982 of the informal unveiling ceremony, attended by a fair number of literary people from Edinburgh and beyond. It was a significant occasion, for happily there is now a growing interest in Susan Ferrier and her work.

When a brief account of her life was published in one of my earlier volumes, it is quite possible that then many readers were being made aware of the 19th-century Edinburgh lady novelist for the first time. After nearly more than a century and a half she might well have faded into obscurity. But this has not been so, and perhaps for one major reason. In 1982, to mark the bi-centenary of her birth, a most comprehensive exhibition of documents, photographs and

132

artefacts relating to her family, her work and the lady herself, was mounted by the National Library of Scotland. The exhibition was all the more illuminating on account of the great deal of hitherto unknown material contributed by one of Susan Ferrier's relations, Judge Irvine, and the exhibition catalogue, still available, is a most valuable document not only for its information concerning Miss Ferrier's background and life, but also for the stimulating and authoritative assessment of her work by Dr Ian Campbell, Reader in English Literature at Edinburgh University. In a review of her three novels Dr Campbell concludes that despite their limitations these did not restrict them to kailyard or to a narrow popularity in their own time but gave them a considerable enduring appeal. Thus, there is now probably more revived interest in Edinburgh's 19th-century lady novelist than when the appearance of her first work, *Marriage* (1818), earned for her the title of "Scotland's Jane Austen". In December 1984 her second novel *The Inheritance* (1824) was reprinted and it is possible that her third work *Destiny* (1831) may also again become available.

When Thomas Carlyle was teaching in Kirkcaldy, Susan Ferrier invited him to East Morningside. Unfortunately, when he was able to call she was not at home and it is not thought that a meeting ever took place. East Morningside House was acquired by Susan Ferrier's father, a solicitor and close friend of Sir Walter Scott, as the family's country house soon after his wife died in 1797, and Susan's three sisters having married she became housekeeper to her father. It was in the fine oak-

Susan Ferrier

Portrait by Robert Thorburn, 1836
In a private collection

pannelled study of the house that, in time snatched from her household duties, she devoted herself to writing. In her diary she provides interesting comments on the Morningside of her day. East Morningside House was the first villa to be built in the district in 1726 and in Miss Ferrier's time was still remote from the city. She wrote: "Except for the Walkers and James on a Sunday, we never see a soul". Again, in her time, the house would still have had its entrance-door facing east, towards "the morning side of the sun", which has been suggested by some local historians as the derivation of the name Morningside. Certainly it is in reference to this house that the name of the district first appears in the records. The east-facing doorway which was built over when the west wing was added in about 1850, has now been restored

133

following other interior alterations to the house and is in use.

Indicative of a developing interest in Miss Ferrier and her work, by the kind courtesy of the present owner, groups of people are able to visit the house and enjoy the exhibition of "Ferrierana" which is laid out. Susan Edmonstone Ferrier, as a person, was something of an enigma; she was described by her close friend Sir Walter Scott, to whom she was a great help in his failing health, as "Simple, full of humour, and exceedingly ready at repartee and without the affectation of a blue stocking". Scott indeed wrote that he retired from the literary field happily confident in those who would succeed him and not least Susan Ferrier. She died on November 5th 1854, and is buried in the family tomb in St Cuthbert's churchyard.

DAVID DAVIDSON

THERE are two fine villas in Clinton Road, East Morningside House and Avallon, while it is overlooked by two others, The Elms and Clinton House, both of which are actually entered from Whitehouse Loan. Until 1962, there was another impressive house, which completed the group. This was Woodcroft, in Clinton Road, which amid much regret and protest was swept away and replaced by the towering modern block housing one of Scotland's busiest STD telephone exchanges, while retaining the name of the former mansion-house. In the original Woodcroft, which he built for himself and his family in 1858, there resided until his death in 1900 in his eighty-ninth year, Lt-Colonel Davidson, a man who is of interest not only in his own right but also on account of his close friendship with Jane Welsh, as she was called when he first knew her, and, subsequently, of course, Jane Welsh Carlyle, following her marraige to the famous "Sage of Chelsea". On occasions, as had been mentioned elsewhere, she resided with her aunts not far from Woodcroft at the corner of Church Hill.

David Davidson was born in Haddington in 1811 and lived there for sixteen years. His early life and his subsequent career are described in great detail in his autobiography *Memories of a Long Life*. He attended Haddington Burgh School, as did Jane, daughter of the local Dr John Welsh, and although she was ten years older than he they became close friends. His *Memories* provide several interesting anecdotes of his Haddington days. He recalled that the celebrated Edward Irving, who later became an assistant minister to Dr Thomas Chalmers in Glasgow, taught at the Burgh School. He also remarks that Thomas Carlyle, following his marriage to Jane, subscribed generously towards the building of Knox Academy. He recalled accompanying a friend on horseback on an errand to Saltoun and how, when he became tired from riding, he was left for a short time at Grant's Braes to rest at the home of Gilbert Burns, brother of the famous Robert, and there met his family. His family's doctor was Jane Welsh's father and he remembered as a small boy hearing of the unexpected death of Dr Welsh from typhus fever which he had contracted from a patient.

After twenty years in India, David

Davidson, with the rank of Lieutenant-Colonel, returned to Edinburgh and, after a short residence in the country, came with his wife and family to Edinburgh, desiring to build a house as a permanent home. Davidson comments that he "preferred the city's southern suburb, almost completely unbuilt upon, with excellent sites". He was introduced to the celebrated architect David Bryce and submitted to him his own drawings. Bryce, apparently very busy at the time, passed the plans to his colleagues Walker and Paris, having made only one modification of Davidson's plan, altering his "Elizabethan elevations" to "Old Scotch", "for which Bryce was famous". "I selected an admirable site on the ridge running eastward from Boroughmuirhead, on which the Scottish army was encamped before marching to Flodden: commanding a view of Blackford, the Braid and Pentland Hills, stretching behind the other like the scenery on a stage, all possessing historic associations, and being thus in themselves an education for my children. The plot contained five acres, and being surrounded by fine trees on three sides, I named it Woodcroft. Mr Bryce resolved to open a quarry in the grounds and furnished an abundance of fine sandstone as hard as Craigleith and of a beautiful pinkish colour. He also introduced a mode of building – of which this was the first specimen, but which has now been largely adopted, – of laying the square-dressed stones on their natural bed, and, being split with wedges, the outer surfaces present no marks of the chisel." Dr John Brown was greatly taken with the house, – 'the best', he said, 'in Edinburgh and

Lt-Colonel David Davidson
From "Memories of a Long Life"

built of the rock on which it stands'. "Imitation is the highest form of flattery, and so two houses were shortly built to the east, of the same stone, and much on the same plan. Having myself had a home round which my most pleasing associations lingered when in a far-off land, I had wished my children to have the same; and this has been pleasantly realised. One writes from India, 'I shall never feel myself really at home till I get to Woodcroft'".

Once settled in Woodcroft, Davidson became very much involved in two spheres of activity. Firstly, he was prominent in the raising of the Queen's City of Edinburgh Rifle Volunteers Brigade, and indeed invented some type of telescopic lens to improve marksmanship. He was, incidentally, a very good shot himself. He commanded the leading brigade of rifles at the Royal Review in Holyrood Park in 1860. His other great interest, as one who had left the Established Church of Scotland at the Disruption and joined the Free Church, was evangelism, a movement whose development nationally was contemporaneous with that of the rifle volunteers. Large rallies were held in Holyrood Park and these were directed from evangelical mission premises in Carrubber's Close, in the High Street. Davidson was involved in organising mass meetings in the Corn Exchange, in the Grassmarket, addressed by the famous evangelists Sankey and Moody.

David Davidson, although, as already noted, very much younger than Jane Welsh, never forgot those early days when they both attended the Burgh School in Haddington, and indeed upon his return to Edinburgh from India after twenty years' absence, and although she was now married and residing in Chelsea, made contact with her again, corresponding with her frequently, and constantly referring to their early friendship at Haddington. These reminiscences Jane Welsh Carlyle seemed at first to enjoy, then when he appeared to indulge in rather excessive nostalgia, she suddenly bade him cease writing in such vein. Nevertheless she did visit him at St Margaret's Cottage in Greenhill where he lived with his family temporarily until Woodcroft was completed, and it was she who suggested the motto above the new villa's main entrance, which had been on a lintel of a door in Haddington: "*Meliora semper cogita*". This Davidson readily adopted. He in turn

had visited the Carlyles in their Chelsea home, there on one occasion meeting Alfred Tennyson. His attempts to press his evangelical Christianity on Thomas Carlyle led to much lively debate and correspondence.

SIR DANIEL AND PROFESSOR GEORGE WILSON

ELM Cottage West, its name carved on a large stone on the front wall at 1 Blackford Road, with the adjoining Elm Cottage East, not now indicated as such, at No 3, was originally one house, built in 1852. Here lived two brothers, each distinguished in quite different fields, who earned a prominent place in the history of Edinburgh. Daniel Wilson, the elder brother, who was also a most accomplished artist, is famous for his classic work *Memorials of Edinburgh in the Olden Time*, and other achievements in the literary world, while his brother George enjoyed a high reputation in the sphere of science and was the first Director of the Scottish Industrial Museum.

Sir Daniel Wilson

SIR DANIEL WILSON

DANIEL WILSON was born in Edinburgh on January 3rd 1816 at 5 Calton Hill. His father, Archibald, had come to the capital from Lochfyneside a few years before, in 1812, and married Jane Aitken, daughter of a Greenock surveyor. The father became a tea dealer in Greenside Street in the city, and later a spirit merchant at Regent Arch, until his death in 1843. He had a very large family and his income was low. Of his eleven children most died in childhood. Daniel recalled "the frequent sad days of serious illness and death's dark shadow again and again". He believed that the frequent playing of his brother and himself in the fresh breezes of Calton Hill safeguarded their health. One daughter who did survive became sister-in-law to the celebrated Victorian novelist Mrs Oliphant.

After attending a small school nearby, run by a Mr. George Knight, Daniel attended the High School and was a pupil there when it moved from the Old Town to Regent Road. He with his younger brother, George, showed early signs of an intellectual bent and when not yet in their teens, with two young friends founded a "Juvenile Society for the Advancement of Knowledge" which issued a weekly "Journal". Whatever its standard, it was an early sign of the distinguished scholarship both brothers were later to show. Of this "Journal", Daniel was the editor and illustrator, the latter another early indication of artistic ability later to become highly developed. A small museum which they set up in their home was the early pointer to one of George's future enterprises.

Upon leaving the High School, Daniel became apprenticed in sketching and engraving to William Miller (subject of another article), the acknowledged master engraver whom Turner regarded as a craftsman without equal. Such was the training Daniel Wilson received and his own talent, that at times the work of the master and pupil could not readily be distinguished. Wilson broke off working with Miller to attend Edinburgh University, specialising in English Literature and in 1837, went to London to work with MacMillan the publisher as a literary adviser and editor. When he returned to Edinburgh in 1842, he brought with him a testimonial from MacMillan of the highest praise for his expertise over a wide range of subjects.

In Edinburgh, he opened in business as a printseller and artists' colourman in West Register Street, and later Hanover Street while residing at Broughton Place. This occupation now brought him into contact with very distinguished artists, notably Charles Kirk Sharpe who was also a great antiquary. It was from Sharpe that Wilson obtained much material for his classic work *Memorials of Edinburgh in the Olden Times*. This book, a masterpiece within its class, was originally conceived simply as a large collection of his sketches and engravings, especially of places then no longer in existence or about to disappear, with large captions. However, as Wilson's sources increased and his researches widened and deepened, the intended captions became the text and his own greatly enlarged number of etchings and engravings the principal illustrations.

The first edition appeared originally in twenty-four serial parts during 1847, printed and published by Hugh Paton, and in two quarto volumes in 1848. Paton had produced *Kay's Portraits* ten years earlier. Apart from the tremendous amount of research behind Wilson's book, its other striking feature was his own illustrations, over 120 of them. The book was acclaimed "a model of local history". Edinburgh's other great historians such as Maitland and Arnot, in comparison, were criticised for their rather too "objective coolness", lacking representation of the human scene. Only Robert Chambers, whom Wilson greatly admired, was said to have fully conveyed the pathos of the Old Edinburgh story. Wilson's "Memorials" were written as a labour of love — he received no remuneration for the first edition and indeed in a profits and loss agreement with Paton, he shared in the initial deficit.

In 1848 Daniel Wilson was appointed Secretary to the Society of Antiquaries of Scotland, providing him with even greater scope for his researches and leading to his friendship with the notable biographer, David Laing. As an ardent lover of Old Edinburgh and as secretary of the Society of Antiquaries, Wilson led protests against "the great vandalism" of removing the Trinity College Church to make way for the building of the Waverley Station. He attended the last service in this beautiful church on Sunday May 14th 1848, remarking upon "seeing there the magistrates who had sold it to the spoilers and were now attending with incongruous ostentation". In 1851 Wilson's *The Archaeology and Pre-Historic Annals of Scotland*

appeared, which was destined to be another classic. A year later, Wilson and his family took up residence in the east part of the sub-divided Elm Cottage, No 3 Blackford Road, built by his uncle. His sister Jessie, and his brother George, who was unmarried, occupied the west part.

But Daniel Wilson's stay at Elm Cottage was short. In 1853 he was appointed Professor of History and English Literature in the University of Toronto. Much of the revision of his Scottish books was carried out there, and yet another classic, his *Reminiscences of Old Edinburgh* was actually written in Toronto. Also while so far from Edinburgh he was outraged to learn of a great deal of plagiarism of his *Memorials*, both text and illustrations, and of a reprint which had taken place without his knowledge or consent. Such was his continuing love for Edinburgh and Scotland that he tried to return, unsuccessfully applying for the Chair of History at St Andrews University, which he had hoped his friend Robert Chambers' influence might have helped procure for him. In 1881 Wilson was elected President of the University of Toronto, previously declining the Principalship of McGill University, Montreal, and other high Canadian educational posts. In 1888 he was knighted, and three years later he learned with the utmost pleasure that Edinburgh Town Council had admitted him as a Burgess and Guild Brother "in recognition of his distinguished services in historical and literary research". He undertook the voyage back to Scotland and on August 21st 1891, in the City Chambers, received the Freedom of Edinburgh. In Sir Daniel's speech he confessed to prizing his native city's

Professor George Wilson

Photograph by J. G. Tunney
By courtesy of the National Galleries of Scotland,
Edinburgh

supreme honour more than his knighthood. He returned to Toronto and died there on August 6th 1892, aged 76.

PROFESSOR GEORGE WILSON

As we have seen, during their early home background and boyhood the lives of the brothers Daniel and George Wilson were very much alike, in that they both received early tutoring from a Mr George Knight, together attended the High School, and collaborated in founding a juvenile "learned society". But after entering the University their paths led in quite different directions.

Furthermore, their personalities, and indeed their physiques, seemed to have differed greatly. While both shared equally a thirst for scholarship and learning, Daniel, the elder, appears to have been more of an extrovert and quite robust in health, travelling a great deal, including crossings of the Atlantic. He lived until the age of 76. George was more sensitive, introverted and of deeply religious devotion and outlook, yet a man of science. From early life, however, he was plagued by ill-health and he died when not much over forty. Daniel's world was that of libraries, literature and his art studio; George's that of his chemistry laboratory and his "dear museum".

George Wilson was born on February 21st 1818, with a twin brother who died some years later. In 1832 he became a medical student and also undertook part-time work in a laboratory at Edinburgh Royal Infirmary. He studied chemistry under the noteworthy Thomas

Charles Hope, and *materia medica* under the highly distinguished Sir Robert Christison. In 1837 he was admitted to the Royal College of Surgeons but "fell head over heels in love with chemistry" and became Christison's assistant. He spent a short time in London with his elder brother Daniel, finding work in a laboratory and also becoming a friend of the famous David Livingstone. He returned to Edinburgh in 1839 and took his Doctor of Medicine degree the next year. However, the clinical aspect of medicine did not appeal to him and he was appointed one of the first lecturers in chemistry to the Royal College of Surgeons in what became the "extra mural" medical school. Coincidentally with the beginning of his lecturing career, he described himself at that time as "bankrupt in health, hopes and fortune". A slight injury to his left foot, complicated by severe rheumatism, required amputation at the ankle. This was carried out by the famous surgeon, Professor James Syme, in January 1843. At a time when there was much controversy surrounding the possible introduction of anæsthesia into surgery, certain surgeons considering this "a needless luxury", Wilson, after the amputation by Syme without an anæsthetic, wrote to Professor James Y. Simpson, the famous pioneer of the anæsthetic use of chloroform, strongly supporting his work and describing "the black whirlwind of emotion, the horror of great darkness and the sense of desertion by God and man" that swept through him during the operation.

Shortly after his surgical ordeal, George Wilson also contracted tuberculosis. However, despite so much ill-health he persevered and his success as a lecturer gained him engagements with the Edinburgh Veterinary College, the School of Arts, the Scottish Institution and several private schools, along with analytical contract work. In 1845 he was elected a member of the Royal Society of Edinburgh and also became President of the Royal Scottish Society of Arts. Wilson carried out much original chemical research and published very many papers. He wrote a life of Henry Cavendish, whose work he sought to vindicate. In November 1853 he published a first series of papers in the *Edinburgh Journal of Medical Science* on colour blindness and did much experimental work in this field, especially with railwaymen and sailors, in relation to identifying signal colours and port and starboard lights. Subsequently, the Great Northern Railway adopted his recommendations for the screening of railwaymen for certain duties, and other bodies followed suit. The famous James Clerk Maxwell contributed an appendix to a book by Wilson on his colour blindness studies.

In 1855 Wilson was appointed director of the Scottish Industrial Museum, founded the previous year, and later the same year became Regius Professor of Technology at the University. His inaugural address "What is Technology" – a debatable subject at that time – concerned the correlation of the sciences. It was widely published. George Wilson's enthusiasm for "his dear museum" as he called it – the ultimate fruition of his schooldays hobby with his brother Daniel, is described with a wealth of personal details about his life in his *Memoirs*, published by his sister, who kept house for him at Elm Cottage and who nursed him in his final illness. The Scottish Industrial Museum was ultimately to become the Royal Scottish Museum in Chambers Street over the period of a century.

Considered in 1858 for the University Chair of Chemistry following Professor William Gregory's death, Wilson might well have succeeded him had not ill-health forced his withdrawal. By 1859 he was a very sick man, and following pneumonia he died on November 22nd of that year at the age of only 41. Wilson was a man typical of so many of his confrères of the 19th century – dedicated to his profession and also deeply religious, concerned about great contemporary theological issues (in his case the "mysterious problem of evil") and devout in his writings and in his life. Though of quiet and withdrawn nature, he was widely respected and loved by colleagues and students alike. He was accorded a public funeral at the Old Calton Burial Ground on November 28th 1859.

9 · MORNINGSIDE VILLAGE

SIR DAVID YULE

THE Old School-house in Morning-side Road, opened in 1823, served the old village and surrounding district until 1890. For a long time attendance was free; then, about the 1850s, it was managed solely by Mr George Ross, advocate, of Wood-burn House in Canaan Lane, who expected parents who could do so to pay a small fee: hence the school for some years was known as "The Ross Subscription School". Morningside also had a number of small private fee-paying schools. One of these was Baillie's School, which occupied a large villa-type house in what was then Marmion Terrace. In the archives of the City Public Library Edinburgh Room is preserved a small prize certificate label from a book, headed "Mr Baillie's School". The prize was awarded to Robert T. Patterson for Map Drawing in July 1877, and is signed "James Baillie, Headmaster." William Mair in his valuable little book *Historic Morningside* suggests that the little school became or was absorbed into Gillsland Park School in Spylaw Road, but this could not be verified. After its closure Baillie's School eventually became the studio and shop of the noted photographer, Yerbury, at one time at 92 Morning-side Road.

Mair refers to a former pupil of Baillie's School, Sir David Yule, as having become a "Merchant Prince" in Calcutta, establishing jute and paper industries and developing large tea estates. Through the initial assistance of the India Section of the British National Library in London, and then especially through the kind interest and most helpful provision of historical material by Mr W. J. Knight, Deputy Secretary of the London firm of Yule Catto & Company, a great deal of detail has been made available concerning the small boy who once attended Baillie's School and was to become, in his day, one of the wealthiest men in Britain and to earn the title "The Squire of Hanstead".

David Yule was born in Edinburgh on August 4th 1858 and after a short period at the little Morningside school attended the High School from the age of ten, leaving in 1874, aged sixteen. He may have attended Edinburgh University for a year. The Yules had once been in the service of the Comyn family – the Earls of Buchan – and adopted the latter's coat of arms. A William Yule had ventured to India in 1772, and another member to Madras in 1799 but it was David Yule's uncle Andrew who founded the family business in Calcutta in 1863. Possibilities for industrial development were limitless. India was just opening up and the Suez Canal provided great new opportunities. While Andrew Yule developed the Indian connection, his elder brother George looked after the London interests. Andrew was recalled to London and George went out to Calcutta – taking

142

seventeen-year-old David Yule with him. George Yule soon gained prominence in the public life of India, becoming Sheriff of the city in 1886 and President of the Indian National Congress in 1888 (a truly unique distinction). His remuneration as Sheriff he donated to the welfare of the children of Calcutta.

The business steadily prospered. Before long George Yule owned two jute mills, a cotton mill, three tea companies and an insurance company. He retired in 1891 leaving David, then aged thirty-three, in sole charge of the fast-developing Yule Indian industrial empire. The next year George died in London, leaving his nephew in full control in Calcutta. A few years later the number of jute mills had doubled; there were fifteen tea companies, four coal companies, two flour mills, an oil mill, a railway company, and a shipping company. In 1902, David's other uncle, Andrew, also died, and he was now sole director of the London and Indian companies. He opened very impressive new offices in Clive Row, Calcutta.

In 1900 David Yule had married his cousin, Henrietta Yule, and had set up a fine house in Calcutta, but the Indian climate did not suit her and he acquired Hanstead House at Bricket Wood in Hertfordshire. It was in this somewhat majestic residence that David, reducing the time he spent in India, lived whenever he could. In 1903 their only child, Gladys Meryl, was born in Hanstead House. By this time David Yule had brought employment to nearly 200,000 Indian people and introduced great advancements in agriculture, forestry, fisheries, roads, schools, hospitals and dispensaries.

These benefits to the Indian people were widely acknowledged. In 1911-12 when King George V and Queen Mary toured India, they visited David Yule's jute mills and other properties, and it is not surprising that he was awarded a knighthood, which was conferred upon him at Government House, Belvedere.

Sir David Yule

During and following the First World War the Yule Indian interests were virtually limitless and new companies were constantly created. The war over, David Yule, who had been in India for most of fifty years and was not as fit as he once was, felt concern for the future of his two companies, in London and Calcutta.

His two brothers had pre-deceased him; he had no heir, and now he sought a close colleague and ultimate successor. The man he chose was to become one of Britain's greatest financial experts. He was Thomas Sivewright Catto, son of a Peterhead shipwright, who by 1918 had an international reputation in financial affairs. Sir David Yule, with little hesitation, offered him the future chairmanship of both his companies and in 1919 the new firm of Yule Catto & Company Ltd. was founded. This was but another stage in the saga of Catto's impressive career. He had already served as Governor of the Bank of England and during the Second World War was to be appointed financial adviser to the Chancellor of the Exchequer in Churchill's Coalition Cabinet.

In 1919, when Thomas Catto took over from Sir David Yule in Calcutta, the latter returned to England fairly promptly. He took up residence at Hanstead House, living the life of "the Squire", with his wife and daughter, and he greatly developed the estate. Retaining a nominal interest in Yule Catto & Co., he developed other minor business interests and regularly would take a local 6 a.m. train to London. In 1922 he received a baronetcy, taking the title Sir David Yule of Hugli (a river in Bengal). He returned briefly to Calcutta in 1925. In 1926, when aged 68, he purchased *The Daily Chronicle* from Sir David Lloyd George and later acquired two Calcutta newspapers. Occasionally he visited Scotland.

Finally, Sir David Yule embarked on building a new Hanstead House, with his wife and daughter temporarily residing in a cottage. But he did not see his dream house materialise, for he died on July 3rd 1928. At his own request he was buried in the grounds of his estate, and his tomb remains inscribed with lines by Kipling praising hard work, which Sir David had certainly made his own. Following her husband's death, Lady Yule, only fifty-three years of age, inherited his vast estate, of £20 million. She was soon reputed to be Britain's wealthiest widow. Lady Yule undertook many long-standing ambitions, such as the laying out of a formal garden at Hanstead "to make it as an ancestral home the envy of all England", and also planned a Japanese garden. During the severe depression of the 1930's and even earlier, especially in shipbuilding, Lady Yule ordered a £250,000 miniature luxury liner from John Brown's at Clydebank, duly launched in July 1930. It undertook many distant cruises before its sale to King Carol of Roumania. It once carried his crown jewels on board. Subsequently it became a floating hotel on the Danube. In the grounds at Hanstead, Lady Yule installed a zoo, an Arabian horse stud, and took up cattle breeding. Another of her interests was film-making and she did much to develop the British film industry in the 1930s. With her daughter she had controlling financial interests in the British National Film Company at Elstree and the National Studios. Later she backed theatrical productions. On July 14th 1950 Lady Henrietta Yule died, twenty-two years after her husband. By her own request, part of her ashes were scattered over the Buchan countryside and her urn was interred in Sir David's tomb.

After her mother's death, Miss

Gladys Meryl Yule, sole heiress, continued to manage the family's financial interests and estates. She was a particularly skilled horse-woman and until 1939 rode in a circus routine at Olympia. In 1955 she gave over much of her land for early research into spoilation, pollution and ecology. In 1957, Miss Yule, having resumed horse-racing, saw her entry "Floss Silk" win at Sandown. Soon afterwards she suffered a heart attack. A week later "Floss Silk" ran again at Lingfield and, against all advice, its owner watched the race on television. The horse won, but the delighted Miss Yule collapsed and died not many hours later. With her death, as the Yule family history comments, it was indeed the end of an era, with some of its beginnings at the little school at Church Hill. After India gained independence in 1947 the Yule interests there had gradually come under State ownership and today Yule Catto of London is a public company, dealing in rubber and oil in Malaysia, producing materials for the building industry, and involved internationally in chemicals. The fine Yule "ancestral home" at Hanstead Hall many years ago became a college run by an American organisation for the training of young people in social studies and responsibilities.

ARCHBISHOP COSMO GORDON LANG

"IN 1868 there was another move, to Morningside, near Edinburgh, at that time a quaint country village, with villas and quiet lanes and no houses beyond it. The real scene of my childhood was the garden of Bank House, Morningside . . . I suppose it was quite a small garden, but it was my world, from the age of four to nine. It was my *own* world, where my imagination for once had its unclouded day. It was a world of make believe. Lessons there were, even for a while at an old dame's school. Brothers there were, three of them. Sometimes I made the younger, next to me, the unwilling and mystified vassal to my dreams. But the world I remember is the garden – the trees behind which robber-knights were stalked and slain; the earth under a shrub where on a cold day, unknown to all, I sat self-stripped indulging in all the pathos of a beggar child: the bundle of sticks on which I stood enduring the fancied flames of a Christian martyr; the great black roaring cat, who was to us the Devil walking about seeking whom he might devour . . . these were the years never to be repeated when I was master of my own realm, the glorious realm of imagination, the land of make-believe".

So, in very much later life, wrote a man who was destined to become a prominent national figure in Church and State, the Very Reverend Cosmo Gordon Lang, Archbishop of Canterbury from 1928 until his death in 1945. These early boyhood years he had spent in a Morningside garden remained vividly with him. In 1868 the Reverend John Marshall Lang, for a short period minister of a newly-built church in the Anderston district of Glasgow, was appointed to the charge of Morningside Parish Church, opened on the brow of Church Hill thirty years before. With

Archbishop Cosmo Gordon Lang

his wife and four young sons he took up residence in the then manse, Bank House, or Morningside Bank as it was originally known, at the south corner of Albert Terrace (the old Doo Loan) and Morningside Road, a fine villa built in 1790, set in its romantic old-world garden and commanding a magnificent panoramic view southwards over Morningside and towards the Pentland Hills. Sub-division of the house took place in 1860.

In 1873, when Cosmo was aged nine, his father returned to Glasgow as minister of the important Barony Church. In 1879 the boy entered Glasgow University. Three years later he visited London and Paris. He was profoundly influenced by Westminster Abbey. In 1881 Cosmo Gordon Lang entered King's College, Cambridge, but after a few

months moved to Balliol College, Oxford. Balliol had a long tradition of students who had been sons of the Scottish manse. Cosmo Gordon entered fully into the many student societies and other related activities at Oxford. In 1885 he was elected President of the Oxford Union. A period followed of deep soul-searching and theological discussion with his contemporaries and distinguished Dons. The outcome was that he forsook a career in law for which he had qualified, and in 1888, soon after gaining a Fellowship of All Souls, Cambridge, he joined the Church of England, entered upon studies for the priesthood and was ordained in 1891.

Lang's progress within the Church of England was steady. In 1909 he was consecrated Archbishop of York and nearly twenty years later was appointed to the supreme office of Archbishop of Canterbury. The new primate was involved in most of the significant movements within the Church of England and in 1930 planned an important conference on Ecumenism at Lambeth. It was in the mid 1930s, however, that he became involved in the great issue, with moral implications, which caused something of a crisis in the country. This was the announcement by King Edward VIII that he had decided to marry the divorced Mrs Simpson and that he was abdicating the throne. The announcement of the abdication was made on December 10th 1936. While Archbishop Lang was obviously very much involved in the crisis, which raised problems primarily for the decision of the Prime Minister of the day, Stanley Baldwin, and the Cabinet, it is a matter of note that while he was consulted at the highest levels and in fact made an important broadcast, according to one principal biographer he neither influenced nor attempted to influence the course of events. Archbishop Cosmo Gordon Lang died on December 5th 1945, aged 81.

While one of the boys who had enjoyed the pleasures of an old Morningside garden rose to the highest position within the Church of England, his younger brother, Marshall, who had entered the Church of Scotland ministry, enjoyed the parallel, if somewhat different, distinction of being elected Moderator of the Church of Scotland, in 1935. If it might seem that the Lang family chronicles appear rather ponderous and unduly solemn, an incident of great humour found its place in their pages during the General Assembly of the above year at a session over which the Reverend Marshall Lang was presiding. The "fraternal delegate" of the Church of England that year was none other than the Moderator's own brother, Archbishop Cosmo Gordon Lang. The proceedings which followed are in the official records. The Moderator, in welcoming the Archbishop said: "Your Grace. . ." The remainder of the sentence was drowned in applause and laughter. The Moderator continued: "It is a very singular pleasure to welcome you to the floor of the Assembly, not only as one I have been familiar with in past years" (renewed laughter), "but as representing the great sister Communion of England". The Archbishop rose to speak. He said he had not come prepared with any address worthy of the Assembly or its tradi-

tions. "I must content myself," he continued, "in the fewest possible words, in saying with what satisfaction I find the choice of Moderator this year has rested upon one of whom at least I can say that he belongs to a highly respectable family, and that he has maintained its traditions of respectability, orthodoxy and fidelity to the Church of his fathers more successfully than his elder brother. (Laughter). With all my heart I pray that God's blessing may continually rest upon the Church of my fathers".

HANNAH C. PRESTON MACGOUN

WHILE the 19th-century rural seclusion and pleasant atmosphere of Morningside made it an attractive and congenial residence for many artists (principally male) over a long period, none produced more attractive work than one of the few ladies, whose home was at Banner Villa. This was one in the short row of semi-detached villas in what was originally Banner Place, taking its name from the legend attached to the Bore Stone next to the Parish Church, and becoming No 69 Morningside Road. Unfortunately, few reviews or published assessments of Miss Macgoun's work were discovered; and equally regrettably not many details could be found to cast light on her as a person. Only her work (and a great deal of that) remains.

Hannah Clarke Preston Macgoun was born on June 19th 1864, at Banner Villa, one of a family of three brothers and four sisters. Her father, Robert William Macgoun, a native of

Greenock, was a graduate of Glasgow University, and after ordination to the ministry served at Dumbarton and Ayr before his appointment to Morningside Parish Church in 1864. He married Isabella Clarke of Comrie in 1853 and died in 1871.

James L. Caw in *Scottish Paintings Past and Present – 1620-1908*, commented upon how she had profited technically by much study of certain Dutch Schools and continued: "Her drawings are marked by a pleasing union of breadth and delicacy of tone and local colour. Her draughtsmanship, if not very constructive, is gracious and expressive and her handling of water colour bold yet refined. But it was her sentiment for the incidents of home life, and especially for the ways of children, which forms the most attractive quality in her art. Sincere and sensitive, her water colours, whether of Dutch or Scottish children, informed of a tenderness of feeling and a quiet joy in the soft rounded forms and radiant faces of childhood which make them charming in a feminine way, and give one more real pleasure than much work of a more pretentious kind ..." Very many people who are familiar with Miss Macgoun's copious book illustrations such as in certain editions of Dr John Brown's Scottish classic *Rab and His Friends*, his *Pet Marjory*, and (especially illuminating as regards her studies of children) his own book on the subject *The Little Book for Children*, will appreciate just how observant and very precise Caw's assessment was. These are only a few of the very many books whose authors sought and enlisted her talents.

Hannah C. Preston Macgoun
Self portrait, 1887
By courtesy of the National Galleries of Scotland,
Edinburgh

Quite by chance and rather surprisingly, considering Hannah Macgoun's Scottishness and kirk background of the Morningside manse, the present writer discovered her work in another book by a writer resident quite close to her, in the Greenhill district. The book is a large one: *Folk Songs of the Tuscan Hills*, written mainly in Italian. It contains four fine examples of Miss Macgoun's child illustrations. These had been especially commissioned by the authoress, Miss Grace Warrack, of "Aros", St Margaret's Road, Greenhill, a member of a prominent Edinburgh family. She obviously had a most detailed knowledge of Tuscany. Unfortunately, Miss Macgoun died on 20th August 1913, just before the book was published. A member of the Royal Society of Watercolour painters, Hannah

Preston Macgoun exhibited her work regularly at the Royal Scottish Academy from 1880 and such exhibitions continued for a few years after her death. Her studio was at 130 George Street.

MARY CARLYLE

CHURCH HILL and its immediate vicinity, as already noted, have associations with Jane Welsh Carlyle and in lesser degree with her famous husband, Thomas. The house of Jane's aunts and of her friend Colonel Davidson, perhaps not surprisingly in view of the lapse of time, have disappeared. More unexpectedly, it may seem, it is a house of relatively more modern origin and style, in Newbattle Terrace, which has the closest associations, certainly with the "Sage of Chelsea", for here at No 30, in a terraced villa, resided his niece Mary Carlyle Aitken, who after Jane's sudden and tragic death in London in 1866, became, if not with the fullest freedom of choice certainly with the utmost patience and devotion, her uncle's housekeeper and constant companion, nurse and amanuensis, until his death on February 5th 1881.

Three documents provide invaluable and most interesting detail of Mary Carlyle Aitken's twelve years of care for her uncle at his Chelsea home, Cheyne Row. One is by her husband, a series of *Jottings on Alexander Carlyle's Life and Work – by Himself*, in typescript, which he continued to keep after her death; another, *A Lady Who Deserves to be Remembered* by Mabel Davidson, adjunct-Professor of English in Randolph-Macon Women's College, Lynchburgh, Virginia, U.S.A., written in 1923; and the third, the record of an interview with Mary Carlyle at 30 Newbattle Terrace, by a journalist from the *Westminster Gazette* in 1895, fourteen years after Thomas Carlyle's death. From all of these a quite remarkable story emerges.

Mary Carlyle Aitken was the daughter of Jean Carlyle, youngest sister of Thomas Carlyle, and was born in Dumfries in 1848, where her father was a house-painter. After Jane Welsh Carlyle's death in 1866, Thomas, who, as one writer comments, had always proclaimed his love for silence and solitude, in fact found that he could not bear to be alone. For a short time his doctor brother John lived with him at Chelsea and tried to look after him, but rather unsuccessfully. Jane's cousin Maggie likewise proved unacceptable; then in July 1868, during his annual visit to Scotland, Carlyle – it is not on record with what means of persuasion – succeeded in bringing his niece back with him to Chelsea. There she remained until his death nearly twelve years later, caring with the most admirable patience for "the dyspeptic Polar bear" as he had often described himself to Jane. Actually, as emphasised for example by Froude, Mary dismissed this image of her uncle and instead praised his kindness and consideration.

One visitor described Mary as "cool, grey, quiet, unobtrusive, in comparison with the colourful glow of Jane". Her grateful uncle described her as "A wise little thing, honest, I think, as spring water, pretty to look upon and shines here

Mary Carlyle Aitken with (left to right): Dr John Carlyle, Thomas Carlyle and Provost Swan of Kirkcaldy

By kind permission of the Carlyle Society

like a small taper breaking the gloom of my new element". After discovering the sights of London, Mary settled to her task. Not only had she the domestic duties to deal with but her uncle was revising, re-arranging and indexing the 34-volume Library Edition of his works, which took two years. Her assistance was invaluable. She was "highly intelligent, swift, taking his dictation (for which his temperament made him quite unsuited) in copy-book handwriting". As his own writing steadily deteriorated and then became impossible to decipher, she wrote down for him from his "tem-

pestuous rhetoric" his *Early Kings of Norway.* His copious correspondence was another mammoth task, as also accompanying him in his carriage, to a certain degree, on the London social round, and, ever his nurse, sometimes during his insomnia accompanying him on sudden impulsive midnight strolls.

Each summer they made a visit to Dumfriesshire, and during the summer of 1879 Carlyle stayed on for some time with his dying brother, Doctor John. On August 21st of the same year Mary was married, in her mother's house, to her Canadian cousin, Alexander Carlyle, whom she had met in Dumfriesshire on previous summer visits. Thomas Carlyle attended the wedding, apparently in better health and good spirits. The young married couple spent a short honeymoon at Moffat, intending soon afterwards to return to Chelsea to act as housekeepers. But their privacy at Moffat was short-lived. Her uncle, so accustomed to her constant care, could not spare her, even for a few weeks, and on September 4th, with a friend, pursued the couple to their Moffat hotel. After Dr John Carlyle's death, on September 16th, all three returned to London. In the following summer the couple's first child was born and named Thomas. The parents feared the baby's crying might disturb the now very weak uncle. But the younger Thomas was extremely quiet and the elder took great pleasure and interest in his namesake, sitting by his crib for hours, philosophising on "this odd kind of article, entering the world as he was about to leave it". On January 1st 1881 Thomas Carlyle took his last drive with Mary, and just over a month later, on February 5th, in his room, surrounded by souvenirs of Jane, he died.

Thomas Carlyle, a distinguished and successful author in his latter years, was a very wealthy man, and he twice gave considerable sums of money to his devoted niece. Likewise in his will she was generously remembered: "To whom also, dear little soul, for the loving care and unwearied patience and helpfulness she has shown to me in these last solitary and infirm years. . ." Originally Carlyle had arranged to bequeath all his moveable estate at Chelsea to his brother John, but he, of course, had pre-deceased him. For some time Alexander and Mary Carlyle remained at Cheyne Row. Alexander, a graduate, was a qualified teacher in Canada and acquired a post teaching the "natural sciences" at a young ladies' school in Chelsea. One of his best pupils was a niece of Disraeli. After other similar posts and the family having moved to Wimbledon, Alexander returned temporarily to Canada.

A second boy, Oliver, was born. After a short visit to Edinburgh and Burntisland, the Carlyles again returned to London, Alexander editing many of Thomas's papers. Indeed both Mary and he did much to counteract the effect of the hastily published biography of Carlyle by Froude which they considered not only false but almost libellous. In 1890 they returned to Edinburgh, where the boys attended George Watson's College. Next a short stay in Mauchline, with the boys attending Ayr Grammar School. Alexander Carlyle was now skilled in various arts and crafts and gained various awards. On September 1st 1894, in order to ensure the continuity of the boys' education, they bought the house at 30 Newbattle Terrace and young Thomas and Oliver returned to Watson's.

Soon after they had settled at Newbattle Terrace Mary Carlyle rather reluctantly agreed to be interviewed by a journalist from the *Westminster Gazette* and the report of this describes the house at Newbattle Terrace as stored with precious relics from the Carlyle home at Chelsea. The vast collection, including furniture originally from Jane Welsh Carlyle's home at Haddington, brought to Edinburgh at their first home in Comely Bank and later to Chelsea, also portraits of Carlyle, of famous contemporaries, innumerable books including signed first editions by distinguished authors — all were there to be sorted out and eventually some items to go to Carlyle's birthplace at Ecclefechan and to Cheyne Row when the house there became a museum. On May 30th 1895 Mary Carlyle died of pneumonia and Alexander sadly writes of "this great calamity". Remaining at Newbattle Terrace, the boys continued their education and their father undertook much more work on Carlyle's papers and the disposal of some of these to the Scottish National Library.

In 1901 Alexander Carlyle returned to Canada, where he re-married. His second wife, Lilias McVicar, died in 1929. The previous year his younger son, by then Dr Oliver Carlyle had died from a chronic condition contracted during the First World War. He left two daughters. Thomas, the elder son, had apparently died earlier. Alexander appears to have continued working on Carlyle's papers well into late life, his brief, informal, unpublished memoir having been written in his 88th year. It lists his many published articles on Thomas and Jane Welsh Carlyle. Despite such an extremely busy and demanding life and the vast task confronting her in dealing with her uncle's papers and moveable estate, Mary Carlyle found or made time to pursue at least one personal interest. She compiled and arranged with brief notes *Scottish Song – A Selection of the Choicest Lyrics of Scotland*, published in 1874, with a preface dated March 1874 and written at Chelsea, in the midst of her house-keeping and other tasks. Rather confusingly, Mary Carlyle is some-times referred to by her unmarried name, Mary Carlyle Aitken, and at other times as Mary Carlyle, her married name.

WILLIAM "SHAKESPEARE" MORRISON

ALTHOUGH in doing so we are anticipating our later account of Canaan's notable residents, while already in Newbattle Terrace it seems appropriate to linger a while in that street. Known originally and for long as Cant's Loan, a very early route travelling the ancient Burgh Muir from the "wester hiegait" (now Morningside Road) to the "easter hiegait" (now Dalkeith Road), the derivation of the later name New-battle Terrace still has historical associations with the Forbes family of Greenhill and Pitsligo and the Marquis of Lothian's family seat of Newbattle Abbey. Continuing in this context of previous centuries is the classical early 19th-century Canaan villa, originally named Canaan Grove at No 82 Newbattle Terrace. Indeed here, in 1813, there resided John Wood, a very notable land surveyor and "town planner". At the beginning of the present century, however, there resided in Canaan Grove one whose distinction conveys us rather sharply from the historical associations of this his boyhood home into a very different era of the relatively modern world, albeit of nearly half-a-century ago. This was William "Shakespeare" Morrison who became one of the most celebrated Speakers of the House of Commons during a particularly colourful and lively period in the history of that institution.

William Shepherd Morrison – always known (although it has never been clear why) as "Shakespeare" or more simply "Shakes" – was not only to earn a place in the annals of South Edinburgh and, of course, so much further afield, but also in those of his school. In October 1899 "Shakes" Morrison entered George Watson's College, then at Archibald Place, a year or so after his elder brother Sandy. The latter became a school "all rounder" while "Shakes" confined his interests more to the College Literary Club and in this, with his great friend and future political colleague, David Maxwell Fyfe, learned the art of oratory and the thrust of debate, which were later to stand them in good stead.

"Shakes" Morrison began his Edinburgh University studies in Arts and Law in 1912, and before long became prominent in student activities. But the pleasures of university life were soon cut short in exchange for service on the battlefields of the First World War. Sandy, the elder brother, was killed at Loos in 1915, aged 25. "Shakes", having joined the Royal Field Artillery in August 1914, was thrice mentioned in despatches, wounded at Neuve Chapelle in 1915, and awarded the Military Cross for rescuing a Highlander in broad daylight under heavy enemy gunfire. By the end of the war he had attained the rank of captain.

Returning to the university, now amidst mature students of more serious mood and more realistic debating themes than hitherto, "Shakes" confessed to feeling privileged in being able to resume his university education. Before leaving

William "Shakespeare" Morrison
(Lord Dunrossil)

By courtesy of "The Watsonian" and Mr James Allan

in 1920, having graduated Master of Arts, "Shakes" had been President of the Union, Senior President of the SRC, editor of *The Student* and president of two other University societies. He earned the reputation of being a first-class chairman. He was called to the English Bar in 1923. After unsuccessfully contesting the Western Isles in 1923 and 1924, he eventually was elected Member of Parliament for Cirencester and Tewkesbury in 1929, remaining so for 30 years. In 1935 began a succession of government posts: Financial Secretary to the Treasury, followed by Minister of Agriculture, Minister of Food, Postmaster General and Minister of Town and House Planning. While he seems not to have shone particularly in any of these high posts, often seeming more concerned with advancing his legal career, Stanley Baldwin is reported to have regarded him as "the stuff of a future Prime Minister".

"Shakes" rejected the possibility of high political office in 1951 when he was elected Speaker of the House of Commons, the first Scot in this post for 116 years. There was the unusual situation of a contest for the position, but Morrison having Churchill's strong support was elected comfortably. His great friend of their Watson's College days, Sir David Maxwell Fyfe, by then Lord Kilmuir, became Lord High Chancellor. Thus two "F.P.s", presiding over both Houses at Westminster, was a rare honour for the college. Lord Kilmuir considered "Shakes" the best Speaker he had ever served under, which was no merely partisan comment since it was an assessment widely shared. The Speaker's powerful Scottish voice and accent, which he was proud to retain, and his emphatic pronunciation of the r's in his calls for "Order . . . order" apparently could bring immediate silence. In those days, after the Second World War, with skilful attempted manipulation of the House's procedures, and parliamentary giants of debate for example in oral clashes between Churchill and Aneurin Bevan, or the high drama and noisy scenes of the 1956 Suez crisis, the former President of the Edinburgh University Union required all his experience as well as his powerful and impressive physical stature and vibrant personality to dominate the frequent uproar, with firmness, yet with the utmost fairness and toleration, never losing control.

The strain of eight such years in the Speaker's Chair, with record numbers of all-night sittings, took its toll. In 1959, the end of his second spell in office, on medical advice he announced his retiral. At the time, with characteristic humour, he remarked that "for a Speaker his increasing deafness was not an unmixed evil in the occupants of his Chair". Morrison accepted a peerage, choosing the title Viscount Dunrossil of Vallaquie (in the Island of North Uist). Anxious to continue in public service he was appointed Governor-General of Australia, not without some critical Labour Party reaction concerning the salary and pension involved. Their new Governor-General soon proved most acceptable to the Australians. He made a point of visiting every province, and once, at a large meeting, urged his audience to retain their native accents – as he had done – and not to ape a 'Queen's English' style. But his Australian appointment was short-lived, just over a year. He died in Canberra in February 1961.

The son of a farmer of North Uist, Morrison was a fluent Gaelic speaker and a player of the fiddle and the bagpipes. The latter, he once said, he played in his imagination during the ceremonial of the daily Speaker's Procession in the House of Commons, which he found embarrassing. In the midst of the tempestuous debates and dramatic scenes of the Commons perhaps "Shakes" Morrison's power and strength to calm it all came from his own inner thoughts, which, as a poet, he once expressed:

154

Earth sings with many voices,
And all of them are sweet:
The great song of the high road,
The fierce drone of the street;
But still the finest music
She has for such as me
Is when the ancient Island
Rolls down in quiet machair
To the ever-singing sea.

ANDREW MYRTLE COCKBURN

THE official naming in 1984 as "Cuddy Lane" of what was known by that name locally over a century ago, immediately south of the Old School-house, and also shown on certain early maps as Rosewood Place, has created much curiosity and varied reactions among local residents. There has been a renewal of interest in the village school, which for nearly seventy years was attended by children from the immediate vicinity or from more distant Lothianburn and Swanston.

Considerable information concerning the school was published in an earlier volume, as also regarding the people involved in its foundation and in the support it had continued to receive from 1823. Reference was made to the "maister" or "dominie" in the school's latter years before South Morningside School was opened in 1892. This was Mr Andrew Cockburn. Sadly the death occurred in 1984 of Mr Cockburn's daughter, who had been still living in Morningside and who most patiently and courteously had on several occasions attempted to recall the details of her

father's career before and during his service as "maister". Thus a last link with the early educational life of the village has been lost.

Mr Andrew Myrtle Cockburn
By courtesy of the late Mrs M. Wilson

For a period parents who could do so were expected to make some financial contribution by way of fees, and Mr Cockburn's daughter always greatly regretted that she had no record of one parent, the father of several children attending the village school, who was an artist and who over a number of years was unable to contribute except by presenting to her father at regular intervals a series of paintings of Morningside and the neighbouring district. Unfortunately all of these paintings had disappeared save one, but this unfortunately was not signed, thus giving no clue to the artist's identity. Many artists resided in Morningside during the mid-19th century and onwards. Some of their work is extant and in private ownership, and while it is possible that the parent who paid his children's school fees "in kind" might have been a Mr F. Dove Ogilvie who resided in Belhaven Terrace and who painted a charming picture of the old Braid Iron Church at the corner of Braid Road and Cluny Gardens around 1883, and also the original Volunteer's Rest at Canaan Lane (undated), the artist's actual identity cannot be confirmed with any certainty.

ALEXANDER FALCONAR

FOR a considerable period Morningside village was very much aware of, and almost centred around, "the big house", Falcon Hall. The large stone-pillared gateway to its entrance driveway was situated on the east side of the village "high street", where today stand numbers 195 and 197 Morningside Road. It is rather ironical and indeed regrettable that despite the prominence of the mansion-house, several illustrations of which remain, little or nothing could be found on record concerning its original builder and first owner, Alexander Falconar or his son-in-law, who eventually inherited the house and estate, Henry Craigie. On account of their close involvement in the life of the village, these men are presented in this context rather than within that of Canaan which included the Falcon Hall estate, although doubtless that is where they more properly belong.

Alexander Falconar, who built Falcon Hall in 1815, naming it so as a play on his name, was the eldest son of William Falconar, one-time Adjutant of Fort St George in Madras, and was born in Nairn. He appears to have been appointed a "writer", or solicitor, in Madras in 1789. A year later he was appointed secretary to the Madras Public Revenue Department. In 1794 he was Persian translator to the Madras authorities, and later Gentoo translator. Indeed Falconar seems to have become competent in various languages and wrote guides for these. In 1809 he became Chief Secretary to the Governor of Madras. In the India Office Library and Records Section of the British Library in London, there is a considerable collection of Falconar's papers, including a letter book relating to his career in India from 1787 to 1796. Inventory papers relating to his estate, especially Falcon Hall, are in the Scottish Record Office, West Register House, in Edinburgh.

In 1792, in India, Alexander Falconar married his cousin, Eliza Davidson, whose father, a solicitor in the East India Company, was a native of Cromarty and became Governor of Madras. Eliza Davidson's father had married Elizabeth Pigou, daughter of Frederick Pigou, an East Indian Company director. While unfortunately no portrait of Alexander Falconer could be traced, one does exist of his wife, Eliza Davidson, at the age of about 15. She is seen seated, in a white dress, beside her younger sister, Mary, who is kneeling with her folded arms on her sister's knee. The picture was painted by Tilly Kettle, the first English artist to go to India, where he resided from 1769 to 1776, producing very many portraits of British officials and their families, including Eliza Davidson's father and mother. Kettle was born in

London in 1735, the son of a house-painter, and much influenced by the work of Allan Ramsay. The painting of the Davidson sisters is in the Dulwich Art Gallery and was reproduced in Volume XV by the Walpole Society in 1926-27.

Miss Eliza Davidson (right), the future Mrs Eliza Falconar of Falcon Hall, with her younger sister, Mary

By kind permission of the Governors of Dulwich Picture Gallery

In 1811 Falconar retired from his Indian post, at the age of 44, reputedly with considerable wealth, soon afterwards returning to Scotland and purchasing Morningside Lodge in nearly 10 acres of land on the Canaan estate from the widow of former Lord Provost William Coulter. In 1815 Falconar greatly altered and embellished what had probably been a much simpler style of villa. Situated approximately at the junction of Falcon Court and Falcon Road West, apart from the main driveway from Morningside Road there were other small entrances to the estate. Falconar placed stone falcons above the driveway entrance pillars; the gates had iron-work versions painted in gold, and there were many more stone ones above the house's main pillared frontage and elsewhere above its walls. Figures of Nelson and Wellington flanked the main entrance. Interiorly the house was equally impressive and quite luxurious in décor and style. Falconar, from his Indian earnings, spared no expense.

Alexander Falconar had fourteen children, several of whom died at an early age, many daughters surviving. Soon after taking up residence in Falcon Hall, the residents of "the big house" of Morningside became prominent in its life and generous benefactors of many developments. The original subscription list for financing the building of Morningside Parish Church – Morningside's first – opened in 1838, was headed by Falconar and five of his daughters. Likewise he gave much financial support to the village school-house. At its annual concerts and prize-givings, Christmas soirées and summer outings, prizes and treats were provided by the Falconar daughters. One donated the cost of the chancel of Christ Church at Holy Corner. A familiar sight in the village was the Falconar yellow horse-drawn carriage emerging from the main gateway and conveying members of the family into town. Alexander Falconar, who died on December 10th 1847, his wife who pre-deceased him by almost 16 years, and three of his children, are buried in the large tomb in the west division of Greyfriars churchyard.

157

HENRY CRAIGIE

ALEXANDER FALCONAR is said to have kept strict vigilance over the affections of his many daughters and the number of these who married is not known. One who did, however, was Miss Jessie Pigou Falconar who married Henry Craigie, a Canadian Writer to the Signet, on July 23rd 1839. As with Falconar, little could be traced concerning his son-in-law. He was the fifth son of John Craigie of Quebec but when and why he came to Scotland could not be discovered. In the context of Falconar's reported close watch over his daughters, Henry Craigie appears to have been the only man who broke through, not only succeeding in marrying Jessie Pigou Falconar but also eventually, after his father-in-law's death, inherited the house and the estate.

One writer has recounted the origin of Craigie's good fortune. During a Royal Scottish Academy sale suddenly a section of the floor gave way close to where Falconar was standing. Craigie, who was nearby, swiftly caught Falconar's arm and saved him from an accident. Craigie was presumably invited to Falcon Hall, met Miss Jessie and eventually married her. After inheriting Falcon Hall, Craigie continued residing there with his own family and four of Falconar's daughters until his death on April 19th 1867.

Craigie was also a generous benefactor in Morningside, particularly towards elderly people in need. The parish church also benefited from his considerable support and he is commemorated by a stained-glass triptych in the south transept which

Memorial stained glass windows to Henry Craigie in Morningside Parish Church

From William Mair's "Historic Morningside". By courtesy of Morningside Parish Church

illustrates six corporal works of mercy. It is believed the artist incorporated Craigie himself in the scenes. The windows were donated by Craigie's widow in the year of his death. She died eight years later. Both are buried in a tomb surmounted by a very large monument, a few yards south of the tower in Newington Cemetery. Unfortunately, on account of the monument's broad expanse and exposure to the wind, it became weakened and finally blew down during a gale in 1931. Three of Craigie's daughters are buried in the Falconar tomb in Greyfriar's. Regrettably no portrait of Craigie could be traced.

JAMES GRANT

A WRITER of quite prolific output in many spheres of literature, but in the context of the present book most notably the author of the undoubted classic and monumental work *Old and New Edinburgh*, is reputed by one biographer to have been born in Morningside on August 1st 1822. William Mair in *Historic Morningside* writes that Grant resided for some time in Springvalley House, whose location is commemorated by a stone-sculpted plaque at the entrance to the stairway between Nos. 43 and 45 Springvalley Terrace, dated 1907, presumably to indicate the final demolition of this villa. These places of birth and residences are difficult to verify, since the Edinburgh Street directories of the period of Grant's birth do not list streets and their residents in detail, but in the Edinburgh Post Office Directory for 1824-25 a Lieutenant John Grant is listed under "Morningside" and since Grant's father was of this name and held an army commission, this may explain the indication that Grant was born in Morningside.

The records relate that James Grant was an eldest son and that his father held a commission in the 92nd Regiment of Foot (The Gordon Highlanders). His mother was a relation of Sir Walter Scott and certain other prominent families. His grandfather, James Grant (1743-1835), was a noted advocate and antiquarian. From these various family influences James Grant perhaps inherited his interest and competence in antiquarian studies and for literature generally. After his mother's death in 1833 Grant's father obtained a military post in Newfoundland, and took his three sons with him. They were brought up in barracks surroundings. In about 1840, having returned from Canada, James Grant himself obtained a commission in the 62nd Foot Regiment. After a few years of army life he returned to Edinburgh and worked for David Rhind, a noted Edinburgh architect. After spending his days as a draughtsman Grant devoted all his spare time to writing, and in the course of his life-time, more precisely between 1845 and his death in 1887, he actually produced approximately seventy novels, completing one to three regularly every year, some in three volumes. Fifty-six were historical romances, often with a military background, set in Scotland. Many were translated into French and German.

Grant also wrote several books on Scottish history, expressing strong Jacobite sympathies. These, too, he gave vent to politically through an organisation – the Association for the Vindication of Scottish Rights – and he even enlisted the support of Duncan McLaren, Lord Provost of Edinburgh from 1851 to 54, subsequently a Liberal Member of Parliament, to compile what was really an early version of the later Scottish National Party manifesto. Grant published a book on *The Tartans of the Clans of Scotland*. He also became something of an authority on army uniforms and was at times consulted by the military authorities. Books ranging from *An Illustrated History of India* to *British Heroes in Foreign Wars* indicate the breadth of his study and interest. To Edinburgh readers of today, however, James Grant is probably best

CASSELL'S

Old and New Edinburgh:

Its History, its People, and its Places.

BY

JAMES GRANT,

AUTHOR OF "MEMORIALS OF THE CASTLE OF EDINBURGH," "BRITISH BATTLES ON LAND AND SEA," ETC.

Illustrated by numerous Engravings.

―――

VOL. I.

―――

CASSELL & COMPANY, LIMITED:

LONDON, PARIS & MELBOURNE.

[ALL RIGHTS RESERVED.]

Title page of James Grant's classic "Old and New Edinburgh", published 1882

known, perhaps to some known solely, for his prodigious, copiously illustrated classic, *Old and New Edinburgh*, published in 1882, at first by Cassells in instalments and then eventually in various numbers of volumes, and finally in three volumes. Of *Old and New Edinburgh*, over 30,000 copies were sold in the United States of America and Canada. It remains one of Edinburgh's much-sought-after standard source books.

Grant married Christine McDonell Browne, eldest daughter of the Reverend Dr James Browne (1793-1841) a former Church of Scotland minister who had become a well-known advocate, journalist and author and a convert to Roman Catholicism. Grant had two sons – Roderick, born in Edinburgh on October 28th 1860, and James, who pre-deceased his father. Roderick eventually became a Catholic priest and was appointed a Canon in the Diocese of Brentwood in 1927. He died on October 15th 1934 and is commemorated by a stained-glass window of the Saints of Scotland in the church which he built at Ingatestone.

James Grant himself, who with his family had moved in later years to London, joined the Catholic Church and devoted the last years of his life to working among the poor. Despite his impressive catalogue of publications, his novels were seldom great successes, and in his more serious work, including his *Old and New Edinburgh*, as was not uncommon, he did not earn a large amount in royalties, often sustaining losses rather than profits from sales in fact. Indeed, Grant died virtually penniless at his London home on May 5th 1887, aged 64. His funeral service at St Mary's Church, Bayswater, was attended by very many clerical, military and literary figures. *British Authors of the Nineteenth Century* described Grant as ". . . a modest, genial man, whose novels were vivacious, picturesque and written in vigorous prose, but for the most part superficial".

DAVID DEUCHAR

NO DOUBT as long as the interesting circumstances of the early "discovery" of the world-famous portrait painter Henry Raeburn are recalled, reference will always be made to the Morningside man who was responsible. This was David Deuchar, who owned and resided in Morningside House from 1795 until his death thirteen years later. That the memory of Deuchar should tend to dwell always in the reflected glory of Raeburn is perhaps inevitable. And certainly to have "discovered" such a genius in itself merits the utmost acclaim. Unfortunately, it has somewhat tended to conceal Deuchar's own not inconsiderable talent as an artist, and while the standard biographical sources, such as the *Dictionary of National Biography* and artistic journals do praise him for his own work, it has been a privilege to obtain a great deal of original material and comment on Deuchar through the kind interest and assistance of one of his descendants, remote perhaps but authentic, Major Alexander Deuchar, a great-great-great-grandson.

From the material made available to me by Major Deuchar it has been possible to acquire much more insight into David Deuchar's life, and indeed the quite ancient lineage of the family which can be traced back to David I of Scotland in the 12th century, and which is the subject of several books. David Deuchar was born at Kinnel, Forfarshire, in 1743 and died at Morningside House in 1808. His father, a farmer, had suffered various hardships during the 1745 Jacobite Rebellion and came to Edinburgh in the same year. For some years he had been interested in mineralogy and had amassed a great collection of Scottish pebbles, garnets and other gems. These he kept in barrels concealed from possible raiders and he brought them with him to Edinburgh. Pebble buttons and other items he made were then very fashionable and Deuchar established himself as a lapidary at Croft-an-Righ near Holyrood, drawing means of power from the strongly running streams there.

Young David Deuchar, when old enough, entered his father's business and then set up his own premises, eventually obtaining a Royal Appointment. However, etching, which had initially been a hobby, became his principal activity. In 1788 he produced a series of etchings of the *Dance of Death* after Holbein which attracted much attention. In 1803 he published another series from many of the great Dutch masters. He had also developed painting in oils, modelling in clay, and the production of pen-and-ink portraits. A well-established artist, he was moreover an authority on antiquarian matters.

Deuchar's "discovery" of the young Henry Raeburn has perhaps become quite well known. The 17-year-old George Heriot's School foundationer had become apprenticed to Deuchar's friend, William Gilliland, a goldsmith with premises in Parliament Close. Several times, as Deuchar passed through his friend's shop, he noticed young Raeburn hastily pushing something into a drawer to conceal it. On another occasion Deuchar noticed the boy gazing into a mirror. Good-humouredly he asked him if he was admiring his handsome features. Raeburn owned up. He was drawing a self-portrait. No doubt in the course of conversation which followed, he produced the other items from the drawer – more of his work. Deuchar, himself no mean artist, recognised the touch of genius. He arranged to give Raeburn free tuition twice a week. His real vocation obviously being other than that of a goldsmith, he resigned his apprenticeship and through Deuchar's introduction became a pupil of David Martin, a leading Edinburgh portrait painter of that time.

David Deuchar at age 30

Miniature by Henry Raeburn 1773
By courtesy of the National Galleries of Scotland,
Edinburgh

In 1773 Raeburn did a miniature portrait of David Deuchar, and in return, as a token of esteem, Deuchar did a pen-and-wash miniature of Raeburn. Mr Stanley Cursiter, RSA., wrote of the portrait of Deuchar: "Miniature, head and shoulders, clean-shaven, face slightly to the right. . .". Unsigned and on the back was a label: "David Deuchar, Esq., of Morningside by Sir Henry

Raeburn, being the second portrait done by him during the time he was an apprentice with Mr Gilliland [sic], Jeweller, Parliament Square". Of Deuchar's reciprocal portrait of Raeburn, Mr Cursiter commented: "The head is in profile showing a boy in a three-cornered hat . . . It is curious to turn from the drawing to the later self-portrait and see how Deuchar caught the character of the features we know so well . . . here we have a valuable cross-reference establishing the link between Raeburn and Deuchar at the time, as well as a new portrait of the artist".

David Deuchar's first wife, Marion Sheil, died in childbirth and in 1776 he married Christian Robertson, daughter of an Eddleston minister. Deuchar bought Morningside House in 1795 shortly after the death of its probable builder and first owner, Lord Gardenstone. The house stood a little back from the roadway between what became Springvalley Gardens and Morningside Park, approximately on the site of the present-day supermarket. The property amounted to 33 acres and the garden was apparently beautifully laid out with fruit trees and rare plants. Deuchar had twelve children from his second marriage, of whom seven survived him. The terms of his will were rather unusual and indeed caused not a little ill-feeling in his descendants. He left £3,000 to each of his seven children but nothing to his wife. He bequeathed Morningside House to his youngest son, William, then aged 14, decreeing that the property should *ascend* from younger to older sons rather than descend by age as traditionally. The only explanation offered for his wife's exclusion was that contrary to David

Deuchar's wishes she had retained friendship with her brother whom her husband disliked and he had warned her of the consequences.

Following Deuchar's death, such was his vast collection of paintings, prints, etchings and other *objêts d'art* that from February 25th 1810 the sale of these, "in Mr Ross' saleroom in Drummond Street", lasted three weeks, with two sessions daily. Much of Deuchar's work and possessions still remain with his present-day descendants.

In 1871 Morningside House, which earlier had become the property of another David Deuchar, of the Caledonian Insurance Company, was sold, and Harlaw House at 24 Morningside Park built in 1874. Here David Deuchar resided until 1881, when he sold the house to Morningside Parish Church as its manse for £3,230. In early maps of the later Deuchar era Morningside Place of today is shown as Deuchar Street. One of the original David Deuchar's sons, John, provides an interesting link with another distinguished Morningdale resident, Professor James Syme. John Deuchar was lecturer in chemistry both in Edinburgh and Glasgow and reputedly the first in Scotland ever to have lectured to ladies on the subject. In Edinburgh he taught in a classroom in Lothian Street, the extra-mural premises of the university. One student who conducted experiments in John Deuchar's laboratory was the young James Syme, who there discovered a method for dissolving crude rubber, which he, under self-imposed ethics as a future medical student, did not exploit commercially. However, Charles Macintosh of Glasgow did so, and produced the celebrated raincoat bearing his name, "making a fortune", which Syme commented upon but remarked that his dedication to medicine was more important.

ANNIE S. SWAN

IF Mrs Eliza Kirk's popular cookery book of the early 1900s, *Tried Favourites*, was to be found in the kitchens of very many Scottish homes, there is a good chance that in the living room, or at the bedside, might be found copies of the books of another widely popular Scottish lady writer whose themes found romance in the kitchen and in the characters and daily round of life. This was Annie S. Swan, who resided with her husband for a short time after their marriage in the early 1880s at 201 Morningside Road, at the north corner of Steel's Place.

Annie S. Swan was born at No 52 Kirkgate, Leith, on July 8th 1859. In her early youth, her father moved the family to a farm near Coldingham, then to Gorebridge where he grew potatoes, but not very successfully. Nevertheless, she was sent to a small private school for girls run by Miss Jane Shore in Haddington Place in Edinburgh and later to Queen Street Ladies College. By this time Miss Swan's family had returned to Edinburgh, residing at Maryfield, near Easter Road. There were seven children. The future novelist often recalled the hard way of life she had once experienced on the farms, with very early rising. She attributed her ability to discipline herself and to work hard – at her desk – to these laborious years. Then she had also met a wide variety of colourful characters, later to feature in her novels.

The early talent which young Annie S. Swan showed as a writer was not encouraged by her father, who thought "Writing was not real work", though with the rest of the family he did enjoy reading her stories aloud and he did meet the cost of her first novel *Ups and Downs*. She began having articles accepted in local newspapers and awards for stories published by the *People's Journal* and *People's Friend*. Indeed it was to readers of the latter that she became most widely known. Her early novels were *Aldersyde* and *Carlowrie*, which received very good reviews. Some of her work, which she sent to Gladstone, was greatly praised by the famous Prime Minister and she became one of his admirers, also devoting herself to the Liberal Party and to the cause of Scottish Home Rule.

The death of her mother at a relatively early age deeply affected Annie S. Swan. She had been much attracted to her parent and indeed "used" her mother as a central character in much of her writing. In December 1883 she married James Burnett Smith, a schoolmaster at Star near Markinch in Fife. The wedding ceremony was in Darling's Hotel in Edinburgh. After a short time of living at Gorebridge and Markinch, Mr Burnett Smith acted upon a long-standing ambition and began to study medicine. He and his wife moved to Edinburgh. For two years from June 1886 they lived in a flat at 201 Morningside Road; while Mr Burnett Smith pursued his medical studies, his wife, retaining her maiden name of Annie S. Swan, contributed to newspapers and magazines to supplement their very meagre income. Indeed in her autobiography she wrote: "We had to do some tightening of the belt in the Morningside flat, once the venture [her husband's studies] was entered upon, but we never looked back". In Edinburgh the Burnett Smiths made many friends in intellectual circles, especially with Patrick Geddes and his wife in their house in the Lawnmarket. Mrs Burnett Smith also became a close friend of Priscilla Bright McLaren, sister of the radical Member of Parliament, John Bright, and wife of Duncan McLaren, Lord Provost of Edinburgh in 1851-54 and later Member of Parliament for South Edinburgh. Although Priscilla Bright was one of the pioneer suffragettes and an ardent feminist, Mrs Burnett Smith was not converted to her cause.

After two years in Morningside and a period at Victoria Terrace in Musselburgh, following upon Mr Burnett Smith's graduation and his setting up in practice as a general practitioner in Camden Town they took up residence there and in other parts of London. They moved in the leading literary circles of the metropolis and Mrs Burnett Smith was especially friendly with S. R. Crockett and J. M. Barrie. Tragedy struck when their son was killed in an accident on the eve of his return from Eton. Then Dr Burnett Smith himself died in 1927, his health having been adversely affected during service in the First World War.

After her husband's death Mrs Burnett Smith paid many visits to the United States, addressing large meetings and appealing for economic assistance for Britain, and especially food, after the war. She was awarded

Annie S. Swan

Reproduced from "My Life, An Autobiography".
Published by Ivor Nicholson & Watson Ltd, 1934

a C.B.E. She still continued to write, and indeed at 70 years of age was still turning out 3,000 words a day. She remained actively interested in politics and could look back on a highly successful literary career, and even a few theatrical successes, along with friendships in so many spheres of life. The secret of her success as a novelist was her presentation of characters and themes common in the "ordinary" person's everyday life. She died at her home at "Alder-syde", Gullane, on June 17th 1943.

"THE CANNY MAN"

THE sequence of the "institutions" which arose in Morningside village

was: Denholm's smiddy, perhaps just before 1800, the local inn at the corner of Cannan Lane at much the same date, the school-house in 1823, and the parish church in 1838. The original cottage-type village inn, eventually known as "The Volun-teers Rest", it is believed, may have been owned by a lady whose name is not on record. Two water-colour paintings remain of the early hostelry, sometimes known as "The Rifleman", and these were by the Morningside artist whose signature is also on a painting of Braid Iron Church which once stood at the east corner of Braid Road and what became Cluny Gardens. He was Frederick Dove Ogilvie who resided in Belhaven Terrace. In about 1870 the inn was acquired by Mr James Kerr, the original "Canny Man", and has remained within his family's ownership ever since. In 1871 Mr Kerr opened the then new and renamed "Volunteer Arms" at the corner of Canaan Lane and Morningside Road. At the rear the original inn made way for the stables and outhouses which still exist.

James Kerr was born in Hertree, near Biggar, where his father was a blacksmith. As a young man he came to Edinburgh, obtained work with Usher's brewery in St Leonard's and before long was appointed their head horse-driver or drayman. For some time Kerr had lodgings in the Castle o' Clouts, the very old and rather famous public house in Dalkeith Road, precipitately demolished some years ago. After the opening of the new "Volunteer Arms" in Morning-side Mr Kerr engaged the celebrated landscape painter, Sam Bough, then resident nearby in Jordan Lane, to paint two inn signs, of a kneeling

Johnny Kerr – "The Canny Man",
with pony and trap at stable behind
"Volunteer Arms"

By courtesy of Watson Kerr

rifleman, one on canvas, the other on an oak panel. The Kerr family today insist that Bough was commissioned to do this work, and it was not the repayment for drink obtained on account. The name "Volunteer's Rest", then "Arms" – and indeed the earlier "Rifleman" – arose from the fact that members of the Edinburgh Rifle Volunteers on their way to and from the shooting ranges on the Blackford Hill chose the inn as their rendezvous.

James Kerr was a great lover of horses, as the interesting collection of antiques in the present-day bar confirms, with pictures of horses, hunting-horns, harness buckles etc. For long the inn's proud boast was its

"Golden Drop" whisky and this, reputedly, was named not from its appearance but after a famous racehorse. Kerr's widely-known nickname – "The Canny Man" – still used today by many for the modern bar, is also associated with horses and not with any suggestion of his being "canny" or "mean" in another connotation of the word. Rather, it is said, that when the many carters who had come in from the farms south of Morningside and stopped in the village, simply to rest or wait while their horses were being attended to in Denholm's smiddy, they would enjoy a refreshment and pass the time in the "Volunteer Arms". However, if any showed signs of over-indulgence, Kerr, thinking of the remainder of their journey on horseback, would issue the salutary warning: "Ca' canny, man!" ("Go easy, man!"). And the phrase stuck. It stuck also to James Kerr's son, John, who duly succeeded his father as "mine host" and became the second "Canny Man". While no portraits could be traced of the original "Jimmy Kerr", one of his son, also an ardent horse lover, is reproduced here. John Kerr died on February 14th 1941 and is buried in East Preston Street Cemetery.